High Hills and Wild Goats

High Hills
and
Wild Goats

LIFE AMONG THE ANIMALS
OF THE HAI-BAR WILDLIFE REFUGE

by BILL CLARK

LITTLE, BROWN AND COMPANY
BOSTON   TORONTO   LONDON

FIRST EDITION

PHOTOGRAPHS BY BILL CLARK

LIBRARY OF CONGRESS CATALOGING-IN-PUBLICATION DATA

CLARK, BILL, 1943–
    HIGH HILLS AND WILD GOATS / BY BILL CLARK. — 1ST ED.
        P.   CM.
    ISBN 0-316-14600-5
    1. NATURAL HISTORY — ISRAEL — HAI-BAR RESERVE.   2. WILDLIFE
CONSERVATION — ISRAEL — HAI-BAR RESERVE.   3. ENDANGERED SPECIES —
ISRAEL — HAI-BAR RESERVE.   4. HAI-BAR RESERVE (ISRAEL)   I. TITLE.
QH193.18C57   1990
639.9′5′0956949 — DC20   89-12348
                                                                  CIP

10 9 8 7 6 5 4 3 2 1

BP

Published simultaneously in Canada
by Little, Brown & Company (Canada) Limited
PRINTED IN THE UNITED STATES

To the memory of Major General Avraham Yoffe

That which happens to men also happens to animals; and one thing happens to them both: as one dies so dies the other, for they share the same breath; and man has no preeminence above an animal: for all is vanity.

All go to one place; all are made of dust, and all return to dust again.

Who knows for certain that the spirit of man goes upward to the heavens and the spirit of the animal descends downward into the earth?

Therefore I perceive that there is nothing better than that a man should rejoice in his own works, for that is his share in life — for who shall bring him to see what shall be after him?

— Ecclesiastes 3:19–22

Contents

High Hills
and
Wild Goats

Welcome

THE SIDE GATE at Israel's Hai-Bar Arava National Wildlife Reserve is a special restricted-access portal, which is closed to the general public. It is open only to staff, nature wardens, their family and friends, and special guests. Those who enter the reserve by this side gate receive a personal greeting and are given access to the fascinating behind-the-scenes activities that make Hai-Bar one of the most unusual and important wildlife reserves on earth.

As you open this book, I would like you to feel that you are entering that side gate at Hai-Bar. You are warmly welcome, and I'll try my best to make your visit among these pages as stimulating and instructive as an actual sojourn at the reserve. Your armchair expedition to Hai-Bar is based mostly on the field notes that I kept while serving as chief curator of the reserve from 1980 through 1982. Although my involvement with Hai-Bar extends back to 1972 and continues to this day, those curatorial years, when I had day-to-day responsibility for hundreds of endangered animals, were the most memorable.

Like so many other aspects of Israel, Hai-Bar's raison d'être is as ancient as the opening verses of the Book of Genesis and as modern as the most advanced concepts of genetic theory and environmental conservation. The three reserves of Hai-Bar are modern Israel's effort to return the animals of the Bible to the Land of the Bible.

Most of the animals of Hai-Bar are critically endangered. The spectacular white oryx (*Oryx leucoryx*), for example, once ranged for more than a million square kilometers across the Middle East. But hunting parties exterminated it throughout its enormous desert range. The last wild white oryx was killed by trophy hunters in the deserts of Oman in 1972.

Fortunately, a few dozen of these beautiful antelope survived in zoos and private reserves around the world, and this captive population formed the only hope of rescuing a species that the King James version of the Bible translates as "unicorn." Today, restoration programs for the white oryx antelope are being conducted in Oman, Jordan, and, of course, in Israel.

Another Hai-Bar animal is the African wild ass (*Equus africanus*), which may be even more critically endangered than the white oryx. Several Bible scholars believe it to be the *arod* of Hebrew Scripture, and biologists agree that it is the wild ancestor of our common domestic donkey. Once, this species was spread throughout North Africa, from Morocco clear across to the Red Sea and up into the Middle East. Today, a mere remnant of this lovely equine's wild population is thought to survive in remote parts of Somalia and in Ethiopia's Danakil Desert. But as a result of the political and military explosiveness of the region, there have been no recent studies of their conservation status. It is considered very tenuous. A mere three dozen pure-blooded animals of this species exist in captivity as a hedge against the extinction of the wild population. Hai-Bar Arava, with its twenty-two African wild asses, has nearly two-thirds of the entire world captive population of this species.

The Mesopotamian fallow deer (*Dama mesopotamica*) is generally acknowledged to be the *yachmur* of the Hebrew Bible. It is also presumed to be extinct in Nature, and its only hope for survival as a species is the careful conservation and propagation of its captive populations. The last known wild habitats of this stately and elegant deer — which once ranged widely through the scrub thickets of the maquis forests of the ancient Fertile Crescent — were the brush and swamps around Shatt al-Arab, which lie between Iraq and Iran. This region has been a vicious battleground, subjected to intensive bombings, military clashes, and even poison gas for years. The fate of its rare deer population is unknown. In all probability, however, the *yachmur* no longer survives in Nature.

Other Mesopotamian fallow deer may survive in older protected reserves in Iran, but there have been no reliable conservation reports coming out of that country since the Islamic Revolution took control. Today, the only members of this species known to exist for certain are a couple of dozen animals scattered through European zoos and twenty-eight living in a protected section of a wild Mediterranean oak and pine forest habitat in a Hai-Bar reserve atop Mount Carmel in Israel.

There are many other rare species being protected and restored to Nature by Hai-Bar — ostriches, ibex, onagers, gazelles, addax, wild goats and sheep, griffon vultures, falcons, and owls. In recent years, a new predator restoration program has been started, and projects involving desert wolves, caracal, sand cats, leopards, and others are under way.

Most of the work is being done at two Hai-Bar reserves in Israel. Hai-Bar Carmel is devoted to the forest animals, such as the deer and wild goats and sheep. It embraces about four square kilometers of verdant forest near the peaks of Mount Carmel and overlooking the Mediterranean. Hai-Bar Arava is a thirty-five-square-kilometer tract of natural desert habitat reserve for the desert species — wild ass, antelope, ibex, ostrich, and some predators. In this larger reserve, located just forty kilometers due north of the Red Sea port of Eilat, is a twelve-square-kilometer fenced area, where much of the animal work reported in this book was done.

A third Hai-Bar reserve is located on the Golan Heights. The land here has been set aside for wildlife work, although the facility has not yet been built.

Hai-Bar is an integral part of the Israel Nature Reserves Authority and therefore cooperates with the 280 nature reserves scattered around the country, while benefiting from the expertise of hundreds of nature wardens and scientists working with the Authority. Thus, a biologist living in the northern Arava Valley is captive-breeding fennec foxes for restoration to Nature, and the nature wardens assigned to the great desert crater of Makhtesh Ramon, in the central Negev Desert, spend part of their time monitoring the progress of the wild asses that have been released there as part of the Hai-Bar program.

There are compelling genetic reasons for preservation of many of these species, which are the wild progenitors of today's domestic livestock. Just as the African wild ass is the ancestor of the donkey, so the wild goats and sheep are the wild ancestors of today's domestic breeds, and the wolf is the wild ancestor of all the dogs. The North African wildcat, which also inhabits Israel, is the progenitor of nearly all the house cats of the world. Indeed, most anthropologists agree that the great majority of today's common domestic animals were first tamed during the Neolithic period, or Late Stone Age, in the Middle East. The preservation of the ancestral species of domestic livestock is very important today because modern biology has developed techniques for tapping the genetic resources of wild populations to enhance the health, disease-resistance, fertility, strength, size, and other aspects of the domestic types.

Another important consideration is biological diversity, or "biodiversity." If you look at a map of the Eastern Hemisphere, you will notice that Israel is the keystone in the only land bridge that physically connects all of Eurasia to Africa. It is physically impossible to find a land route between one of these great landmasses and the other without crossing through Israeli territory.

This funnel has been of vital importance to the distribution of species throughout the world. Consider, for example, the horse family, which evolved in North America. The family spread out across the continent and crossed the Bering land bridge during the Ice Age. Wild horses then thundered across Eurasia, while the populations they left behind in America died out. Some of these horses turned south and crossed via the Israeli land bridge into Africa, where they evolved into three species of zebra and one species of wild ass. Many other species followed this route.

But the Israeli land bridge did not have one-way traffic. Many species of plants and animals crossed northward, out of Africa. Many of our own human ancestors, having evolved in Africa, ventured northward across the Israeli land bridge to disperse across the face of the planet. Indeed, only the black African can claim not to have had an ancestor who visited the Land of Israel — at least as a tourist — so very long ago.

This land bridge is still very important to conservation, for plants and animals are still migrating across it. Some move with hardly perceptible slowness. But others make the trip twice a year! Many of the Eastern Hemisphere's birds — and most of its large soaring birds like eagles, pelicans, and storks — migrate twice annually across this useful land bridge.

Because Israel connects two continents, there is a constant biological influence from both directions. Add to this the extremely varied topography of rugged mountains, broad plains, sea coasts, rolling hills, and the Great Rift Valley, which descends more than 1,200 feet below sea level, and then consider the varied climates (from hot desert to humid wetland to subalpine) and the many vegetative systems and numerous other biological factors, and one realizes that little Israel — barely the size of New Jersey — has one of the richest ecological heritages on earth.

Israel's plant and animal life is extremely diverse, and fortunately much of it is protected. Nearly 20 percent of the country's land area is classified as nature reserve. Another 12 percent is national forest. Yet another 10 percent embraces national parks, recreation areas, and other protected sites.

Hai-Bar was created to assist in preserving this magnificent treasure by reintroducing rare native species that have been locally exterminated, thus restoring the vitality of Israeli ecosystems to maximum integrity.

The conservation and biological merits of the Hai-Bar program are very considerable indeed; equally important, however, is its cultural significance in establishing the biblical context of the protected species, as fundamental elements in a cornerstone of our civilization. They are part of the heritage of the Western world.

People who identify themselves as being part of the Western heritage preserve the Hebrew Bible as a great source of law, ethics, tradition, and morality. Long before modern states got around to drafting codes that prohibit murder, theft, and perjury, the Bible had clearly defined these acts as crimes. And long before the modern world recognized our responsibilities to society and, indeed, to Nature itself, the Bible set forth clear outlines of behavior.

The writers of the Bible, however, sometimes couched their wisdom in symbols, similes, and metaphors involving animals. And to understand the full meaning of these writings, we must understand something of their frame of reference.

What did Solomon mean when he admonished a married woman to "be as a loving deer" (Proverbs 5:19)?

And what did the patient Job mean when he wrote: "For vain man would be wise, though man be born like a wild ass's colt" (Job 11:12)?

And what did Jeremiah mean when he prophesied: "Hazor shall be a dwelling for jackals" (Jeremiah 49:33)?

There are hundreds of such passages scattered throughout the Bible, and full comprehension of them requires at least a basic appreciation of Israel's native wildlife.

Four decades ago, many people were skeptical about the survival prospects for the newborn State of Israel. And ever since that time, Israel's survival has been, at best, tenuous.

Through the years, Israel has been forced to face extremely difficult challenges — dangerous military threats, oppressive economic boycotts, incessant political crises, massive immigrant absorption, serious social unrest, and numerous other hazards. These challenges have been all the more onerous because of Israel's lack of natural resources. The land area is small, the soil is poor, and the rainfall is scant. Mineral wealth is negligible. Israel has no valuable resources except its people.

Yet with this single, human resource, Israel has flourished. It has met each challenge and emerged stronger. And despite innumerable problems, Israel has managed to devote a large measure of its energies to very positive ends. It has built great universities, hospitals, and world-class museums. It has cultivated internationally admired symphony orchestras and virtuoso musicians, fine artists, and literary talents.

In a part of the world that knows starvation because of drought and mismanagement, Israel has mastered the desert, feeds itself, and exports more food per capita than any other country on earth. In a region that is ruled almost entirely by dictators, generals, feudal monarchs, and dogmatic religious fanatics, Israel is the only true democracy — and not merely a political democracy but also a social democracy. Those who wish to live the communist ideal on a kibbutz are free to do so, and those who are intent on exercising capitalism to the full extent of their talent and energies are equally free. And those who seek a middle road of free enterprise mixed with social welfare may also take that path through life.

Above all, a great ethical imperative imposes a potent influence on an Israeli's relationship to the Land itself. It is a very complex relationship, involving ancient traditions and modern realities. It is a relationship that recognizes responsibility as a prime motivation for action.

Israelis care about their Land, and they feel profoundly accountable for it. Admittedly, the media is flooded with reports about divisiveness in Israel on any number of political or social issues — but this dissension is merely an expression of intense concern for the Land and its future. Israelis may hold diverse opinions and fight furiously on behalf of their points of view, but there is near unanimity that the Land itself is inviolable.

A national consensus exists on restoring the nation in its ancestral Land. Much has been achieved in four decades — cities built, agriculture established, commerce initiated. The magnitude of the consensus, however, extends beyond development to embrace the physical environment.

In the centuries before the establishment of modern Israel, the Land itself had been subjected to terrible abuse. Nearly all forests had been cut away. Pastures had been overgrazed. Wildlife had been ruthlessly exterminated. Water reservoirs drained. Soil eroded.

Modern Israel is rejuvenating an exhausted Land. This restoration process involves a comprehensive approach to conservation. Forests must be replaced and grazing controlled; wildlife must be assisted in recovery and water and soil be conserved.

Nature conservation is an integral element of restoring the Land to the ecological integrity it once had and which it still deserves. The Hai-Bar program is a key part of this process. Hai-Bar, therefore, is an ethical expression of caring for the Land. It is a statement that, despite all the problems and hardships of the Middle East, Israelis can, and do, assume full responsibility for the rehabilitation of Nature and, in the process, are setting a high standard for professionalism, idealism, and results.

Now, let us enter through that side gate of the Hai-Bar Arava reserve and see what has been developing beneath the desert sun.

High Hills and Wild Goats

HERE, read this," the burly general ordered. He handed me a Bible opened to the one hundred and fourth Psalm, and pointed to the eighteenth verse.

" 'The high hills are a refuge for the wild goats,' " I recited.

"Which high hills?" he snapped.

I shrugged hesitantly.

"Which wild goats?" he inquired, in a near whisper.

I stared passively at the floor.

"You have much to learn," the general said. "And you *will* learn!" He was right on both counts. He would be my mentor, my motivator, throughout the educational process.

My first meeting with General Avraham Yoffe occurred in July, 1974, while I was on a six-month visit to Israel with my wife, Judy. I found the general in the ramshackle Tel Aviv headquarters of the Israel Nature Reserves Authority. He impressed me with his decisive and confident manner and with the warmth of his expression. He smiled with his whole face.

So I wanted to learn about Israeli wildlife conservation, he mused. "Surely you want to see the Hai-Bar," he said. "But that's some distance down in the desert. You would do well to acclimatize yourself, as I wouldn't want your enthusiasm to be burnt up in a case of heat prostration. Besides, Hai-Bar is the main course. I think you should start with an appetizer!" Avraham Yoffe loved to speak in culinary metaphors. His waistline demonstrated that his interest was more than linguistic.

"I want you to see those high hills," he said, "and those wild goats. The next time I ask you about the one hundred and fourth Psalm, you'll be able to answer me from first-hand experience." The high hills, he told me, were an oasis in the Judean Desert called Ein Gedi, and the wild goats were actually ibex, wild caprids related to common goats. It was most important that I visit this nature reserve as an introduction to Israel's native fauna. "When you get there, look for Asaf Rosenberg," the general said. "He's our warden. Tell him I sent you, and he'll show you around."

A week later, I returned to the general's office. The sunburn on my face was healing, and so were the bruises on my left arm. I had lost several pounds. "Now you understand something about those high hills?" he asked. "Yes, sir," I said — and indeed I did, for I had climbed into the desert mountains and experienced in just a few days an unforgettable sequence of exertion, thirst, incredibly beautiful landscapes, abundant wildlife, the taste of apprehension along the faces of tall, sheer cliffs and, at the end, exhilaration.

"And you've seen a few wild goats?" he asked.

"That I have," I said. Indeed, I'd seen more than a few. The greatest excitement of all had been seeing those magnificent ibex in their natural habitat. They were enchanting creatures of astonishing grace and agility. Well muscled and powerfully built, with the males carrying a formidable pair of horns, the ibex were masters of the desert mountains. They could sprint nimbly across the cliffs with the greatest nonchalance.

"And did you like it there?" the general inquired.

"Oh, yes," I replied. "Very much indeed."

"And you can appreciate, if only just a little bit, how important the Bible is to the education of a nature conservationist in Israel?" he asked.

"Without question," I said. "If anything, the Bible can be something of an understatement. By my definition, Ein Gedi is something more than simply 'high hills.' And the ibex certainly are more wonderful than mere 'wild goats'."

Avraham Yoffe sat at his desk staring blankly into space. In a few moments, his eyebrows rose and his lower lip protruded in an almost pouting expression. "Your wife was born here in Israel, yet you make your home in America. Have you thought about *aliya* (immigration to Israel)?" he asked.

"We have spoken of it," I said. "But this trip is only a long visit for us. Perhaps in the future."

"We are creating our future today," the general said. "And your visit to Ein Gedi has helped to create *your* future. You were influenced by it. And I want to create a greater influence, because I think you may be useful to the purposes of Hai-Bar. We have more than two hundred other nature reserves."

"Are you suggesting . . . ?"

"You have many years before you," he said. "Visit the reserves at every opportunity. And be mindful of the three 'opens.' Stay in the open — outdoors. Keep your eyes open — use all your senses to the fullest. And most important, keep your mind open. Try your best to understand everything you experience.

"I suspect you're anxious to go to Hai-Bar," he said. "I'll give you a note introducing you to Mike Van Grevenbroek, our curator there. I believe you will like him."

Saying good-bye to Judy, who remained in our rented Jerusalem apartment, I faced five hours of glaring sun, parched air, and oppressive heat along the road to Hai-Bar. The trek across the desert was onerous, even in the relative comfort of an Egged bus. But the Negev Desert had a spectacular landscape, with ever-changing vistas, and even the casual traveler would find the succession of panoramas an awe-inspiring experience. Broad grasslands stretched out to the horizon, dotted by scattered tribes of Bedouin tending flocks of sheep and goats. Low-slung black tents made of goat-hair fabric were seen along the undulating ridge lines. Wealthy Bedouin had white Peugeot pickup trucks parked outside their tents, and occasionally even a television antenna could be seen poking anachronistically from the peak of a nomadic home. Many Bedouin, however, made do with a few camels grazing by the door flaps of their own tents.

The terrain became more rugged. Uneven hills strewn with rocks and boulders dominated the landscape. The road twisted and turned along a serpentine track. A few bits of vegetation sprouted down in the valleys, but the hillsides were barren.

Midway across the desert, just south of the town of Mitzpe Ramon, the road dropped into a steep descent that traversed many switchbacks as it plunged to the floor of an enormous crater. This was Makhtesh Ramon — about four hundred square kilometers scooped from the belly of the desert.

The walls surrounding Makhtesh Ramon were nearly a kilometer high and, in many places, almost perfectly vertical. The floor of the crater was a rugged badlands that supported a modest variety of desert vegetation. Observant botanists would realize that, somewhere along the descent, they had crossed a major geobotanical border. Just a few kilometers north, the landscape was typically Asian, with plants related to those found in the desert areas of Syria, Iran, and Afghanistan. But to the south, the vegetation was more typically African and akin to that found in the Sahara.

Farther on, the bus rolled across stark landscapes with jagged mountains, through labyrinths of ravines and gorges, and out onto broad, barren plains so hostile that even the Bedouin avoided them. The heat was overwhelming. The sun's intensity, streaming in through the bus window, was painful.

By early afternoon, the bus was thundering down the Arava Valley, part of the Great Rift Valley, which runs between the Dead Sea and the Red Sea on Israel's border with Jordan. A few settlements of pioneer Israelis along the way were trying to eke out a living growing irrigated vegetables under the relentless sun.

The bus ride ended at Yotvata, a kibbutz lying close against the border near a gasoline station and a small snack bar. Leaving the bus, I asked the service station attendant, "Where's Hai-Bar?"

He pointed southward. "'Bout three kilometers. That way," he replied. We both squinted in the indicated direction, but there were no signs or evidence that a major nature reserve actually existed there. "Believe me!" he exclaimed. "Only 'bout three kilometers!"

Lifting my pack, I trudged off down the road, making doubly sure to keep my orientation. Just in case there was a problem, it would be wise to know the direction back to that filling station. But somehow, simply being out of the bus and in the open air made the desert less oppressive. Surely, the sun was just as intense, and the heat just as suffocating, but there was an appealing quality to the atmosphere, a "desert seasoning," which made the dry heat less pernicious, more benevolent, perhaps even agreeable.

Before the roof of the service station disappeared from view, I caught sight of the reserve's northwestern corner and followed its protective fence southward. As I walked along the outside of the fence, I noticed quite a few tracks on the ground, going in the same direction ahead of me. They appeared to have been left by several very large wolves.

Glancing into the reserve as I walked along, I caught glimpses of the extraordinary wealth of wildlife living there. A half dozen addax antelope — beautiful creatures with their elegantly spiraled horns extending harplike above their heads — reclined in the shade of an acacia tree. A flock of ostrich drifted by, pecking at some unseen objects on the ground. A herd of onagers, or Asian wild asses, walked across the desert, not 200 yards away.

Arriving at the work area within the hour, I called "Mr. Van Grevenbroek!" through the chain-link fence gate. My cry brought a tall, muscular Dutchman out from behind a prefabricated shed. He was stripped to the waist, barefoot, and deeply tanned. "Who's there?" he called.

Introducing myself, I produced the note from General Yoffe. "Hold on to that for a while," he said, "my hands are too dirty. Come in. Come!" He swung the gate open and I set foot within the Hai-Bar Arava National Wildlife Reserve for the first time.

"Do you mind a little work?" Van Grevenbroek asked while we walked toward the shed. "No. Not at all," I replied. "Good! Then put your bag down in the shade there and come with me."

We walked a bit farther until we reached a wagon with one wheel missing. "Now, we've got to lift that wagon high enough to slip this wheel back on its axle," he said in a self-assured tone. "That looks like a pretty heavy wagon," I observed. "How much do you think it weighs?"

"Dunno. Maybe a hundred kilos or so," he replied. A bit of mental arithmetic told me that such a wagon weighed 220.46 old-fashioned American pounds, or so. "How were you going to lift this?" I inquired. "Dunno. Probably curse it and kick it until it surrendered," he said. We put our backs against the wagon and lifted until it was just high enough to rest the wheel-less axle on a stout log.

"Not too bad," the Dutchman said, slipping the wheel on the lifted axle. "How are you at stacking hay?" I shrugged. "Anybody Av'ram sends down here wants to learn something about Hai-Bar," he said, "and the way to learn something is to do it. You want to learn about Hai-Bar?"

"For sure," I said.

We walked to a small, one-room bunkhouse, which held two cots and a massive table cut from the cross section of a tree about four feet in diameter. A few books lay on a nearby shelf beside an empty wine bottle corked with a half-burnt candle.

As we drank thick, steamy, black coffee, we talked a bit. I told him of my interests, and he seemed generally agreeable to letting me stay on for a few days. "You can stay here overnight, if you like, or there's a youth hostel in Eilat that doesn't cost very much," he said. For the first night, I preferred Eilat. I wanted to see a bit of the town on the shores of the Red Sea.

"There's not much left to do here," he said. "The time to see the animals is in the morning, before it gets too hot. We can do that tomorrow. You got swimming trunks?" I had. "Then put them on!"

"By the way," he added, "just call me Mike."

We jumped into Mike's Renault for a quick tour of the reserve to make sure everything was secure for the evening and then headed out onto the main highway for a forty-kilometer ride to Eilat. Entering the town, we made a beeline for the seashore at North Beach. "It's the only sane way to end a workday in the desert," Mike said. And we jumped into the sea to let all the day's heat, dust, grime, and dryness simply float away. The Red Sea, despite its hostile desert surroundings, is crystal clear and soothingly cool.

Refreshed, we drove a few blocks up into the town, to 637 Patio, Mike's home. Here, I was introduced to his boys, Angus and Bobby, and his wife, Agnes — each of them as blond as the Dutch Boy on the paint can. "Marcel needs some help," Agnes said.

Marcel Moore, also known as Itzik, and perhaps by several other aliases, is part of the Eilat local color. He's an entrepreneur with vast dreams, which sometimes actually bear fruit. Merkaz Moore — the Moore Center — an apartment house and retail shop complex in Eilat, is one of his more notable accomplishments. So is Gan Ha-Muzika — The Music Garden — the only shop in Eilat where high-quality musical instruments could be purchased.

Marcel's emergency involved moving to a new apartment. Throughout the day, he had been shuttling back and forth in a battered old jeep, moving all his worldly possessions one box at a time. He had them nearly all moved when we arrived, but he had saved the best for last.

"Marcel, meet Bill," Mike said. "Now, what do you need?" Marcel smiled and pointed to a refrigerator and then pointed to his jeep. "*Ya Allah!*" Mike exclaimed. "I hope you have some cold beer in it."

"Not a chance," said Marcel, "but. . . ." Whereupon he produced a half-empty bottle of Johnny Walker Red Label scotch. "An excellent substitute!" Mike pronounced, twisting off the cap and swallowing a big gulp before passing the bottle around. "Maybe we ought to get the refrigerator moved before the bottle's empty," Marcel suggested.

We all put our shoulders against the appliance and in moments it was hoisted into the back of the jeep. Mike leapt into the driver's seat, Marcel jumped in alongside, and I squeezed into the back. "The starter's busted," Marcel warned, "so you'll have to jump-start it. But you won't have to do that for a few blocks, because we're going downhill most of the way."

Coasting quietly down the hill, the old jeep emitted a few rattles and groans until Mike jump-started the vehicle amid a cloud of dark smoke and a thunderous roar. "Yeah, well it didn't have a muffler when I bought it," Marcel explained. "I suppose it didn't have any gasoline in it when you bought it, either," Mike snapped back.

The motor ran for a few blocks, until Mike turned a corner to a downhill street, whereupon he switched the motor off again and we coasted another block and a half to Marcel's new apartment. "Well done!" Marcel exclaimed. "I knew if I could get a stingy, tightwad Dutchman to drive I wouldn't need any more than two teaspoons of fuel."

"Hantarish!" Mike spit back. "You needed a Dutchman because only a Dutchman has the brains to move this pile of junk you call a jeep from one place to another in one piece!" They continued, insulting each other with each breath, and working together like the closest of friends. The refrigerator was moved, as were the washing machine, sofa, and uncounted other personal belongings. After the work was done, we rattled off to a falafel stand near the beach and bought some supper.

Dropping me off at the youth hostel, Mike made arrangements to meet me at five o'clock the next morning. Sleep claimed me quickly. The night was restful. And 5:00 A.M. came all too soon.

I emerged from my morning grogginess somewhere along the road north of Eilat, and by the time we got to Hai-Bar, I was wide-awake and enthusiastic. There was a large truck and trailer waiting at the gate when we arrived.

"And now you will learn the meaning of a day's work in the desert," Mike said. He was right. The truck and trailer carried fourteen tons of alfalfa hay driven down overnight from an Arab farm in the Galilee. The hay had a nice dark color and sweet aroma. Mike yanked a few handfuls at random from the bales, sniffed the hay, and rubbed it between his fingers to see how it crumbled. When he was satisifed that the hay was well cured, he swung the gates open and called the truck and trailer into the reserve. Fourteen tons of hay — seven hundred bales at twenty kilometers per bale — were hefted from the truck and wagon and arranged in a neat cube on the desert floor in about two hours.

"You'd better start drinking much more water than you have been," Mike said. "In the desert here, you won't realize how much you perspire. Most of the sweat evaporates quickly, as soon as it comes from your pores. It's hard to estimate just how much water your body is loosing.

"And keep an eye on your urine. If it gets dark yellow, you're dehydrating and need more water. Headaches are another symptom of water loss. Drink, and drink some more."

I followed his advice reluctantly. The water at Hai-Bar was tepid and reeking with minerals. It tasted horrid.

Finishing with the hay-stacking, and dispatching the truck back north, we threw ourselves into the next task — supplementary feeding. "There's enough natural food out there for the animals to browse and graze," Mike told me, "and they do eat quite a bit of it. But we must supplement that diet for a number of reasons."

First, he explained, is reproduction. One of the objectives of Hai-Bar is to create nucleus herds of native wildlife and then encourage them to reproduce in large numbers so the offspring can be reintroduced into parts of Israel where they have been wiped out. There's a very close correlation between good nutrition and good reproduction. And while the natural foods of the desert are quite nutritious for desert animals, supplements like alfalfa hay increase their vitamin and protein intake, ensuring that they always have good reserves of nutrients in their bodies.

"It's the same in Nature," Mike said. "Take the ibex, for example. Those which live in truly barren habitats, where there is little food of low quality, generally have low birth rates, but those living in good habitats where they have lots of high-quality vegetation usually have high birth rates."

Also, he explained, nearly all of the Hai-Bar animals came from zoo stock that were acquired after several generations of eating zoo foods like hays and concentrated pellets. "You can't simply take an animal off zoo food and change the diet to natural foods without running into serious digestive problems. Most of these animals couldn't handle radical changes in their diets, so the shift has to be gradual."

"Then there's the matter of saving the natural vegetation in the reserve," he added. "We have eight square kilometers within the main area, and there's plenty of natural foods here. But in all this vegetation, there are certain preferred foods. Without supplementary feedings, the animals would browse their preferred foods too heavily and destroy an important element of the vegetation." This had already happened with several types of wild grasses that once grew in the reserve. The onagers — or Asian wild asses — liked the wild grasses so much that they ate them all within a few months, even though supplementary feeds were available to them.

The lesson in Hai-Bar nutrition practices came as we loaded about a quarter ton of hay into the wagon that we had repaired the day before. With the wagon latched to a tractor, we drove off into the reserve, distributing bales of hay to various feeding sites in the desert.

We passed by a herd of scimitar-horned oryx, well named, for their horns sweep back from their heads like great curved scimitars. As we spread the food and the animals came to eat, Mike had the perfect opportunity to count his charges and to see if they suffered any ailments.

"Six, seven, eight, nine, ten, eleven . . . and there's the young one . . . twelve," Mike said, as the addax drifted in toward the hay. "I count all the animals every day," he said. "In herd animals especially, if one drops out of the herd and doesn't come to eat, it's a sign of trouble."

Mike studied the addax carefully and pointed out a female that had a few ticks on the lower parts of her neck. "We'll have to take care of that a bit later," he said. "We don't have the proper equipment to do it right now. Those ticks can carry blood parasites. And if one animal gets infected with them, it can spread to the whole herd. So we'll have to take care of it as soon as possible."

Farther along on the morning rounds, we came across a flock of ostriches and a herd of onagers — tough-looking equines that appear perfectly at home in this open desert scrub. In the distance, we saw a herd of African wild asses — a different equine species. "We'll put food out here for them and then move away," Mike said. "They're new here, and very wary. They won't come within three hundred meters of us."

We spread the hay in an open area and then retreated to a rise about three hundred meters away. While Mike counted and inspected the animals through his binoculars, he told me that the African wild asses were recent arrivals from the Danakil Desert in Ethiopia. They were some of the few truly wild animals in the reserve.

The African wild ass is the ancestor of the common domestic donkey — although by no means does it have a subservient temperament. It is fiercely independent and maintains a solid herd integrity. Among all the equines, I think it is the most beautiful — large and well proportioned with a long, erect mane and ears. The body color is mostly a soft rose-grey, which looks almost like velvet, and the lower half of the legs is white with black zebra stripes.

This particular herd has been captured in the wild by Jurgen Shultz, who mounted an expedition on behalf of the Catskill Game Farm in the United States. But once the animals were all captured, crated, and ready for shipment, U.S. veterinary authorities refused to authorize their import to the United States. They feared that the animals might carry African horse sickness, a deadly viral disease; if the animals were brought into the United States, the disease could spread among the very expensive horse breeds of America.

Avraham Yoffe had received news of the stranded animal shipment and consulted a few veterinarians. It was unlikely that the animals were infected with African horse sickness, they said, especially since they had been confined for several weeks and none had demonstrated any symptoms. Blood tests could confirm their state of health once they were brought to an Israeli quarantine station.

Being a national hero and a major general in the Israel Defense Forces gave Avraham a certain amount of influence with the Israeli military establishment. And he used this influence (or *protekzia,* as it is known in Hebrew, or sometimes simply "Vitamin P") to wheedle a C-130 Hercules transport plane out of the air force "for just a few days." The aircraft was fueled to capacity, a crew of air force men and nature wardens were loaded, and they all took off for Ethiopia, where eight African wild asses — one of the rarest, most endangered of all the wild equines — were loaded into the airplane and whisked back to the Negev Desert. After a brief quarantine, a few blood tests, and other veterinary work, the animals were released into the Hai-Bar reserve to form the nucleus of a conservation program.

The only large mammals native to Hai-Bar are the two types of gazelles that live there. When the reserve was enclosed with the large fence, to exclude the wild wolves and hyena that live in the region — and thus protect the semitame animals within from predators — Israeli conservationists learned that they had also fenced in populations of dorcas and Arava gazelles. The dorcas gazelle is a lithe, reddish-brown animal with S-shaped horns. It is recognized as severely endangered by most conservation authorities around the world.

The Arava gazelle, however, is even scarcer. It's an extremely rare subspecies, or race, of the common mountain gazelle, which is found in the richly vegetated hills and mountains of northern Israel. The Arava gazelle is specially adapted for life in the desert and can tolerate the more intense heat and lack of water much better than its northern cousins. It's a gray-brown animal, with horns much straighter than those of the dorcas, and it has a distinctive chocolate-brown mark right above its nose. In all the world, only about forty Arava gazelles are known to exist — and they all live in the Arava Valley in the vicinity of Hai-Bar.

"There's no need to feed the gazelles," Mike said. "They've been here since before the reserve was created, so they've lived in balance with this habitat and won't destroy the vegetation. They might come and nibble some of the alfalfa hay if the larger antelopes don't eat it all, but, generally, the gazelles are so well adapted to this area that it isn't wise to interfere with their way of life."

After the last of the hay was distributed from the wagon, we returned to the work area, where there were several smaller paddocks with animals confined in them for various reasons. One large paddock had an onager that was a notorious troublemaker with the herd and had a history of frequent fighting with the others. In Nature, he would become either a dominant stallion or an outcast, but here at Hai-Bar, the situation was resolved simply by removing him from the herd and enclosing him in a private paddock. Another paddock housed a female oryx antelope recovering from a goring wound. Her neighbor, in the next paddock, was a male addax with an eye problem. "Once they've recovered," Mike said, "I'll release them back to their herds. But I don't know about that onager. He's just incompatible."

One large paddock was a nursery enclosure for young ibex. In the center of that paddock was an enormous pile of boulders, where many of the young kids — then about three months old — were climbing and jumping. "These were Ein Gedi ibex," Mike told me. "The oldest ones here were captured in the wild at Ein Gedi a few years ago and were brought here to form a breeding herd. And as you can see, we've been quite successful. But tell me, where else on this planet would a pile of stones be warmly accepted as a charitable contribution?"

Mike explained that the copper miners at Timna, about eight

kilometers to the south, contributed one hundred tons of boulders to the Hai-Bar paddock so the young ibex could have stones for climbing. "It gives them good exercise," he said, "and develops their agility."

With the main animal chores done, we gathered some rope, buckets, and food concentrate, and a bucket of dissolved Ambush, an acaricide proven effective in removing ticks from addax antelopes. The search for the female addax took the better part of an hour, as we tracked the herd from its feeding site to a watering area and then into a thicket of acacia trees, where they were resting. We drove around to the northern edge of the thicket, and Mike crushed a bit of the food concentrate and tossed it out into the sand. The breeze carried the scent of the food to the herd, and a few animals rose to investigate what might be eaten. But the infested female stayed quietly reclining among the thorny trees. "Not a chance today," Mike said, with the voice of experience. "If we try to go in after her, she'll only run away and scatter the herd. It's better to wait a day or two and try to catch her at a morning feeding."

We did catch the female addax — two days later. Mike's technique was quite simple. He scattered hay over a much larger than average area, to spread out the herd during the feeding. We then drove casually and very slowly through the herd, stopping here and there to pour a bit of food concentrate on top of the small piles of hay. Coming near the infested animal, Mike tossed a large measure of concentrate on the ground. She saw it and started drifting over to nibble at it. As soon as she was in range, Mike deftly tossed a lasso over the points of her horns. The rope dropped down to the base of the horns, and as it did, Mike pulled the loop snug and then quickly wrapped his end of the rope several times around a peg on the hay wagon.

The addax struggled against the rope for a few minutes, but she wasn't strong enough to pull a tractor and its wagon, and soon she began to tire. When she relaxed, she left a bit of slack in the rope, and Mike quickly pulled this taught. Gradually, taking up a bit of rope at a time, we drew the addax closer to the side of the hay wagon until she was only about a yard away.

Mike passed the end of the rope to me saying, "Now, you hold this snug. Don't let her pull back. Not a centimeter!" He then grabbed the bucket of Ambush and slipped from the opposite side of the wagon. "Talk to her," he instructed me. "Talk to her and keep her attention on you." And he circled around the far side of the wagon.

"Nice addax," I said to the grunting, snorting, struggling beast. "Nice addax."

In an instant, Mike leapt out from the far side of the wagon and splashed the entire contents of the bucket directly on the lower neck and chest area of the addax, soaking her thoroughly. "Ha!" he exclaimed with an air of success.

"Now comes the hard part," Mike warned as he climbed back into the wagon. "Tossing a rope over her horns was easy enough. But now it's snugged down tight around the base and won't be so easy to get off." We went back to the reeling-in routine, pulling the antelope — inch by inch — closer to the wagon. Gradually, her head was brought flush against the side of the wagon itself. "I'll grab her head and hold her immobile," Mike said, "and you slip the rope off over her horns. If the rope's too tight, cut it with the knife." He then slipped down from the wagon again and walked around to the far side of the addax, deftly grabbing the base of her dangerous horns.

Standing on the right side of the addax and facing in the same direction, Mike wrapped his left arm across the top, around, and then under the animal's neck. Simultaneously, he pushed his right thumb into the side of her mouth, slipping it through the diastemma — the empty space between the molars and incisors that exists in all ruminant antelopes. With this hold, Mike gained maximum control over the antelope, while I loosened the knotted rope. The addax had pulled so hard against the rope that the noose was pulled very tight around her horns and was worked loose only with great difficulty. But in a few moments it began to slacken, and eventually I had the loop opened and lifted off.

"Now comes the best part," Mike said. He released the addax and jumped clear. The animal galloped away and rejoined her herd." She'll be clean tomorrow at feeding time," Mike said. "There won't be a tick left on her."

The first week at Hai-Bar was not entirely adventure. Mike put a heavy accent on maintenance, and I spent much time scrubbing out watering tubs, helping to repair gates, cleaning out empty paddocks so they'd be ready to use at a moment's notice, and doing many other chores.

But it was all a great joy and an inspiration. I found a tremendous sense of freedom working in the vastness of the open desert and also a tremendous sense of purpose. Out there, we were actually helping endangered species to survive and to be restored to their native habitats. This was the "front line" of conservation — where the solid, productive work was accomplished and where results can be seen and counted.

There was an emotional, romantic attraction in the bright sky and vast expanse of desert, in the craggy distant mountains, and in the arid heat. I began to fall in love with the desert.

637 Patio

I RETURNED to Hai-Bar several times during our stay in Israel, and each time I became more attached to the place. But the calendar turned, and we had to return to the United States, taking our newborn son, Joe, with us.

In the States, we settled down to a conventional routine. We purchased an old house on Staten Island and converted the attic into a studio where Judy could pursue her career as a painter. I found some nine-to-five work, first editing a community newspaper, and later working for Friends of Animals. It was fulfilling work, for I had long been committed to FOA's policies for protecting animals. Steeljaw leg-hold traps are indeed very cruel and nonselective and ought to be abolished. Sport hunting is a contradiction in terms — there can be no sport in killing a defenseless animal. Bludgeoning seals to manufacture coats, and slaughtering elephants to produce ivory jewelry and knick-knacks, are indeed obscenities and should be discouraged.

Yet, despite my devotion to these causes, I found my heart lay out in the bush. The urban routine oppressed me. And New York in particular seemed to generate its own type of unnerving intensity.

Friends of Animals chased me out of the office from time to time — once to the Bering Sea to look at seal populations and gather information on the commercial slaughters that were conducted

there. Other times I ambled down to Georgia swamps to study
relations between the timber industry and wildlife conservation and
up the Connecticut coastline to help migrating geese steer clear of
areas where hunters lay in ambush.

Judy, Joe, and I also made several visits to Israel during the
1970s. Judy's whole family lived there, and, of course, I seized
every opportunity to visit Hai-Bar.

During these years I learned that real nature protection requires
a proper education. It is not enough to say that it is "wrong" to
manipulate habitats in order to increase populations of hunted
species. One must be able to demonstrate why such policies are
wrong and to provide sound alternatives for reform.

This meant I had to get some more education, so I enrolled in
New York University's graduate school. I specialized in biology and
delighted in each course. One semester I pursued protozoology and
studied large populations of microscopic animals whose existence
was confined to a single drop of water. Another semester brought
me a class in field biology and ecology, and our teacher, Professor
Alfred Perlmutter, revealed to us the other end of the habitat
spectrum. The Atlantic Ocean became our "laboratory," and we
studied every manner of fish and clam and seaweed.

All the while, I kept in contact with Hai-Bar. While in the
United States, I helped with some publicity and fund-raising and
even with the acquisition of several animals from American zoos.

Avraham Yoffe also kept in contact with me. We corresponded
often. And when I went to Israel, or he came to the United States,
we would visit one another. I was flattered by the interest he took
in my work, my schooling, and my peripheral help to Hai-Bar. At
each meeting, he would tell me that New York City was no place
to raise a child, and I was inclined to agree. He persistently urged
me to pack up the entire family and move to Israel and we were
encouraged to do so also by many friends and family members as
well.

Judy and I talked about moving several times. Certainly, New
York was a center of the art world and important to her career. But
there were other considerations, and it was a difficult decision to
make.

On a warm day in June 1980, Avraham Yoffe called me at home. "Mike Van Grevenbroek has left Hai-Bar," he announced. "After a decade of working with wildlife, he has decided to become a farmer and raise ostriches. I now have a recently retired military officer running the place, but this is just an interim solution. He is not making wildlife his career."

"I want to offer the job to you," the general continued. "I know you love Hai-Bar, that you've worked there as a volunteer, and that you've been helping from the outside since nearly the beginning of things. So now it's yours for the asking. I only require that you agree to stay on for at least one year. Why don't you talk it over with Judy and let me know as soon as you can?"

It was like an earthquake. Taking over at Hai-Bar meant uprooting my family and moving seven thousand miles east, from all the sophisticated living of New York to the blistering-hot, provincial desert town of Eilat. It meant selling a house, severing all sorts of social relationships, and numerous other changes.

But it would be for the good. Judy was born in Tel Aviv and had at least some inclination to return to Israeli life-styles and hear Hebrew as the language of everyday life. Joe was just coming to school age, but I couldn't afford to send him to a private school in New York, and I was apprehensive about sending him to public schools. Reports of hard drugs and violence, even in the elementary schools of New York, were frightening. Judy and I agreed it would be better to educate him in a more secure and socially stable system.

We moved quickly. In a matter of weeks, all arrangements had been made, we had set up house in Eilat (at 637 Patio, where Mike had lived until he decided to become an ostrich farmer), Joe was enrolled in *Kita Aleph* (first grade), Judy was invited to teach art classes at the town's cultural center, and I was riding a sorrel mare around the desert looking for broken fences.

There was a brief change-over period after I arrived, but soon I assumed full control of the reserve. I was provided with three helpers. Nathan Minkovski brought a pair of broad, strong shoulders to the reserve, along with a strong commitment to wildlife conservation and a penchant for practical jokes. Eran Krystal was more thoughtful and gentle. He seemed absolutely

compatible with the stillness of the desert. Shmuel Bin-Nun
worked as our gatekeeper and spent his days controlling the flow of
tourists in and out of the reserve.

We worked as a team through the Israeli work week from Sunday
to Friday, and on Saturdays, we took turns going to the reserve to
perform the essential chores.

Actually, I was most enthusiastic about going to Hai-Bar on
Saturdays because of the delightful holiday atmosphere. Sometimes
I'd pile the whole family, plus a friend or two, into the reserve's
Peugeot pickup truck on Saturday morning, and we'd spend the day
tending animals, having a picnic, and relaxing in the sunshine.

Frequently, I'd take Joe and one or two of his classmates to
Hai-Bar on Saturdays, for this was a child's paradise, and Joe could
show off his donkey-riding skills.

Often, Joe and I would be alone at the reserve on this one-day
Israeli weekend, and these became very special days for us. I wanted
to encourage a positive attitude toward wildlife, and Nature in
general, in my son, and I figured the best way to do this was simply
to let him be among all the animals and desert habitats of Hai-Bar.

He soon learned how to split a bale of hay and spread it in feeding
racks. And he learned how to measure out a bucket of concentrated
feed and then apportion it to the several animals we had to keep in
smaller enclosures. He found tremendous happiness in tending the
smaller animals, especially the occasional orphan, which were
hand-reared and fed with baby bottles. Happily, he learned to
distinguish white oryx antelope from scimitar-horned oryx antelope
before second grade — a zoologist in the making!

Not every Saturday at Hai-Bar was a delight, however. I recall
one day, after I had been there only for a short while, spent loading
hay into a wagon.

I was there with Joe, and while I stood atop the haystack,
heaving bales into the wagon below, I watched him disappear into
a small enclosure where we kept Lightning, Joe's donkey.

I continued tossing forty-four-pound bales of hay into the wagon
until I heard a terrible cry right beneath me. Joe had decided to
sneak up on me and had been very successful until he crawled into
the wagon that was being loaded with hay. A bale I had tossed hit

squarely and threw him against the steel frame of the wagon. He landed directly on his chin.

A quick wash revealed a nasty gash. It was obvious we'd have to rush to a doctor. Wrapping Joe's head in at least ten feet of gauze bandage, I lifted the frightened child into the pickup truck and raced south to Eilat.

Driving into the Eilat hospital parking lot, I rushed Joe into the emergency room, and, to our astonishment, we came face to face with Zohar Ohanna, the girl next door. Zohar was exactly Joe's age and shared a desk with him in their classroom. Every school-day morning either Joe would stop by her house or she would come by our door, and they would walk to school together. In the afternoon, they would return home together and do homework. And there were quite a few Saturdays which they spent together at Hai-Bar. They were the best of friends.

At that moment, as Joe stood holding yards and yards of gauze against his bleeding chin, Zohar was doing precisely the same thing. It seemed she had sailed over the handlebars of her bicycle and received a wound identical to Joe's.

Both children were treated by the same physician, who that morning laced ten stitches — five each — beneath their youthful chins. The two received identical lollipops and were instructed to return at the same time to have their stitches removed. The next morning, as they sat at their shared desk, the entire class had a delightful time speculating what on earth could have happened to these children sporting identical bandages.

Joe was one of the more popular youngsters in class, not necessarily because he was bright or particularly good at sports but rather, I suspect, because he came from such an interesting home.

637 Patio was well known around Eilat as an unusual residence long before we arrived. The small building was owned by the Nature Reserves Authority, and for a decade before we moved in, Mike Van Grevenbroek had tended all his sick, lame, and lazy animals there. At one point, Mike and his wife, Agnes, were hand-rearing more than two dozen ibex kids in their back yard, which must certainly have been a full-time job plus. To start with, they had to sterilize, fill, and feed more than one hundred bottles of

milk daily. And then there were the cases of diarrhea and runny
noses, and all types of misfits and problems.

On another occasion, Mike came home with a little kitten he had
acquired from a sailor stopping over in Eilat's port. Peter, as the cat
was called, was an adorable creature, with soft fur, faint spots, and
a lean, greyhound-like stature. He was also lively and scampered
energetically here and there about the house. One peculiarity of
Peter's was that, unlike those of other cats, his claws could not
retract. Thus, when he ran across the tile floors, he created a
staccato click-click-click-click-click-click.

Only one cat in all the world has nonretractile claws, and as Peter
grew up, it became evident to anyone who peeked through the
vertical slats of the front gate that this cat was indeed a proper, if
unusually friendly, cheetah.

With such a cat roaming about the house, the Van Grevenbroeks
were one of the few families who never gave a second thought to
purchasing locks or any other gadgets to protect their home from
burglars.

Thus, when we arrived, 637 Patio already had a well-established
reputation for being something of a wildlife sanctuary itself. We, of
course, fitted right into the pattern. My work was intimately
involved with the care of wildlife, and Joe had a very natural child's
fondness for animals. Judy, too, had a weakness for animals, an
interest cultivated over many years. Even as a child, she tended pet
monkeys, which she let swing freely through the trees of Tel Aviv.
And as a high school student, she had worked part-time taking care
of animals after school in the Tel Aviv Zoo.

We had a neighbor named Gita who worked as a secretary in the
local office of the Society for the Protection of Nature in Israel. One
day, soon after we moved in, Gita told me that a stray shepherd dog
had been found abandoned in the Sinai Desert. The animal had been
brought to the Society's local field study center. Perhaps I would be
interested in adopting him?

I drove out to the center and found an enormous shepherd lying
in the shadow alongside the building. When I approached, he
climbed to his feet, laid his ears back, and lifted his lips to show
some very impressive teeth. I could see that he was quite thin and

uncared for; and despite the aggressive features of his face, the rest of his body displayed signs that he was actually afraid. His back was arched, and his tail was drawn between his legs. He seemed prepared to run away at the slightest provocative gesture.

I decided to avoid making any provocative gesture. Walking around to the center's kitchen, I negotiated a nice piece of raw chicken from the cook. Back by the dog, I sat down in the shade just five or six yards away and tossed half of the chicken piece on the ground midway between us.

The dog stared at it and then at me. But he was reluctant to move immediately. So we sat and passed a quarter hour. At this point, it might be useful to mention that through quite a few years of working with many species of animals, I have learned that the most valuable technique that can be applied to working with animals is relaxed, yet disciplined, patience. The worst sort of catastrophe occurs when something is forced upon a reluctant animal.

We sat for another quarter hour. Eventually, the dog stood, stretched, looked around, and step by step moved toward the piece of chicken. I watched without moving. When the dog was within reach of the meat, he snatched it quickly and backed away before eating it.

It must have tasted quite good to him, because within another five or six minutes he came to my hand to take the rest of the meat. From that moment, we started building a friendship that lasted through the six years that remained of his life.

I brought the dog home and began to call him Whyah, a Cherokee word that means "wolf" — and certainly this large, gaunt canine did look very much like a wolf. After talking with a number of people and assessing a number of factors, from the sores on his feet to the flow of international politics, I decided on the most likely scenario of this dog's earlier life.

At this time part of the Sinai had been returned to Egypt as the result of the Camp David Peace accords, and Israel was preparing to return the remainder of the peninsula. During the Israeli occupation of the Sinai, there had been a relatively relaxed attitude toward visiting the region. Nearly anyone could wander nearly anyplace.

This attitude attacted a number of young people, especially from

western Europe and the United States, who built small shacks along
the beaches and adopted an easy life of playing music and trading
with local Bedouin tribes. Many of these settlements kept
animals — chickens, donkeys and, of course, dogs.

I suspect Whyah had lived in one of these settlements. He
probably shared in the carefree life along the beach for a year or two
until peace was made. But soon after the peace agreement was
signed, the beach people learned that the Egyptians had no
intention whatsoever of letting the relaxed atmosphere continue. As
soon as the Egyptians reoccupied the western beaches of Sinai, all
the squatters were cleared away. The holiday was over. Many just
picked up their belongings and returned to Europe or America —
minus the animals they had acquired.

It's my impression that Whyah was one of these animals
abandoned in the desert. He had become entirely dependent upon
human generosity to provide him with food. And when that
generosity vanished, he suffered.

He wandered a considerable distance for a long time, or so his
sore feet and gaunt condition suggested. But otherwise he appeared
to be in good health and just the sort of animal that would be useful
from time to time in my work.

At home, we brought the dog into our family, tended his sores,
and began a program to train him in basic obedience. He soon
became absolutely devoted to the family.

Through the coming years, Whyah would not let a stranger enter
our front gate without approval from a family member. But once
that stranger won family approval, the dog became very friendly. At
Hai-Bar, Whyah quickly learned how to playact the role of an
aggressive alpha wolf in a program I devised to help our wild
equines prepare for life in the wild. But this same dog could also lie
beside a newborn gazelle and protect it from any harm, or care for
a newborn ibex as if it were his own pup.

We certainly had ample opportunity to observe the antics of ibex
kids. The infancies of J.R. and Buba demonstrate.

There was a palpable unease in the air when I entered Hai-Bar
early one morning in mid-March. The animals were restless and
paced about nervously. There were vultures circling overhead.

I went straight for the place directly beneath the densest concentration of vultures and found the problem. A female ibex was lying flat on the desert sand. She had died only moments earlier, while giving birth to the first ibex kid of the season.

When I arrived, her kid was only partially born, with just his head protruding from her birth canal. He struggled weakly.

I finished the delivery immediately, cleaned the newborn, gave him a brief physical examination, and as everything seemed in order, I set him in the sun to dry. I then dashed back to my medicine cabinet and found several sterile syringes. With these, I returned to the corpse of the mother ibex and began to milk her.

The mother's first milk is called colostrum and is vital to the survival of her infant. It is through this first milk that the newborn receives important immune globulins that protect it from many diseases, particularly enteric problems such as diarrhea and digestive disorders. From one perspective, a newborn without colostrum could be as vulnerable to infection as an AIDS victim.

Drops of colostrum trickled down into the open end of the syringes until I had milked more than forty milliliters into five syringes. From all the signs, I presumed the ibex had died only minutes before I arrived, and I thought her milk would still be good.

Setting four syringes in a pan of evaporating water, in an effort to begin the cooling process, I took the fifth syringe and brought it to the newborn. Slipping the plastic tip into the corner of his mouth, I slowly began to feed him the rich and vital fluid.

At about this time, my helper Nathan walked into the ibex enclosure. His eyes widened as he took in the situation. "Quick, Nathan, collect those four syringes and take them to Yotvata," I asked. "Put one of the full syringes in a refrigerator, and put the rest into the freezer. Carry them with care, as if some lives depend upon them. And while you're there, call Judy and ask her to run to the Mashbir department store and buy some baby bottles, nipples, and a sterilizing rack."

As Nathan rushed off to the kibbutz, I continued feeding the infant, drop by drop, from the plastic syringe. The newborn was weak and did not feed with any vigor. Nevertheless, I deliberately kept the feeding at a rate even slower than he could have managed because I didn't want the slightest risk of his vomiting a drop of this precious fluid.

The optimum time for an infant to nurse on colostrum is within six hours of birth. After twelve hours, it is virtually worthless, because the newborn's intestines quickly lose their ability to absorb the immune globulins.

It took me nearly a full hour to feed ten milliliters of colostrum — no more than three teaspoons — to the infant ibex. But every last drop of it went down and stayed down. With this job done, I set the kid down into a niche among the rocks piled in the ibex enclosure and went to work on one of the less appealing aspects of wildlife conservation.

Nathan and I set up an autopsy table outside the ibex yard but within sight of the niche where I had placed the newborn. We had to perform a postmortem examination of the dead animal, and I wanted to keep the infant in view at all times.

The examination passed without revealing anything significant except that the ibex was quite old and most likely had died from exhaustion during delivery. When we were done, Nathan and I hoisted the carcass into the back of the Peugeot pickup, and Nathan drove it out into the unfenced western part of the nature reserve. There he set the body on the earth, said a few words, and left a few wildflowers upon it. It fed eagles and vultures, wolves and foxes, through the following days, for all these feed upon carrion.

As a general rule, I prefer to leave carcasses in that area. Wildlife feeds wildlife. Our practice of saying a few words and leaving some flowers are signs of respect for the dead creatures, which, we must accept, are our distant kin.

Meanwhile, I busied myself with a number of chores in the work area, all the while keeping a watchful eye on the newborn. A few does late in their pregnancies passed by the youngster, but their interest appeared to be little more than curiosity. It was very unlikely that any of them would want to adopt him, for they would soon have infants of their own to tend. It was clear that this youngster would be my responsibility for quite some time.

Late that morning, I assigned Nathan the task of being the kid's watchman, while I drove to the kibbutz to fetch the refrigerated colostrum syringe. Returning, I warmed the syringe and its contents in our coffeepot and then brought it to the newborn ibex. This time, the infant seemed much stronger than he had at the first feeding, and he pulled at the syringe with considerable vigor. But I was as miserly as before with the colostrum and fed it only one drop at a time. It took more than a half hour to complete the feeding.

With that accomplished, I finished up a few chores around the reserve and prepared to go home early. "You're the boss this afternoon," I told Nathan. "I've got to go back to Eilat and take care of this little one." But I did nothing of the sort, for when I got home, Judy literally confiscated the infant ibex from me. I knew from the start that this kid would grow up to be an absolutely spoiled brat. And I was right.

The kid had his own little padded crib, which was set in our bedroom. Judy put him on a diet of pure cow's milk and plenty of tender loving care. Our own dinner was provided by giving young Joe a few shekels and sending him off to buy falafal for the family.

The infant slept precisely three hours from his 10:30 P.M. bottle until his 1:30 A.M. concert. *Gweee, gweee, gweee,* he sang from his crib.

"He wants to eat," Judy muttered from the depths of her maternal wisdom.

"Fine," I replied. "You can feed him."

"Yes, I will," she said. "Just as soon as you warm the bottle in the refrigerator and bring it to me."

Dutifully, I shuffled off to the kitchen, fetched the prepared bottle, heated it in a pan of water, and shuffled back to the bedroom. "Here," I said, passing the newly warmed bottle to Judy, who had the baby ibex comfortably nestled down on my pillow. No matter. I didn't need a pillow anyway. I lay down, yawned once, and slipped into unconsciousness.

At 4:30 A.M., I felt Judy poking me in the ribs. In the darkness, I could hear that innocent *gweee, gweee, gweee.*

"I know, I know, you'll feed the cute little darling if I run off to the kitchen and fetch the bottle and heat it and bring it here," I muttered as I stumbled out of bed. I recall stubbing my toe on the way out of the room.

Nobody got a full night's sleep that week. But the little ibex grew in strength and vigor. During the second week, I started to bring him to Hai-Bar with me each morning, and release him among the other ibex so he could spend at least part of those important formative days with his own species — and indeed, with ibex his own age, for by now other does were giving birth to their kids, and the ibex enclosure was alive with scampering newborns.

Sometime during the second week, the little ibex began to sleep through the night, and we all rejoiced.

Two days after my first full night's sleep I came home from work with another newborn ibex, and we started the whole process of middle-of-the-night feedings all over again. The second kid was a female, and she was as white as Santa Claus's beard.

She was one of triplets. As is normally the case among ibex, when a doe delivers triplets, she immediately rejects one of them for she knows she has only enough milk to nurse two. The odd one — in this case, our little snowflake — is simply abandoned. Fortunately, I saw the triplets within a couple of hours of their birth and could intervene on behalf of the rejected kid.

I retrieved the dose of frozen colostrum stored at the kibbutz, thawed it, and fed it drop by drop to the latest foundling. And then the kid was introduced to the same routine we used for her older step-brother.

The little lady had many names from the start. She was called Snowflake for a while, although Nathan insisted on calling her Tnuva, after Israel's national dairy cooperative. But Judy called her Buba, a Hebrew word that means doll. And that name stuck.

Buba's step-brother didn't have any identity problems at all. He had only one name from the start — J.R. The kid was named after the infamous J.R. Ewing of the popular "Dallas" television series, and, like his namesake, our little kid was constantly creating all sorts of trouble.

It was J.R. who would bound onto our supper table in the evening, grab a leaf of lettuce from someone's plate, and then leap off — often knocking over a glass in the process — to dine on the treat at his leisure.

It was J.R. who sneaked into Joe's room one evening, bounded up on his bed, and was sick on Joe's Mickey Mouse pillow!

It was J.R. whose mischief kept us all working a bit later than usual every day of the week, cleaning, repairing, and tidying up in his wake of destruction. And it was J.R. who kept us perpetually entertained with his precocious and daring antics.

During the days at Hai-Bar, J.R. could sometimes be seen lowering his infant (and hornless) head and charging full tilt into one of the big rams fifty times his size. The large males were amused by the youngster and tolerated him with benevolent indifference.

Buba, on the other hand, was a perfect lady. During the evening, she would leap gracefully as a miniature ballerina to our living room couch and recline, with her legs neatly folded beneath her, beside Joe. That was our music hour — Joe's nightly struggle with violin practice. Buba was the only one who could sit through the discord with any poise at all, for Joe's playing was anything but soothing.

The animals brought a sense of warmth and extended family to our new home, as we launched into the adventure of life at Hai-Bar.

Desert Storm

ALL THE DUST of Saudi Arabia and at least half of the sand seemed to be carried on the harsh southerly wind. We stood and watched in awe, as the desert storm obscured the ancient Mountains of Edom just across the border in Jordan. The advancing great brown shroud would engulf us in a few moments, but we remained outdoors, contemplating this majestic tempest as it loomed menacingly close. I had never seen the hand of Nature moving so dramatically, so solemnly.

The animals also sensed the coming of the great storm, and they instinctively huddled together. Oryx antelope gathered in their herds and lay down on the lee side of large salt bushes. The smaller and more fragile gazelles pressed their delicate bodies close against any defense — low sand dunes, boulders, or the trunks of desert acacia trees — to protect themselves from the imminent onslaught. Ostriches, addax, and ibex also ran for cover. Only the onagers, those incredibly tough and intractable Asian wild asses, stood their ground before the storm.

The dark cloud began to close in on us. The animals, which were scattered among their makeshift shelters only a few hundred yards to the south of us, faded from view, lost within the gritty brown haze. Wind-blown sand pelted my face and hands with a painful sting. I scooped up six-year-old Joe, who was standing close beside me, and we made a dash to our little prefabricated bunkhouse about twenty yards away. We reached the door just in time.

The storm hit like a cloudburst. But instead of a downpour of rain, we were besieged by sheets of swirling sand and dust pushed by a howling gale. The little bunkhouse grew dark, and as I groped around for a flashlight, I heard the corrugated roof groan under the steady pressure of the wind. The whole south wall of the building hissed under the impact of the flailing sand. "Don't worry, Joe," I tried to assure the frightened little boy, "This place was built by a Dutchman!" The roof groaned again, and I wrapped the boy in a blanket and tucked him under one of the steel frame beds, just in case the Dutchman had missed a few bolts.

Wind-driven sand threw itself against the door, and little wisps of it penetrated through the slight crack between the bottom of the door and the floor. But I was more concerned about all the dust that was filtering in. The air was thick with it, and I could feel it collecting on my lips and in my nose. Grabbing an armful of empty feed sacks, I searched along the windward side of the building and stuffed them into every little hole, slit, and crack I could find, until our little shanty was tight and snug.

The storm howled and growled, but the bunk house seemed to be holding its own. "Want to come out?" I asked Joe. "Soon," he replied. The storm continued with unrelenting fury. I went to the window and aimed my flashlight outside, but the air was so dense with flying sand and dust that I couldn't cast a beam against the pepper tree, barely five feet beyond. "Want to come out now?" I asked again. "Just a bit longer," came the apprehensive voice from beneath the bed.

"OK, do what you want," I called back to him. "But I'm going to sit out this storm emptying Coca-Cola bottles and bags of Beezlees. That's the best way I know of to get all this dust off my lips. And you're welcome to join me at any time you choose." That invitation brought him wriggling out from under the bunk before I could get the first bottle opened. "Here, let me do that," Joe insisted with a tone that suggested he doubted his father's competence in such an important matter. "Do you think Lightning's all right?" he asked. "I do hope so," I said. "Donkeys are pretty tough critters, and Lightning has better protection than most of the animals here. We'll check on him just as soon as the worst of this blows over.

We had barely finished our Coca-Colas and the cellophane bag of
Beezlees — a crunchy Israeli snack food — still had a few tidbits
within, when the storm began to break. Within two or three
minutes, the light outside changed from a dark and dusky umber to
shades of sepia and cinnamon and ochre, until the sun broke
through with a brightness that made us squint. "Think it's safe to
go out now?" Joe asked. "I've *got* to check on Lightning."

"It looks all right," I said. "Let's see if we can dig our way out
of here." But no digging was necessary, for there was only an inch
or two of sand piled in front of the door. "Must be that sand is
simply noisier than snow flakes," I thought.

Outside, we found the whole area had survived the big blow
pretty much intact. The only damage I noticed was that the
sign that had once hung by the side gate had been blown from its
hinges and was lying face up on the ground about ten yards away.
Well, at least the birds would be able to read its message —
Hai-Bar Arava National Wildlife Reserve — Israel Nature Reserves
Authority — Please Use Main Gate, Two Kilometers North and
One Kilometer East.

Joe had already sprinted around back, and by the time I got
there, he was carefully inspecting his shaggy, chocolate-brown
donkey. "Is he OK?" I asked.

"Seems to be," Joe said, "except I think his coat just vacuumed
up all the dust from the storm." He patted his pet donkey several
times, and with each pat, a little puff of desert dust erupted.
"You've got enough work here to keep you busy until lunchtime,"
I told Joe. "But before you start working on Lightning, I suggest
you bring him some fresh water. He's probably very thirsty after all
that dust, and his own water tub has turned to mud."

Joe set about tending Lightning — the slowest donkey in the
Negev Desert (except when it was time to eat) — and I had
somewhere around three hundred seventy other critters to check.
Saddling up Whiskey, our sorrel mare, I prepared to make a quick
tour of the reserve. I filled one side of the horse's saddle bags with
a number of hand tools and the other with binoculars and a canteen
of water. "I'll be back in an hour or two," I told Joe. "You keep
working with Lightning and his corral, but keep a watch out for

storms. The wind might change and blow that monster right back here. Or another one might blow up from the south. So just stick close around the bunkhouse and run right inside if the weather turns bad again."

"OK, Abba," Joe said. I swung into the saddle and started moving off toward the south at an easy trot. My first objective was to check the main area's twelve-kilometer fence to see if the storm had blown any of it down. This, of course, was the most important chore after the storm, but it was also the most appealing. I had come to love the desert while riding fence patrol — and was getting paid for enjoying myself!

In all, the Hai-Bar reserve embraces thirty-five square kilometers of desert wilderness, just about forty kilometers due north of the Red Sea port of Eilat. Hai-Bar stretches across the Israeli half of the broad Arava Valley, from the border with Jordan (which is figured at the lowest seam of the valley — where a stream would run, if there was one) and up into the Negev Mountains to the west, with desert peaks rising to about eighteen hundred feet. Only part of this, of course, is enclosed for the wildlife restoration project.

I urged Whiskey along the fence line at an easy trot. She was a spirited horse, and on a day like this — following a major sand storm — she was the best transportation and working companion available. Whiskey could move through any sand dunes that might have drifted across the fence line much more easily than a tractor. Riding horseback was also much quieter, and this let me hear any tell-tale noises that might be expected after such a storm — the cries of an injured bird blown down from its perch by the harsh winds, or the bleating of a young fawn separated from its mother while the dust and sand swirled across the desert.

Whiskey responded to verbal commands to move forward and to halt. With a stout rope and a few levers, I've been able to reset fallen fenceposts in just a few minutes by using Whiskey's horsepower to provide the brawn. More important, however, were Whiskey's excellent herding instincts. She would have made a fine cowboy's steed in the Old West, alert, responsive, energetic. But this day, I was concerned about something a bit more unnerving than stray cattle — my worry concerned wolves.

Israel's desert wolves are incredibly smart and unbelievably numerous. When there was a break in the fence it was a race between me and them to see who found it first. If a wolf got into the reserve, there would be bedlam until I chased it out again. And that was Whiskey's finest talent — with her, I could circle around any prowling wolf and gradually herd the predator back toward the break in the fence or to some other exit point and then chase it out of the reserve. When this is done quickly and efficiently, Nature wins — the endangered species are properly protected, and the wolf is free to conduct its own life back outside, where it belongs. Wolves, incidentally, are also endangered. They deserve, and get, full protection in Israel. It just takes a little wildlife management, and a reliable horse, to keep one endangered species from eating another.

We trotted out across the desert for two kilometers until we reached the main area's southwest corner, where we turned east. Another two kilometers brought us to the most barren part of the reserve. From here and toward the east, the desert is perfectly flat and completely desolate. Not a blade of grass grows out of this plain for another six kilometers — which is more than five kilometers into Jordanian territory.

We turned north for the next four kilometers and followed the fence line, first across the flat desert plain and then into a region of scattered dunes ranging from six to twenty feet high. To our east was a narrow strip of military zone that is patrolled day and night by the Israel Defense Forces. Beyond that is a border fence and then the Hashemite Kingdom of Jordan. The craggy face of the biblical Mountains of Edom was now clearly visible again, for the last of the storm had faded far from view toward the north. Those mountains were magnetically appealing to me — a forbidden fruit lying just across the border — and one day, if peace ever comes to this frontier, I'd love to climb up into their steep and stony peaks.

We turned west again, away from the border zone. This part of the Hai-Bar fence runs along the edge of Kibbutz Yotvata's date palm plantations, and the rich green foliage is always a soothing sight for desert-strained eyes. We wove through a small grove of thorny acacia trees on our side of the fence; at one point I had to dismount and walk on foot, just to make sure the fence was intact as it ran through a dense part of the thicket.

About a kilometer along this stretch I came to the main gatehouse, another prefabricated concrete building, where our watchman, Shmuel Bin-Nun, checked tourists in and out of the reserve. "Shmulik" was a likeable gentleman, nearing retirement. As I approached, he was busily sweeping a good quantity of dust and sand from the little house. "Morning, Shmulik! Taking up indoor gardening?" I enquired.

"Ahhhhh. A window broke during the storm," he replied. "The place is a mess inside. Papers, receipts, booklets, everything's blown all over the place."

"Did we have any visitors inside the reserve during the storm?" I asked. "Nobody," he said. "There hasn't been a single visitor all morning."

"Just fine," I said. "You can admit any tourists who come, though. There's very little damage inside. In fact, it looks as if most of the damage has been sustained right here in your gatehouse. I've got to finish patrolling the fence. See you later. *L'hitraot*!"

"*L'hitraot*, Bill," he called. "How's little Joey doing in all this stormy weather?"

"He got a little nervous when it first set in. But he's fine now. Pampering that donkey of his." Whiskey and I trotted farther west, until we reached the northwest corner, and then turned southward for the last leg of the patrol, in some respects the nicest. Along this route is *Ein Radiana*, a natural oasis with remarkably sweet water. According to current tradition, the spring — or *ein* in Hebrew — takes its name from Diana, the Greek goddess. Most desert springs are terribly brackish and concentrated with bad-tasting minerals, but this one is extraordinarily pure. Around the spring grow scores of lovely palm trees and other vegetation, making the oasis one of the most exotic and enchanting sites in the region. There are also a few ancient ruins, which archaeologists have begun to probe, near the oasis. Historians believe that the ruins are very likely the remains of an old caravansary because it is just about one day's hard ride from the Red Sea — or about two day's drive for a camel caravan — right along the main Arava Valley route that opens the best highway from the Red Sea and all the ports of the Indian Ocean to Jerusalem. Some think it might even be the site of the biblical Yotvata, a camp not far from Eilat, where the Children of Israel rested during the Exodus.

A bit farther along the fence line we returned to the work area. The patrol took a little more than an hour, and as I dismounted from Whiskey, I saw that Joe had nearly finished restoring Lightning and his paddock to first-class shape. "How's the fence?" Joe asked.

"Just the way it ought to be," I said. "There's no damage to the fence at all. But you should see Shmulik's gatehouse. Looks like the inside of a goat's stomach!"

"Want to check the animals now?" was Joe's next question.

"Want to come?" was mine.

I unsaddled Whiskey and turned her loose into the large corral for a rest. Next, it was Daliah's turn, and I fetched the big white mare for a walk across the desert. Daliah's an easygoing horse, not as spirited as Whiskey, perhaps, but guaranteed a softer ride. I slipped only a bridle and blanket on her, not bothering with a saddle for this excursion. Once on her back, I reached down for Joe, and with a quick heft, he was sitting on the big mare with me.

Our tour took us directly to the south end of the reserve, and from there we zigzagged back and forth across the low-growing *alhagi* brush and salt bush, weaving our way northward. With this technique, we never had to look directly into the sun as we searched for lost or injured animals.

We circled around a herd of African wild asses, or *arod* as they are called in Hebrew, and they all appeared quite well. I counted heads and made a note in my diary. Farther along, a few gazelles leapt out from the brush and darted off toward the west, leaving a disproportionately large cloud of dust behind them. Evidently, they had just nestled down into the vegetation for the storm, had become liberally covered with dust, and hadn't moved a muscle until we came along.

The scimitar-horned oryx herds, or *re'em sahara* in Hebrew, were gathered around one of the watering tubs that I had scattered through the desert reserve. They were bemoaning their fate —

mooing like dairy cattle at a barn gate. It seemed that the storm had done the same thing to their tub that it had to Lightning's water — turned it to sticky, oozy mud. We rode over, dismounted, and spilled the mudbath out onto the sand. Fresh water immediately gushed from the hose that was connected to the tub, and we cleaned away all the dirt and mud. Within five minutes, the tub was spic and span, filled with fresh water, and the oryx antelope were happily guzzling its contents.

We continued our lazy zigzag across the desert range, wandering for a few kilometers across an open sandy area, where the highest vegetation is no more than a foot above the ground, and across some parts where the earth is completely bare. Here and there, we passed through occasional thickets of acacia — tough trees of the desert, which in times of severe drought can go without a drop of water for years. Toward the northeast, we wandered into a bit of dune country and noticed that many dunes had fox burrows dug into their bases.

Hai-Bar is a paradise for the foxes. The main protective fence has a wire mesh, which is certainly tight enough to exclude predators such as wolves and hyenas. But the mesh isn't tight enough to exclude foxes, so they can pass in and out of the reserve at will. Mostly, they prefer to be inside the reserve, because here they are the largest predators and have no competition from the larger carnivores found outside. This was fine with me, because foxes aren't big enough to pose a serious threat to the reserve's antelopes, ostriches, and other animals, and they can feast on desert mice, gerbils, and jerboas, which are quite numerous in the reserve.

Throughout our ride, I kept a tally of the animals in my daybook — so many addax, onagers, ostriches, ibex, and oryx. I never tried to tally the gazelles — there should have been about ninety. Our formal gazelle census is taken but once a year, because it is a very difficult task that requires many people and several vehicles. But all the other large animals are quite easy to count, and by the time we had circled through Ein Radiana at the northwest corner of the reserve, all the animals were accounted for.

"Seems to me, these critters can handle themselves pretty well when left out in a sandstorm," I observed.

"And they didn't even have any bunk beds to hide under!" quipped my six-year-old helper.

We trotted back to the work area, released Daliah back into the large corral with Whiskey, and then hitched the trailer to our Massey-Ferguson tractor. After loading sixteen forty-four-pound bales of hay into the trailer and seating Joe atop the stack, we started chugging back out into the reserve to serve a supplementary feeding to the animals.

We linked into the ten-kilometer loop road that runs around the central part of the reserve, and then, about a kilometer from the work area, we turned off the road across a patch of soft sand. I stopped the tractor for a moment, hopped off, and raked over the tractor tire tracks where they led off the road — I didn't want any foolish tourist taking note of the tracks and trying to drive off into the sand. Such expeditions often led to disasters — such as tourists getting all bogged down in the soft sand and my having to pull them out with the tractor. Besides, the tourists could see well enough if they simply stayed on the road and kept their eyes open.

For a while, when I first started to run the reserve, there was a bit of a problem with tourists not seeing any animals. Some of them would drive through the entire reserve, which has more than three hundred animals within its confines, and then complain that they hadn't seen a single critter. At first, I shrugged off these complaints. Hai-Bar, I'd remind them, is a wildlife restoration facility and not a safari park. Our work here was to restore endangered species to the desert and to teach those that had been confined in zoos, safari parks, and other institutions how to live in the wild. Performing for casual tourists was not part of what was expected of these animals, and, generally, I wanted to encourage animals to keep a safe distance from humans. I didn't want our antelopes and wild asses to become tame spongers like the bears at Yellowstone Park in the United States, which have become nuisances in some areas because of their constant begging for treats from tourists.

Although I tried to keep the wildlife and the tourists a respectable distance apart, I also realized that people coming into the nature reserve wanted to see the animals, and it was in the interest of conservation to encourage public support. So I devised a plan to bring most of the animals to a reasonable distance from the tourist road. This was done by creating a hidden tractor path parallel to the tourist road and about fifteen or twenty yards distant from it. Along this path, I distributed bales of fresh grass and alfalfa hay as a supplemental feeding for the animals. The food attracted the animals, and they frequently spent much time along the hidden path — either waiting for food, eating, or ruminating after the meal. This kept the tourists happy, because they could see the animals from just about as close as they are in a zoo but without all those objectionable bars and fences.

Joe and I chugged around the hidden path for a few minutes before reaching our first feeding area. The boy rolled a bale of hay off the wagon, and I cut its binding cords open. The bale was broken apart and tossed around an area of about fifty square yards. A herd of scimitar-horned oryx saw us and began wandering in our direction.

We were back on the tractor and moving before the antelopes arrived. In another kilometer or so, Joe tossed another bale of hay on the ground for me to open and spread around. This time, a herd of sixteen addax antelope were waiting to eat.

Driving along the hidden path, I took special care to follow a very precise route. The path, as laid out, could not be seen from the tourist road, but if I let the tractor wander off the path and didn't follow the route exactly, the way would become widened and eventually visible from the tourist road. And then my problems would start. Tourists, wanting to see the animals even more closely, would begin looking for ways to cross to the feeding areas. Some would get stuck in the sand. Some would frighten the animals. And all of them would crush the sparse and fragile desert vegetation.

I never worried too much about the ones who got stuck in the sand. It was a bit of a project for me to pull them out with the tractor, but it was usually much more difficult for them to get stranded out in the desert and then have to go for a five- or six-kilometer hike to look for someone to help them.

Very rarely, a tourist would insist on getting close enough to the animals to frighten them. Most often, however, the animals had the clear advantage and could keep a good distance from any tourist.

The animals are well adapted to the desert and can move about freely — something which can't be said for most tourists.

Most frustrating were the tourists who drove off the road and crushed the vegetation. Desert shrubs are very well adapted to go for months, and even years, without any water at all. They're also very well adapted to withstand intense solar radiation, extreme heat, and occasional nibbling by wildlife. But they are not adapted at all to the crushing weight of automobile tires. Unlike the shrubs of well-watered parts of North America or Europe, which can recover in days — or sometimes even hours — after an automobile has driven over them, desert vegetation frequently requires months, and sometimes years, to recover.

We followed the hidden path, dropping bales of hay here and there along the way, for about an hour and a half. When the feeding was finished, we drove the tractor out the north gate to pick up fresh alfalfa from Kibbutz Yotvata and to find a little snack for ourselves. Hai-Bar had a number of agreements with the kibbutz, and one of them involved their providing us with about two hundred pounds of fresh-chopped alfalfa every day. But we had to go pick it up, and I drove the two kilometers north along a dusty road to a site where the kibbutz alfalfa chopper dropped our ration every morning at about ten o'clock.

Joe had his own pitchfork and helped me heave the alfalfa into the trailer. It was sweet and cool and green. The little purple flowers were tasty tidbits that we chewed on as we finished tossing the greenery into the trailer. We had, however, a few additional tidbits in mind, and as soon as the alfalfa was loaded, we drove straight to the *miznon*.

The *miznon* is a snack bar operated by the kibbutz along the main Arava Valley highway. It serves a variety of typical snack bar foods — sandwiches, packaged cakes, and so forth — but the local people order Yotvata's best product — yogurt.

Yotvata has one of the finest dairy herds in Israel, and they provide fresh milk and dairy products throughout the southern Negev region. The yogurts, however, are phenomenal and are in constant demand throughout the entire country. Yotvata yogurts can be found as far away as Metulla and Qiryat Shemona on the

Lebanese border — the best milk product in the Land of Milk and Honey.

We ordered a couple of *prigurts* — yogurts laced with fruit. Mine was *toot-sadeh* (strawberry) and Joe devoured his *mishmish* (apricot). And then we bought a couple more.

Back in the reserve, we scattered the fresh-cut alfalfa around several feeding sites. Some of it went to the ostriches, which usually took their share directly from the trailer and didn't waste time waiting for it to be spread on their feed trays. And some of it was reserved for "special cases" around the work area.

Our special cases were the animals confined to individual enclosures that lined one end of the work area. This day we had an addax antelope with her sickly calf — fresh alfalfa would help her to produce a better-quality milk, which would assist in the calf's recovery. The next enclosure had a young oryx calf with his broken leg set in a plaster cast, and the next another oryx recovering from an eye injury.

A bit of fresh alfalfa was a treat for each animal. It was also a bit of extra nutrition, which would help with the healing process and compensate for the loss of natural vegetation that they would have browsed on out in the reserve. We carried the remaining few bucketfuls of alfalfa into the large enclosure populated by our nursery herd of ibex. Again, a ration of this feed was intended to help the nannie produce better milk and healthier kids. And, at the very end, I saved a few handfuls of alfalfa for old Napoleon, an aged oryx antelope living out his retirement in this enclosure.

We had a few more projects, but since it was Saturday, we did only the essential work required for the health and well-being of the animals. Thus, there were a couple of afternoon hours for more leisurely activities — watching the ibex kids butt heads together in mock battles, visiting our "sick, lame, and lazy" paddocks to check on how each ailing animal was mending, and making sure they all had fresh water and clean bedding. At quitting time, we drove a reverse tour of the tourist road to find visitors still within the reserve. As they were gradually checked out, we picked up Shmulik at the gatehouse, locked up, and headed back to Eilat for the end of the day.

Forty kilometers of flat, straight desert highway rolled due south from Hai-Bar to our home in Eilat. Through most of the year, the afternoon ride was suffocating. If we closed our windows, the pickup truck would be like an oven, and if we opened them, it would be like a blast furnace. But the drive also afforded spectacular views of desert scenery as we raced across the *hamada* gravel plains of the southern Arava. The road paralleled the border with Jordan, and forbidding mountains rose to the east and west of us, facing each other as great, craggy stone walls of gritty sandstone, which, in some places, soared more than a kilometer skyward.

We arrived in the Red Sea port city of twenty-four thousand people within a half hour, dropped Shmulik by his front door, and then rolled down to our home.

Joe bounded out of the truck just as soon as the engine was switched off. He sprinted down a narrow walkway to our front gate, leapt up three steps, and bolted across the garden and through the front door, flipping an electric switch just inside the house. By the time I got in, he already had the most comfortable chair pushed to the best position in front of the desert cooler. I quietly accepted my fate and pushed the second-most-comfortable chair into the second-best position in front of the desert cooler. And the great clanking wind machine spilled soothing cool, moist air down upon us.

The Manicure

IRST, I decided to wait through the birthing season. Certainly, with so many infant ibex running around, we should avoid any real rough-and-tumble work with the herd. Then, I decided to wait through the heat of the summer. This project would be a real struggle, and I wouldn't want to risk heat prostration or any other similar catastrophe. And then, I decided to wait through the fall. This was the mating season for the ibex, so their hormone levels were up and they were more ornery and aggressive than ever.

The short desert "winter" — a mere cool spell with a few overcast days and, perhaps, a few odd drops of rain — was upon us. And I sat up late at night trying to think of a reason for putting off this unappealing project. But nothing came to mind. Obviously, I had procrastinated long enough, and now it was time for the showdown. It was time to clip hooves.

Our big male ibex, in particular, tended to suffer from overgrown hooves. In Nature, their normal daily activities keep their hooves worn down to just the right size. But in Hai-Bar, these animals had a somewhat different life-style. There was no need to migrate daily up into the safety of the high mountains or descend to a remote drinking place or leap across ravines to reach a few morsels of food. Here, the ibex had all their physical needs within easy reach.

The young and the female ibex tended to be more active, even within their enclosures. True, they did not have the freedom of the mountains, but they did have several acres of semi-natural desert habitat and a man-made mountain of sandstone boulders to climb upon.

The young kids and females enjoyed their exercise. They spent much time bounding among those big boulders, and I liked to encourage this by tossing hay up among the rocks to make them climb if they wanted to eat. But the mature males had little enthusiasm for such activity. They preferred to relax in the shade, right at ground level, and watch. Sooner or later a breeze would blow a bit of hay back down to them — or if the day was still, I'd eventually give in to their silent protests and provide hay to them right where they wanted it, on terra firma.

Thus, the only ibex that needed their hooves clipped were the lazy males who never climbed upon the rocks and let Nature do her less stressful type of manicure. Some of these males were getting badly overgrown hooves, and I was getting a bit concerned. First, if they ever did decide to climb onto the rocks, they'd very likely fall because their overgrown hooves wouldn't give them proper balance and traction. But more probably, the overgrown hooves would simply begin splitting and cracking, which could be painful for the animal and cause infection of the foot. Enough said. The hooves had to be trimmed back to normal size.

Clipping itself is a fairly easy task. The difficult part is the preclipping negotiations, during which the big male ibex must be persuaded to lie still for their manicures. I'd been through the procedure before and carried a few painful souvenirs — a couple of scars, a chipped tooth, and a bruised ego — it is not an easy operation.

No doubt about it, a mature male ibex is a tough critter. They're members of the goat family and, like male goats, they have little "goatee" beards hanging from their chins. But that's about where the similarity ends. A male ibex can weigh in at about 180 pounds, and he's solid muscle. To add persuasiveness to that muscle, he also has enormous horns that reach back over his head for more than a yard.

Hai-Bar's male ibex are regal, tough, and unpredictable. Conse-

quently, we had named them all after Roman emperors. There were
Caesar and Augustus and Tiberius and Caligula and Claudius and
Nero and Vespasian and Titus and all the rest. And not one of them
was a pushover.

Aided by my helpers, Nathan and Eran, I went into the ibex
enclosure early one morning to study the situation. Noting that
every big male there could use a trimming of his hooves, I advised
my assistants to make sure their Kupat Holim health insurance was
paid up. They both thought this was funny; after all, the ibex all
seemed so tame. How difficult could it be to trim a few toenails?
Obviously, neither of those fellows had ever been involved with a
project of this nature before.

While I began making plans to corner and capture ibex individ-
ually, Nathan said he wanted to try it his way first. Perhaps just a
simple little scuffle would suffice to wrestle the animal to the
ground, where he could be held still by two of us while the third
clipped his hooves. Unlikely, I thought, but why not try it? Brute
force might be used to keep the beasts still while they underwent
their manicures.

Nathan wanted to do the initial wrestling, and we agreed to join
in just as soon as he had a good grip on one of our "trimees."
Nathan was probably the strongest of the three of us, a big,
imposing fellow with powerful arms and a viselike grip. If any of us
could tackle an ibex, he could.

Nathan strolled out to the feed bin and scooped about a quarter
bucket of food concentrate pellets into a pail. He then sauntered
back into the ibex yard and stood about twenty yards away from us,
in an open part of the enclosure. All he had to do was shake the
pellets in the pail and the whole herd came trotting over. As usual,
the females and young arrived first, pushing and shoving each other
to get a handful of feed. And as usual, the big lazy males came last.
But rather than wait their turns, they simply put their heads down
and plowed into the crowd. Tiberius was the first big male to push
his way through to Nathan, and as a reward, Nathan offered him
the remains of the pellets in the pail. The big ibex plunged his face
into the bucket, and Nathan immediately seized one of his horns
and flipped him over.

The herd scattered in all directions, and Eran and I ran to help Nathan. In a few short seconds, Tiberius had regained his feet, but Nathan was still flat on the ground still hanging on to the ibex horn. Tiberius was simply backing away, dragging Nathan as he went.

Eran and I piled on the ibex, and down he went again. But not for long. With all three of us trying to hold him down, Tiberius flexed his muscles and stood up again. We tumbled off his back like raindrops spattering from an umbrella, and with a sudden leap, he broke free.

Tiberius sauntered off to rejoin the herd, while Nathan, Eran, and I lay on the sand, gasping for breath. For some reason, I thought, I recall seeing a similar incident in a kiddie cartoon in which an inveigling coyote tried to corner a quick-thinking, quick-moving roadrunner. . . .

We retreated from the enclosure to lick our wounds, scheme up a new technique for capturing the ibex, and return a newly dented pail to the feed bins. We made two more unsuccessful attempts that day and two more on the following day. Then we decided to get down to serious business and build a proper trap.

Our trap consisted of a newly built pen about six yards long and four yards wide with two gates. One gate opened into the main ibex enclosure. The other opened into a large, sturdy transport crate — the type used to move horses and other large animals. When the pen was completed, we moved a few square yards of stout netting in and set it on the ground. Next, we moved the ibex's watering tub into the pen. Any ibex wanting a drink would have to enter the pen.

We left the arrangement like this for three days. The ibex eventually got used to the idea of wandering into the little pen to get their drink of water, and through the day they'd drift in and out. The big males were very wary, but thirst finally persuaded them that they'd have to enter the little pen for a drink. And they, too, got used to the new arrangement.

When all appeared settled, we added another item. A thirty-yard rope was attached to the gate leading from the little pen to the ibex yard; with a tug of this rope, the gate could be swung shut. The other end of the rope was threaded out through the fence to a hide we built of old crates and transport boxes. Eran volunteered to sit in the hide and keep watch for the ibex. When one of the big ones entered the pen for a drink of water, he would yank the gate shut and lock him inside.

Eran simmered in the hide nearly all day long, but the big males were clearly distrustful. Some people claim animals don't have the power to reason — so perhaps it was all pure coincidence. But as Nathan and I watched from afar through binoculars, we saw the ibex stare at the rope tied to the gate. They also stared at the pile of boxes and crates where Eran was hiding. And they refused to go into the pen to drink.

A truce was called that evening; although the rope was left on the gate, Eran vacated the hide. As soon as he left, all the big male ibex went into the pen to drink.

Next morning, we decided to use a Trojan horse tactic. Nathan and I carried a large crate to the blind and set it down among the rest of the boxes piled there — the crate contained Eran. We walked away casually, but both of us could feel the penetrating gaze of all those ibex.

Eran slipped from his crate into the blind, apparently unnoticed, for only a half hour later, one of the big male ibex strolled into the pen for a drink. Caesar himself! The biggest, strongest, meanest ibex at Hai-Bar!

Eran yanked the rope so hard that he tumbled out of the blind — but hard enough also to close the pen gate with Caesar trapped inside. Nathan and I came racing out from the far side of the work area, where we had been restacking hay that morning, and saw Eran's victory. "Lovely, lovely," I said, congratulating Eran, "let's leave him alone in there for a while. Let him have his drink and calm down a bit. He's probably a bit upset right now."

About twenty minutes later, the three of us walked back to the pen where Caesar was captive and saw him resting near the gate. As we approached, he got up and started backing away. He put his horns down threateningly and turned up his upper lip. I don't know if that's a gesture of warning or of contempt, but he looked as if he meant to put up a fight.

"Maybe you should just dart him?" Eran suggested. "And we can trim his hooves while he's unconscious."

But I decided against that. First, as policy, I don't like to use drugs unless it's absolutely necessary and in the best interest of the animal. Even the safest drugs have certain risks. They tend to upset the metabolism. Besides, Caesar was already prepared for a fight, and this meant his adrenaline levels were up and would neutralize the standard Hellabruyn cocktail we normally use on ruminants.

Also, a bit of hard work would be good for all of us. I believed that Nathan and Eran, by working with a conscious, resisting animal, would learn a bit more about animal handling, would gain more confidence, and would gain greater respect for the ibex. Struggles like the one that would surely come would demonstrate to my helpers that wild animals are incredibly smart and resourceful. Ibex and goats might be classified in the same zoological genus — but there's a world of difference in their intelligence and vigor.

Finally, a bit of hard work would also be good for Caesar, who, despite his strength and intelligence, spent much too much time lying in the shade. It would do him good to use some of his strength and put his body under a bit of stress — he was tough and mature and still quite a few years away from enfeebled senility.

Entering the gate, we spread out at arm's length and slowly walked forward. We intended to gradually drive Caesar back into the big transport box standing open at the far side of the pen. Once he was in there, we could set up a heavy net by the door and then drive him back out again into the net. While he was entangled in it, we could tie him down and blindfold him for the hoof-clipping operation. But there was one hitch. Caesar was not going to enter that transport box.

He skillfully slipped between us and successfully avoided all our efforts to force him back into the box. After being knocked over twice as he nimbly evaded us, I decided to grab the net and try to toss it over him while he moved around the little pen. But Caesar had other ideas.

The ibex made a false dodge past Nathan, but midway through the rush, he swerved and butted him on the thigh. This knocked Nathan over and he tumbled straight into my arms — whereupon I fell over too. As we lay in a heap on the ground, Caesar decided to use us as a trampoline of sorts. He ran at us, and, using our bodies as a springboard, jumped on us and bounded from there over the fence.

He then sauntered off toward the watching ibex herd. They all seemed to be smirking at us. We were clearly embarrassed, and I do believe Caesar was somewhat smug — overgrown hooves and all.

Undaunted, we went back to our usual work; the following day, Eran was smuggled back into his hide, ready to slam the gate shut on any big male ibex who entered the little watering pen. Again, it was Caesar. Perhaps he was a bit overconfident, for he strode into the little pen with his head erect, not even bothering to look around the area before entering. When Eran pulled the rope and yanked the gate shut behind him, Caesar took no notice. Instead, he strolled over to the watering tub and took a long, cool drink.

Again, the three of us marched up to the pen to find Caesar reclining contentedly near the gate. As we entered, he began to back away, lower his horns, and turn back his upper lip in a sneering gesture. We then unfurled our secret weapon. Unrolling a sheet of heavy burlap that stretched from one side of the pen to the other, we marched forward very slowly. The burlap was spread evenly and loosely between us. If we held it tightly, a good butt from Caesar could probably knock one of us over again. But with the burlap held out loosely, his mightiest ram could be absorbed into the folds of the material. One step at a time, our curtain moved forward. Caesar charged, but uselessly. He only tangled his horns in all of our drapery. He backed away.

It took about ten minutes to cover perhaps ten steps. But slowly, slowly, Caesar was backed into the big transport box. Once he was inside, we slid the wooden door shut and locked it. He responded by charging and ramming the door from inside the box. The sound of the impact was explosive, but the door held. Caesar was safely locked within.

In the next step Nathan climbed on top of the box, right above the door, with the heavy entangling net. Eran prepared to open the door, and I stood directly in front but about four yards away from it.

"OK, Eran, open it," I said, and Eran deftly slipped the wooden door out of its slot. Caesar was about four feet into the box, standing still but with his horns poised to charge. Minutes passed and nothing happened. I walked closer to the door, trying to tempt Caesar. I even turned around and bent over to tie my shoe laces, offering the ibex one of the most tempting targets of his life. Still, no deal. And then I asked Eran to go around on the far side of the transport box and pound on it, perhaps driving the ibex out that way. Still, nothing.

Caesar kept us at stalemate for about a quarter hour, but I resolved to wait him out. I sat down on the earth and made myself comfortable, just to demonstrate to him that I planned to stay around for a long while.

I had barely gotten myself comfortable when Caesar charged. "Now!" I called to Nathan, and the big mesh net fell across the transport box exit. Caesar's momentum threw him right into that net, entangling him properly.

The three of us pounced on top of the struggling ibex and with the help of the net, managed to keep him subdued. My first objective was to slip a homemade blindfold over his eyes to keep him disoriented. The blindfold was made out of an old pant leg with a couple of ties extending from the top end. The pant leg was simply slipped up over his muzzle and then over his eyes. The open bottom gave him plenty of air to breathe and the ties at the top secured the pant leg to his horns.

With Caesar's eyes well blindfolded, I went to work securing his feet with my modified clove hitch. For this work, I prefer a well-used, cargo-parachute line. Being well-used, it's very soft and flexible, but because it's made for cargo parachutes, it's made to take tremendous jolting and has great tensile strength. By the time I was done with him, Caesar looked like Gulliver tied down in the land of the Lilliputians.

Clipping hooves is not a very complicated business. I prefer to use ordinary garden shears, sharpened to a good edge, and then a rasp and wood-working files. I shear the hooves a bit longer than natural and then file them down to near-natural size. This is a bit time-consuming, but it also serves as a safeguard against two problems. First, hooves that are trimmed too closely can sometimes bleed and cause the animal discomfort and soreness. And second, the filing gives an opportunity to round the edges of the hooves and thus prevents the edges from splitting and making an entrance for foot infection.

With the job done, we opened the pen gate and jostled Caesar into position so he'd see the opening just as soon as his blindfold was removed. I tossed a towel over his head just before the blindfold was taken off — thus maintaining darkness while the net and ropes were removed. We worked his body out of the entangling net, and then, with all three of us keeping hold just in case he lurched while his legs were being untied, I went to work on the nylon parachute ropes. They loosened quickly and I slipped them off. Caesar knew precisely when his fetters were released. It was like trying to contain a volcano with a garbage pail lid.

Caesar jumped erect and shed us effortlessly. The towel that covered his eyes fell to the ground. He was absolutely free and he saw the open gate. Within seconds he had charged through and, once clear, slowed down to his normal smug saunter as he strolled back to his herd.

During the following two weeks, we captured every one of the muscular male ibex and trimmed their hooves. Our only tough case following Caesar was Caligula, who, as soon as the pen gate slammed closed behind him, immediately attacked it. He rammed it a half dozen times before we could close in on him, breaking it from one of its hinges and seriously weakening the other.

Caligula put up an even greater struggle than Caesar and his fiery temper threw him into such a rage that we were wondering how to design a strait-jacket for an ibex. But even Caligula was tangled by the net and had his hooves clipped.

The whole project was done by Tu B'Shvat, the annual "birthday of the trees" in late January, which traditionally signals the coming of spring in Israel and is celebrated by planting trees. We celebrated by planting the hoof shears in the tool shed, vowing to leave them there for at least eleven months.

Napoleon

NAPOLEON had escaped from exile, and I expected another bloody battle. Horns down and waving, nostrils flared and snorting, the old bull was looking for a fight. The trouble was, he lost just about every fight he started. That's why I had put him in exile — a sort of protective custody to protect him from himself.

Napoleon was a scimitar-horned oryx (*Oryx dammah*), a large desert antelope, weighing in at about four hundred pounds. This species also has a pair of mighty impressive scimitar-shaped horns, which sweep back over their heads for more than a yard. The scimitar-horned oryx is a native of North Africa's Sahara Desert and once ranged from the Nile clear across to Morocco and from the Mediterranean southward for more than a thousand miles. Its range covered about four million square miles — a third of Africa. Today, the species is reduced to a very fragile remnant of perhaps a few-score animals on the border of Chad and Niger.

Israel maintains a population of scimitar-horned oryx in its Hai-Bar program as a hedge against the extinction of the species, and Israeli conservationists hope that some day, if Israel finds peace with those North African countries, the Hai-Bar scimitar-horned oryx will form a nucleus for restoring the species to its native habitats. Meanwhile, a vigorous herd of more than five dozen of these animals thrives within the security of the Negev refuge.

Some years before our story, Napoleon had been the dominant male of the Hai-Bar scimitar-horned oryx herd. He'd strut around the reserve like the king of the desert, waving the two scimitars growing from the top of his head with a certain authority that required respect. Younger males would step aside for him. In fact, they'd jump aside.

Napoleon ruled with an unruly temper. For more than a decade, a single snort from this big bull could put the entire reserve on alert. But then, time imposed a condition that Napoleon couldn't accept. It made him old. His skin wrinkled and sagged. His strength ebbed. His bellowing became more like wheezing.

Although Napoleon was very, very old, and his horns were half their original length — worn smooth by countless battles — he still had the heart of a gladiator and the spirit of the Furies.

For a while, old Napoleon insisted on tagging along with the herd. He wouldn't behave like the other older bulls and go off to live his last days in peace and seclusion. But it appeared obvious to all the younger males that Napoleon's snorting and aggressive gesturing were only hollow threats. They generally ignored him.

Napoleon, however, discovered how to get their attention. He'd just saunter over to a few females and start acting like a romantic old fool. That was usually enough to enrage the younger bulls, and one of them would come charging over to teach Napoleon a lesson he seemed incapable of learning.

Because the horns of this species are curved back, it's impossible for the bulls to attack head-on. Instead, they sidle up from an angle and fight by lowering their heads and swinging those long, sharp horns upward toward the flanks and belly of their opponent. Napoleon knew all about this fighting technique, for in his younger years, he had inflicted quite a few wounds this way. More recently, however, he had been the one doing most of the suffering.

At Hai-Bar, we usually followed a policy of noninterference with animals exercising their natural behavior. In this context, a certain amount of dominance fighting was accepted. We interfered only when something *extraordinary*, such as a threat to the herd's social cohesiveness, happened, or when the life of an animal appeared seriously threatened.

So when Napoleon lost his dominance position to younger and stronger bulls, we left him alone to nurse his own wounds. And when he recovered and again challenged the newcomers and again lost the fight, we left him alone. He gradually recovered and the gashes healed. Soon he was looking for even more trouble.

He must have challenged the younger males a dozen or more times — losing each fight — before he started to sustain serious injury. After one nasty fight, I noticed that he was pretty battered — lame, bleeding a bit, and suffering from a bad goring wound just behind his rib cage.

That was enough for me. He had to be tended.

Catching an injured antelope can be quite dangerous — especially for the antelope. The main hazard is stress, particularly if the animal involved is high-spirited and has spent an entire lifetime with a great amount of freedom. Indeed, stress could be more dangerous to Napoleon than the combined threats of all his wounds. So the old bull had to be captured with as little force as possible, because I doubted that he could take much more strain.

In fact, stress itself is a mechanism that protects animals from extreme pain. For example, when certain antelopes are attacked by big cats, their nervous systems automatically shift into a state of stress, manifesting physiological changes such as increased adrenal activity and other metabolic changes, increased heartbeat, and several other phenomena that usually help normal, healthy animals deal better with a dangerous situation. A stressed animal is usually capable of greater feats of strength and speed and stamina. Its sensory organs are usually keener.

But if the animal is eventually cornered by the big cat, and it becomes obvious that there is no escape, it will slip into a state of shock. This is the nervous system's response to a hopeless situation, and it virtually reverses all of the "keyed-up" aspects of stress. Shock is a state of collapse. Blood flow is severely reduced. The physiological responses become anesthetized, and the animal reacts as if it had been drugged. It exhibits poor sensitivity, sluggish reactions, and, since the processes of shock can reach an irreversible stage, the animal can simply collapse and die without the predator's having touched it. This shock mechanism protects prey animals from the extreme pain of being pulled down and killed by a predator. Thus, some of the most sensitive types of antelopes are hardly aware of their own destruction because of this stress-shock syndrome. The predation of many wild animals isn't really as torturous or cruel as it appears. Mother Nature knows how to protect her children.

I didn't want to stress Napoleon and start a mechanism that could, given his frail condition, easily progress to shock. So I gave up any idea of trying to chase him or allowing him to sense that he was being pursued, which would have gotten his adrenaline up to a dangerous point. Instead, I loaded Hai-Bar's Peugeot pickup truck with my toolbox, a few planks, rope, blankets, water cans, and other equipment, and set out to look for the wounded Napoleon.

He wasn't hard to find. All I had to do was return to the place where I had seen him earlier and then follow his limping, foot-dragging tracks, which wandered out into the desert. He had gotten only a kilometer or so and appeared to be straying aimlessly in a generally southeast direction. My plan was simply to circle around him and then wait for him to approach me. I'd "head him off at the pass," so to say — an old Indian trick I learned in my youth by watching John Wayne movies. But, in this case, I was the one who had to create the pass.

I drove a wide circle across open desert until I came to an area of thorny scrub. I figured when Napoleon reached it, he'd change direction slightly and drift along the edge of the scrub toward me, rather than enter directly into all those sharp edges and tangled growth. Then I could employ my secret weapon — a homemade blowpipe and a dart loaded with a mixture of chemicals known as a Hellabruyn cocktail.

The blowpipe was nothing more than a yard length of aluminum television antenna pipe fitted with a makeshift mouthpiece adapted from a plastic toy rocket. The darts were also homemade and were assembled from parts of syringes, cannula needles, and cork. They were fitted with three-milliliter doses of the Hellabruyn cocktail, the invention of animal workers at the Hellabruun Animal Sanctuary in West Germany. This cocktail is a concoction of xylazine, an analgesic sedative, and ketamine, a common, fast-acting sedative. When injected into an antelope, the cocktail sends the creature off to dreamland in just a few minutes.

I drove along the edge of the brush for about eighty yards and then pulled away from it about ten yards, leaving a "pass" for Napoleon to funnel through as he drifted along the edge of the desert vegetation.

This he did. When Napoleon approached, he could see me relaxed in the driver's seat and not paying any heed at all to him — but actually, I watched every step he was making in the reoriented rear-view mirrors. Confidently, Napoleon ambled along, stumbling through the pass formed by the thorn bushes on his left and the truck on his right.

Just as he passed by, I lifted the blowpipe and aimed it at his backside. A little puff into one end of the pipe sent the dart flying out the other end. It sailed through the air and landed needle-first right where it was aimed — in the muscle known as *biceps femoris,* on the high side of the animal's right rear leg. Napoleon twitched a bit, as if he'd been stung. Other than that, the dart caused him no real concern, and the cocktail injected itself into the large, meaty muscle.

Then came the waiting game. Although modern capture drugs are quite safe — much safer than the old-fashioned cowboy lasso capture techniques — they still must be used properly. One must know, for example, that xylazine can be counteracted by adrenaline. Thus, if an animal is injected with this drug and then chased, adrenaline produced by stress will destroy the xylazine and the animal will not be immobilized. So it is better to sit back, take it easy, and let the drug take hold without interference. Napoleon continued to stumble on, and I watched him closely through my binoculars. About another sixty or seventy yards further along, he stopped and seemed to be a bit woozy. He lowerd his head, and his eyelids appeared heavy.

Still, I sat and watched. After a minute or so, he tried to walk. He was determined to keep moving. And he did get another six or seven steps before he went down, first to his foreknees, then to his hindquarters, and then down completely.

Still, I sat and watched. I wanted him to get into a nice deep slumber before I moved. Once before, I had gotten too close to a drugged oryx shortly after it had gone down and learned, much to my distress, that they can wake up with an explosive alertness at that point. It's much better to make sure they're well beyond the point of no return before getting very close.

Meanwhile, I studied Napoleon through my binoculars and made a number of notes in my diary concerning his wounds and general condition. The gore wound was especially bad. It would have to be stitched up and protected from infection and maggots.

About a quarter hour after being darted, Napoleon was snoring like a timber mill. I drove up behind him, stopped about twenty feet away, and then walked the rest of the way to old Sleeping Beauty. I gave him a little shove from behind — no reaction. Then I gave him a more forceful shove, which only caused a slight shift in his snoring pattern. Walking around in front of him, I began checking his senses. His eyes were closed, tickling the whiskers around his nose produced no reaction, and talking into his ear produced as much response as talking to a stone. Napoleon was tuned into a different world. He was flat-out unconscious: good enough!

Then I drove the pickup around until the tailgate faced Napoleon's sleeping head and prepared to load my unconscious passenger.

Step number one was to blindfold the sleeping giant to protect his eyes and also to keep him momentarily confused just in case he woke up.

Step number two involved tying Napoleon's feet together with a modified clove hitch. This is an excellent knot for hooved animals, since it's just about impossible for them to pull out of, yet it has a little slip device that permits quick release when required. The sleeping antelope was tied just to keep him manageable in case he awoke unexpectedly at an indelicate moment.

In step number three, I removed the dart that still dangled from his flank, swabbed the puncture with antiseptic, and placed the dart with the rest of my equipment in the truck.

Step number four was always the hard part. I slipped two planks under Napoleon, stretcher-style. That way, I had four corners to work with while lifting his 400-pound bulk into the back of the truck. First I lifted one end of one plank to the back bumper and then the same end of the other plank. Next, I lifted the opposite ends, one at a time, to rest on my big toolbox. Then I moved the first ends yet higher, to the bed of the truck. And gradually, Napoleon's snoring carcass was lifted and jostled into the back of the truck, bit by bit until the job was done.

Next, I wedged the spare tire alongside the big antelope, thus keeping him in the sternum position, that is, with his belly flat on the floor, instead of letting him flop over on his side. This is very important with ruminant animals such as antelopes in order to prevent digestive problems. If a ruminant lies down on its side for very long, its four-compartment stomach will tend to spill backwards, one into the other, with stomach acids ending up in the wrong places, upsetting the digestive process. If this goes on for too long, it can make the animal mighty sick, or even kill it. So it must be avoided.

With the antelope still snoring like a drunk on Sunday morning, and properly resting in his sternum position, I opened a liter bag of Hartmann's infusion solution and suspended it from a section of the truck frame that arched over Napoleon's sleeping body. A needle-tipped flexible tube led down from the clear plastic bag to his flanks. I then slipped the needle right under his skin and opened a small valve on the bag to let the lifesaving fluid trickle drop by drop into the sleeping beast. Infusions are important in these situations because they help to prevent shock and also provide a fresh supply of much needed body fluids. Napoleon had lost a bit of blood in his fighting, and if his fluid levels weren't brought back to a good level, he could suffer many different cardiovascular problems. Indeed, fluid levels are ultracritical in desert animals. These species have evolved with such a high degree of water discipline in order to survive in the desert that any upset of their fluid balances can result in devastating consequences.

Finally, I packed several old horse blankets around the antelope, soaked them down by emptying a twenty-liter jerry can of water over them, and checked that everything was secure and there was nothing lying loose to bang against the sleeping Napoleon if we hit a bump. I then drove back to the reserve. Around to the north of the work area is a paddock of about five or six acres. I decided to call the place Elba, since this was where Napoleon would spend his exile. His most recent battering had convinced me, if not him, that the old bull simply couldn't stay with the herd and keep all vital parts of his anatomy in proper working order.

Driving the truck into the enclosure, I stopped beneath a large, shady acacia tree. There I hoisted Napoleon off by reversing the loading process and went to work. The gore wound came first. It was about an inch across, round, and nearly two inches deep. It was pretty dirty and needed a thorough washing, followed by a packing with an antimaggot powder that also promotes healing. No major blood vessels were broken, nor had any organs or membranes been seriously damaged, so he wouldn't require surgery. I stitched the wound closed, leaving just a tiny hole for drainage, and started Napoleon on a regimen of antibiotics and steroids. There were some other nasty wounds, but nothing that required sutures. I just cleaned them up and gave them a good spraying with gentian violet, a good all-around fungicide, bactericide, and anthelmintic that would discourage flies, which can lay eggs in a wound; when the eggs hatch, the maggots feed on the rotting flesh and can cause other complications.

With Napoleon treated, I untied him, unblindfolded him, and left him to sleep in the shade of the acacia tree. Meanwhile, I set about turning Elba into a proper exile for a noble antelope. I secured its eight-foot-high fence, set a feeding rack into place, and installed an automatic watering tub to ensure that he'd have plenty of fresh, clear water twenty-four hours a day.

The enclosure was also home for Hai-Bar's nursery herd of ibex; these sprightly mountain goats would be good company for old Napoleon. The ibex were much too agile to be threatened by Napoleon, yet their presence would afford him a sense of companionship. Social animals that are locked up by themselves, even in very large enclosures, often become neurotic and suffer from the confinement, so it is usually better to make sure there are other animals around them for company. By the time Napoleon sobered up, Elba was a fitting exile. He had everything he needed, if not everything he wanted.

He escaped the next morning.

The escape route was obvious. Napoleon had simply slipped a horn through the chain-link mesh of the gate and pushed the throwbolt open. The gate then swung open and out he went, along with about a dozen ibex. The ibex were easy to catch. It only required a bucket of concentrated food pellets — which they loved above all other delicacies — shaken with a familiar rattle. The Hai-Bar ibex come running to this sound as reliably as a compass needle is drawn toward the North Pole. As I spread the pellets around in the small feeding trays, in bounded the ibex, piling through the open gate to get at the goodies. It was as easy as opening a whole carton of free chocolates inside a playground and waiting to see how many neighborhood children remained standing outside on the street.

Napoleon, however, was a different story. He ate only to sustain his own life. The ibex seemed to sustain life only so that they might eat.

I found Napoleon stumbling around the desert. He evidently had been chasing females again, as usual upsetting the younger bulls and catching the worst end of their outrage. There were new cuts, scrapes, and contusions.

Once more I employed the Hellabruyn cocktail, blowpipe, boards, infusion, blankets, and whatnot. An hour and a half later, we were back beneath the same old acacia tree, with Napoleon snoring and I was painting him with gentian violet again. At least this time there was no need for stitches.

With the medical work done, I put a new two-direction bolt on the gate. This device had to be lifted from a slot before it could be pulled open. Certainly, I thought, no antelope could figure out how to open this bolt.

I was wrong. It took a few days of ruminating, but old Napoleon figured out how to open the two-direction throwbolt by poking it this way and that with his horn pushed through the gate. There was a second escape, and a second recapture, and another round of wound tending.

The gate to Elba began to look like the main entrance to Devil's Island penal colony, with all the chains and bolts and little geegaws I had on it. But, undaunted, Napoleon found another way out. He just sidled up to the chain-link fence, stepped up on a few links, and slipped a horn through one of the slots, about six feet from the ground. With this accomplished, he flopped over backward, and his four-hundred-pound bulk dragged down a whole section of fence with him. He wriggled out from under the wreckage, and with his dozen ibex as escorts, made his break for freedom and another disaster.

In all, Napoleon made eight escapes from Elba, and after each escape, I repaired the damage so he couldn't get out that way again. Before long, the place was as tight as Fort Knox. I was becoming rather exasperated by this ingenious antelope, and after the eighth escape, I finally figured out how to keep him in Elba. All I had to do was give him what he wanted all along.

Napoleon wanted to be dominant! That was obvious. The difficulty lay in trying to persuade the rest of the herd to let the cantankerous old gent have his way. He reminded me of one of those ninety-eight-year-old retired generals who still have vivid memories of charging up San Juan Hill but who don't have the energy now to charge up four steps.

Cogitating about the situation for a day or two, I came up with an idea. I'd convince Napoleon that he could be happy by being dominant over me! He knew me well enough and probably despised me for intruding on his bizarre life-style. And his attitude was just the right one for my plan.

After he had recovered a bit from his eighth major trouncing and was well enough to toddle around a bit, I put the plan into action. One morning I marched into Elba armed with about ten pounds of alfalfa hay and a long bamboo pole. I set the hay in Napoleon's feeding crib and then blocked his way. Nope, he wouldn't eat this morning without a fight. I whacked him across his horns with my bamboo pole — a resounding crack that startled us both. Napoleon was infuriated! Here I was, challenging his authority even in this ramshackle, tumble-down, contemptible, destitute old-age home. The bull snorted and shook his head and prepared for the attack!

Now, Napoleon could only attack about one or two feet at a time before having to stop for a rest. He simply didn't have the stamina to roll on like a locomotive. To avoid being gored, I needed only to step back a pace or two, and old Napoleon would have to stop and catch his breath before renewing his onslaught. I whacked his old horns again. And he snorted, grumbled, and attacked again. It took a quarter hour for him to drive me back to the gate, at which point I dropped my bamboo pole and retreated like a beaten cur.

Napoleon had a remarkable victory! And he celebrated all day long by munching alfalfa hay, sipping cool water, and snoozing in the shade. My geriatric general was on top of the world!

Next morning, we repeated the battle, and Napoleon won again. And so it went. The morning joustings became a Hai-Bar tradition, and, thereafter, Napoleon had no interest in breaking out of Elba. He wasn't interested in females. He wasn't interested in contriving new escape schemes. He was interested only in being boss of his own territory, the lord of his own domain. And as long as Elba was his kingdom and he could assert his dominance, he felt fine. It got so that, when I entered in the morning, Napoleon would come to meet me, slowly pacing his advance and waving his old, worn horns all the way. We became the best of sparring partners.

Age continued its relentless advance, and Napoleon weakened still further. The following winter, he simply couldn't muster the energy to stand in the morning. I had to help him. And he'd permit me the honor of hoisting him up before we had our daily battle. He'd exercise a bit and then lie down until the next morning.

By early spring, he couldn't stay on his feet. Most wildlife workers would have euthanized such a creature. But I could see from his continuing enjoyment of his simple pleasures that Napoleon wanted to live. And as long as he wanted, I would help. In the mornings, I'd jockey him up so he'd lie across a couple of bales of hay with his legs hanging fore and aft. He'd get his daily dose of steroids, which kept him in good spirits, and then we'd have our ritual fight. After a few minutes, I'd back away, dropping my bamboo pole as I retreated. At the end of the day, I'd jockey Napoleon back down to the earth for the evening, massage his legs a bit and then fold them under him. I made sure he always had something to chew on and a low tray of fresh water right next to him.

The ibex living in the enclosure began to give birth in March.

Within a few days, the little kids were bounding all over the place, and, of course, Napoleon became the object of great curiosity. They'd dash over to him and sometimes hop up on the hay bales where he rested. He seemed to like the attention. But the presence of a whole new generation must have been a signal to him. New life had arrived. It was time for old life to pass. He simply turned his head back against his flanks one night at the end of March and passed away.

I lost a friend.

I said good-bye to Napoleon by reading a few verses of Scripture beside his cold remains, verses that confirm a kinship between humanity and all the animals:

> That which happens to the sons of men, happens to animals, and at least one thing happens to both: as one dies, so dies the other, for they have one breath: for a man has no preeminence above an animal, for all is vanity.
>
> All go to one place, all are made of dust, all return to dust again.
>
> Who knows with certainty that the spirit of man goes upwards, and the spirit of the animal goes downward into the earth?
>
> Ecclesiastes 3:19–21

It was springtime in the desert, a lovely season. But the intense heat was only a few weeks away. Napoleon's last days were filled with sweetness and fragrant blossoms, and he left before the harshness of the desert summer descended upon Hai-Bar.

Cornucopia
in the Desert

THE ORDERS came down from the Great Bureaucracy in Jerusalem: "We will make the desert bloom!"

"But why this part of the desert?" I asked.

"Don't ask questions!" was the reply.

And so the botanists of the Nature Reserves Authority embarked on a great scientific study of the desert's potential for floral productivity. Teams of scientists, technicians, and laborers — not to mention the usual assortment of bystanders, meddlers, and malingerers — showed up at the Hai-Bar gate one morning with truckloads of fencing, hoses, sprinkling gadgets, and all sorts of exotic paraphernalia. More importantly, they had large sheets of plans, and orders signed by The Boss himself. There was no way to turn them away.

"Mind if we look at those plans while you're getting organized?" I asked one of the scientists. He was scientifically cooperative, which means he handed me the plans without any discernible emotion. Just cold facts.

My helper Nathan and I unrolled the plans on a big table in the bunkhouse and, much to our chagrin, saw that they called for fencing off dozens of little plots here and there all over the reserve. Across from our south watering area, the Nature Reserves Authority planned to fence off a tract of about fifty by thirty feet. Up in the northwest corner, they were planning on another plot of about forty by sixty feet. Out beyond the ibex nursery they wanted to fence off another rectangle of about twenty by seventy feet.

"We're going to have more fences here than Alcatraz!" I exclaimed. "They want to build little dog runs all over the place!" On closer inspection, I saw that small water hoses connected many of these little plots and that sprinkler irrigation systems were to be set up in many of them. The Project Description revealed the designs of the botanical investigators. They wanted to learn the biotic potential of these little tracts under varying conditions of rainfall — how desert vegetation would respond to additional amounts of water. The tracts without irrigation would serve as control plots that would indicate the desert's natural, undisturbed growth rate on the amount of water provided by normal rain patterns. In these parts of the country, that is usually between one and two inches of rain per year.

Sprinkler irrigation in other plots was to be precisely measured, and would tell the scientists how the desert plants would grow if rainfall increased to five or ten or twenty inches of water a year. Some of the plots were to receive as much water as normally falls on Brazilian jungles!

"Maybe we ought to start reading up on the care of pythons and crocodiles," Nathan observed. "Parts of this nature reserve are going to look like the rain forests of Borneo before long."

"Why do they want to know what will happen in the desert if it gets more water in a year than it has in the past century?" I asked. "Do you think they've gotten advance warning of some change in climate?"

"I'm not sure, Bwana," Nathan kidded. "But when we go back to Eilat today, I'm going to look for a store that sells hip boots and a swamp buggy. Maybe I should look for some shark repellent too."

"Why are they doing it inside Hai-Bar?" I asked. "They've got thousands of square kilometers of empty desert outside. Why put all this junk in our animal area?"

"Because Avraham Yoffe said so, that's why," Nathan replied. "Somebody *schnorred* him into giving them permission to do their master's thesis here. And they were probably such *nudniks* in

Jerusalem that he just signed their papers to get rid of them, and now we're stuck with them."

After reviewing the plans, we drove out to a few of the work sites and watched the laborers putting up their little fences. They were just about four feet high, and were made of galvanized wire squares about six inches across. Australian fencing we call it — not as tough as chain-link hurricane fencing, and not as weak as chicken-wire fence. Nathan began wiggling a few of the fence posts. "Nope, not very sturdy at all," he remarked with a sly smile.

But I was already contemplating all sorts of disasters. What if a herd of fragile animals — gazelles or ostriches or addax — stampeded some night and ran smack into one of these fences? There'd be broken necks and broken legs all over the desert. Or what if lush vegetation began to grow because of the extra irrigation water? The animals would forever be trying to squeeze through the fencing just to get at all the greenery. Lawyers would call it an attractive nuisance! Maybe the extra water would create moist conditions and pools, which could become breeding areas for previously unknown insect pests, and parasites, and bacteria. All sorts of dire consequences could be envisioned.

The project took the better part of a week to set up, and in the end, little plots checkered the desert landscape. When it was put into operation, most of the animals ignored the little plots until one wise ibex learned a certain pleasure could be gained, simply by lying down on the south side of a fenced area while its sprinkler was working. The prevailing north breeze blew fine mist from the sprinklers through the fencing and deposited it as a cooling spray on any critter smart enough to be in the right spot at the right time.

News of a good thing gets around pretty quickly, and within a few days, the whole ibex herd would run over to the fence just as soon as the sprinkler system started up. The trouble was, there was less space in the spray zone than there were ibex wanting to enjoy the spray. They got into a big shoving contest to determine who would get into the best spot, an old Israeli tradition that also determines which fans get the best seats at soccer games, who gets the best seat on the bus, and who gets the choicest vegetables at the market.

One day, Claudius, a big male ibex with a bit of a limp and somewhat innocently muddled behavior, must have decided he wanted a better position for the spraying. He was so insistent that he just put his enormous horns down and pushed with all his might until he got to the front. Slowly but surely, he wedged his way forward. In the end, when there was no more resistance, he lifted his head to see where he was. Paradise. The big male had simply pushed his way through the crowd and through the fence as well, and was standing inside the plot with delicious water spraying all over him. His moment of private bliss lasted about three or four seconds, by which time the rest of the herd realized what had happened. They bounded across the shattered fence, where they all gleefully soaked themselves in the sweet water. Thus fell the first of the botanical bastions at Hai-Bar.

The following day, while Nathan was loading the trailer with hay to feed the animals, I noticed him giving very careful scrutiny to several bales of alfalfa hay. This was our "private stock" — well cured, sweet-smelling, the best hay available in Israel.

"*Nu?*" I asked.

"*Yesh le patent hadash!*" Nathan replied, "I have a new idea!"

He inspected the bales of alfalfa, probed into them, sniffed their sweetness, and then tossed the finest of the lot on the back of the hay wagon. Popping into the tractor's seat, he fired up the engine and drove off into the desert. "See you later!" he cried, as he rolled away pulling a trailer full of goodies.

Nathan returned about two hours later with an empty wagon. "Big catastrophe!" he lamented. "You must come and see what a terrible thing has happened. It is nearly the end of the world!" I jumped on the back of the tractor, Nathan popped it into gear, and off we rumbled toward the southwest corner of the reserve. We pulled to a stop about sixty yards away from one of the fenced-in botanical study zones. It wasn't precisely fenced-in anymore. In fact, a part of the fence looked as if it had been flattened by an armored brigade. Inside, about a dozen onagers calmly munched the fine alfalfa hay.

"An accident," Nathan shrugged. "While I was feeding the animals, a few straws of hay blew into the botanical study area. And wouldn't you know it, a whole herd of onagers wanted to eat that little bit of hay, so they just backed up to the fence and kicked it until it fell over. Then they went into the botanical study area to eat those few straws, just as you see it right now."

"Wind?" I replied. "There isn't enough wind to disturb a butterfly! Few straws? There's a forty-pound bale of hay in there! But I've got to admit that landscape surely looks a lot nicer ever since the onagers rearranged the fencing." Thus fell the second of the botanical bastions of Hai-Bar.

The destruction of the third plot was an outside job. A few days after the onagers had dined better than usual, some unseen tourist driving through the reserve must have noticed all the nice new irrigation equipment going to waste irrigating the desert. He simply helped himself to the goodies and probably put them to better use sprinkling tomatoes and cucumbers at some farm.

I explained my theory of the missing irrigation sprinklers to Nathan, who replied, "Tomatoes? Cucumbers? Why not?" The next day, he showed up for work with little seed packets bulging from his shirt pockets. He had developed a new interest in agriculture.

A few weeks later, the scientists visited the plots to determine how their experiment was progressing. There were a few signs of disappointment over the botanical study zones that had been plundered, but others survived and could be investigated in greater detail. But upon detailed study of those other plots, the botanists found a most peculiar phenomenon. Blessed with a bit of extra water, the study plots were producing tomatoes, cucumbers, and all manner of lovely garden vegetables — a cornucopia in the desert!

"What in hell is going on down there?" Avraham Yoffe growled at me that night on the telephone. "It's a miracle!" I replied. "You ordered that the desert shall bloom, and guess what happened!" We then embarked on a long discussion as to why all those scientists were fiddling around inside a wildlife restoration facility, and the several conflicts of interest in land use. We agreed on a "phased withdrawal of forces" at Hai-Bar; the scientists could go putter around a different sandbox. "From now on," Avraham warned, "if you want garden vegetables, find them outside Hai-Bar."

The following morning, I repeated the stern warnings to Nathan, who solemnly agreed to restrict his agricultural endeavors to the area outside the reserve. His first opportunity came a few days later.

A kibbutznik from Yotvatah came to complain that a porcupine was raiding the kibbutz melon patch. In Israel, all wild-animal damage problems are supposed to be reported to the Nature Reserves Authority so nature wardens can handle the situation. For example, farmers are advised how to build proper fences to exclude all wild animals from their fields and chicken coops, but if an animal does get in, the farmer is not supposed to take matters into his own hands. So the kibbutznik came to Hai-Bar with a request that we give the porcupine the boot.

"What sort of damage is it doing?" I asked.

"About one or two melons a week," was the reply. I could see that it was a serious crisis, and I dispatched my best crisis manager to handle the situation. "Nathan," I called, "take a box trap and set it out in the kibbutz melon fields to catch a porcupine."

Nathan disappeared with the kibbutznik and returned about an hour later. "All set, Bill," he said, "I'll go check the trap in the morning and see if we've caught the porcupine. By the way, here's a melon for lunch." He had returned with two melons — one for each of us — and they were sweet and juicy.

Nathan checked the trap the next morning and returned to the reserve with two more melons and a broad smile. "That porcupine is still on the prowl," he remarked.

After about a week, and about a dozen melons, I went with Nathan to the kibbutz to see how the trap was set. It shouldn't have taken so long to catch a porcupine. We drove into the melon fields, and, at the far eastern end, I saw the trap in a good location. Coming closer, I saw a porcupine inside it. "You've caught him!" I congratulated Nathan.

"I've caught him every day!" was Nathan's response. "Very foolish porcupine, this one. But also very nice. I make sure he has plenty to eat. I'd even pet him if he didn't have so many quills." Nathan explained that there were tens of thousands of melons in the field, and the only reason the kibbutzniks were upset with the porcupine was that he was a messy eater. If the critter had simply snapped a melon off its vine and carried it away to eat elsewhere, nobody would ever have noticed. But instead, the little fellow just dug right into the melons in the open field and made a conspicuous mess of it.

"Now the porcupine is well fed, and we get some sweet melon each day, and the melon field is neat, and the kibbutzniks are happy. What more could you ask for?" was Nathan's sagacious philosophy. "Besides, these kibbutzniks are cheapskates, so it's better that they're generous without knowing it."

Some months later, the melon field produced a terrible crop. Even the porcupine wouldn't eat them. The kibbutz, in all its generosity, donated the entire crop to Hai-Bar, and one morning upon arriving at the work gate, we found several tons of bitter melons piled outside the gate.

"Just what we need," I sighed. "Let's see if we can do anything with this stuff." We couldn't. I tried all sorts of tricks, but not a single animal would eat those melons. And I couldn't blame them. I tried mixing melon chunks with freshly chopped alfalfa and feeding it to the ostriches. No deal — although those big birds did develop an extraordinary technique for pecking all the alfalfa off the sticky melon chunks.

Word got around that there were thousands of unwanted melons sitting outside the Hai-Bar gate, and on my arrival a few mornings later, they were all gone. David Sadeh, the regional manager of the Nature Reserves Authority, was determined to track down the thief. "Thief?" I replied. "Nobody stole those melons. In fact, I'm glad to be rid of them. They'll all be rotting in a week or so, and there will be a million flies all over the place."

Undeterred by common sense, Sadeh launched a major investigation. He followed all the evidence to the kilometer 101 marker north of Eilat on the main Arava highway. Here, a colorful fellow known as Kushi runs a delightful restaurant, rest stop, and hang-out famed for the host's enterprising spirit, extraordinary ambience, and unusual refreshments. One of the delicacies he was selling to passing tourists was melon heavily sprinkled with sugar.

Kushi, it must be known, has a well-earned reputation for innovation and adventure. His best-remembered exploit was "bor-

rowing" a United Nations jeep for about a week, dressing himself
in a European-looking uniform, and flashing a pile of U.N.
letterhead papers at the Jordanian border guards as he drove
eastward from Israel. They saluted him, waved him through their
barricades, and Kushi took a nice vacation, driving hither and yon
around the Hashemite Kingdom. He even drove down to Petra, the
ancient Nabatean city built of red sandstone high in the Mountains
of Edom. But all nice holidays must end, so eventually he drove
back to the border, passed through the Jordanian checkpoint, and
was stopped by Israeli border guards. He was released after some
months in jail. All the local newspapers made him something of a
cult hero.

Kushi's kilometer 101 rest stop is located almost directly across
the border from Petra, and here he has made an eclectic palace for
himself and his guests. For shade, a variety of awnings, Bedouin
tent fabrics, and used parachutes are suspended from long poles.
His restaurant has a similarly eclectic cuisine, depending upon
what's in season and available at modest price (or modest risk!). It
is one of the most relaxing places in the Arava Valley and is staffed
by some of the most interesting people to pass through. Kushi
simply takes on helpers he considers good-natured, intelligent, and
fair-minded. At any time one might find a college student taking a
semester off, or a scholar doing the same thing, or a farmer or two
who want a break from the daily routines of a kibbutz — all sorts
of interesting people who go to the desert seeking a change in their
lives and a relaxed atmosphere.

Kushi's Shangri-La is also home to several goats and sheep, a few
camels, donkeys, kindly stray dogs, some chickens, an abandoned
pet monkey, and who knows what else. It is what Israelis call a
balagan — a caravansary in a perpetual state of casual confusion,
where many travelers meet and cross paths, and where quite a few
simply stop for a few days' rest.

"Oh, no! Those are my melons! I bought them!" Kushi protested.
But Sadeh pressed his case, convinced he had the culprit cornered.
And soon the local police paid a visit to the kilometer 101 rest stop.
Certainly, anyone who would "borrow" a United Nations jeep
would not be above "borrowing" a few melons. There were papers

and charges and visits to the courthouse in Eilat. Kushi fumed and vowed a feud. He was determined to see David Sadeh chased out of his part of the desert, and he had just enough "vitamin P" to do it. Our regional manager soon left for a new assignment somewhere north of Tel Aviv. Kushi's rest stop returned to normal. And Kibbutz Yotvatah planted a new crop of melons.

Saint Patrick

HAI-BAR'S "SAINT PATRICK" is named for Ireland's patron because the saint didn't like snakes. But whereas the Irish saint made his reputation, according to tradition, by casting the serpents out of the land, Hai-Bar's Saint Patrick claims distinction because he eats them. Our snake stalker insists upon a strictly slithery diet. His sole ambition in life is to devour every snake in the Negev Desert.

Hai-Bar's Saint Patrick is a short-toed eagle (*Circaetus gallicus*), an avian species that is commonly known as the snake eagle. One day, this big bird ate the wrong snake, and thereby hangs a very ecological tale.

Saint Patrick was found in the desert near Eilat by one of our nature wardens, who was making routine rounds of the area. The poor bird was discoverd lying on the ground, very weak, just waiting to die. The warden's job was quite easy: he walked up to the bird, wrapped a blanket around it, picked it up, and set it on the back floor of his jeep. The bird made no effort to struggle against its captor. Within a half hour, the warden had the eagle at Hai-Bar and we were giving it an examination. Poison. No doubt about it. The bird had all the symptoms — he was uncoordinated and suffering spasms; there was evidence of diarrhea and extreme weakness.

But how does a snake eagle get poisoned? One might initially think that perhaps he dined on a cobra or viper. But these birds are too smart for that. Besides, there's enough poison in the average cobra or viper in these parts to kill a score of eagles in short order. The strength of poison is usually calculated by ratio of dose to body weight, and the snake eagle weighs less than five pounds. No, if a poisonous snake had caused the problem, the warden would have found a dead eagle. Instead, the diagnosis seemed to lie along the lines of classical ecology. Like the vast majority of poisoning cases, we presume the poison got into our patient through a very normal food chain. He didn't eat a *poisonous* snake. He ate a *poisoned* snake.

Not many people go around poisoning snakes. But they do poison the snakes' favorite food — mice. Mice are regularly poisoned around the world, and in these parts, farmers had been using grains of wheat coated with fluoracetamide to exterminate rodent populations that had been causing problems in alfalfa fields. That's the way I summed it up — the poison went from wheat to mouse, and from mouse to snake, and from snake to eagle — leaving a trail of pain and destruction all along the way.

The eagle evidently had been poisoned for quite a few days, to judge from his weakness, apathy, and very serious loss of weight. He was bony and appeared to be near the very end of his body reserves. In fact, I suspected that the poison wasn't the immediate problem any more, and that the real danger lay in malnutrition. I figured that the poisoned snake made the eagle very sick for a while, and during this sickness he was in no shape for flying. Unable to fly, he couldn't hunt, so he went hungry. As the danger of poisoning began to pass, the dangers of malnutrition took hold, and plain weakness kept the eagle grounded. A close inspection of the eagle also revealed that, like many other birds of prey when they're sick, this poor fellow was infested with lice, which probably made his life miserable.

Most people who work with sick birds know that if the patient is still alive twenty-four hours after being received, chances of survival are fairly good. I went right to work. First, I put the eagle straight into a cardboard carton and set it down in a quiet corner of the reserve workshop. Here, he'd have quiet, darkness, and rest while we made preparations.

Malnutrition was obviously the most serious problem and had to be addressed immediately. Since there weren't any snakes lingering about prepared to volunteer as eagle food, I had to find the next best thing. I persuaded a friendly cook at Kibbutz Yotvata to donate a bit of fresh chicken. Chicken and snake meats are actually quite similar, and both are unlike the fatty red meats of mammals, so this substitution was the most practical choice.

Back at the reserve, I sliced the meat into thin strips, just about the size of large matchsticks, and using blunt tweezers, I fed it to the eagle. The bird lacked either the strength or the will to eat, so he had to be helped. I moistened the small strips with a bit of water, and forcing his hooked beak open, I set them on the back of the eagle's tongue. Rubbing his throat gently produced a swallowing reflex, and down went the chicken. After a light meal, Saint Patrick was lifted back into his cardboard carton for an afternon nap.

Meanwhile, my helper Nathan prepared a small cage for our avian guest. It was a simple, wooden-frame cell, wrapped with chicken wire and bedded down with fresh hay. He made it just large enough for the eagle to sit in; we didn't want the bird wasting his first spurts of renewed energy hopping around to find an escape route.

Before going home that evening, Nathan and I dusted the eagle with a powder to get rid of the lice. We fed him another light meal and then transferred him to the new cage, which stood in the darkened corner of the workshop. Food and rest were what this bird really needed.

Saint Patrick had improved by the next morning and readily nipped pieces of chicken from the tweezers all by himself. But he still didn't have the strength to move around much, so I decided to keep him in that tiny cage a bit longer. Actually, he stayed in there for another three days, until he was showing good strength and had little patience for sitting much longer in the close confines of that undersized chicken coop.

During those days, Nathan prepared the next stage of the eagle's rehabilitation — a larger cage, measuring about ten feet by ten feet. The roof was covered with date palm branches to keep a dim atmosphere and also to protect the bird from direct sunlight. Under normal conditions, eagles thrive in bright daylight and spend many hours soaring under an intense sun. But I wanted this fellow to stay still and rest as much as possible, and the subdued environment in a cage would encourage just that.

Nathan installed several perches in the large cage, each perch being of a different diameter and all arranged so the eagle could hop from one to the other. The different diameters were important for the eagle's feet muscles; if the perches were all the same diameter, the feet muscles wouldn't have much opportunity to flex, and this could bring on cramps. For eagles, care of the feet is especially important, because the feet contain the muscles that operate the talons — and without properly functioning talons, an eagle cannot catch prey to eat. Also, we set a flat tray in one elevated corner of the cage and bedded it with hay, so the big bird would have a place to lie down.

The crowning masterpiece of this raptorial suite was the automatic watering system. The eagle had an ample supply of clear, fresh water twenty-four hours a day delivered to a little bowl installed right by the edge of one of the perches. The key to keeping the pint-sized bowl filled at all times lay in a Rube Goldberg system of fluid dynamics, bent hoses, and complicated hydraulics. There was a bit of modern art in the arrangement, what with all the black plastic hoses, spigots, and fantastically balanced water levels. The contraption could have been confused with a bootlegger's still in the backwoods of Tennessee. But it did work well, and the eagle didn't complain about all those strangely arranged odds and ends and plain junk stacked up right outside his cage.

By week's end, Saint Patrick was well on his way toward recovery. But as he gained strength, I noticed that the poison was still influencing him. In the larger cage, for example, he sometimes misjudged short distances while hopping from perch to perch — a sign of loss of coordination caused by the poison.

At the end of the second week, Saint Patrick was transferred to our large aviary — an enclosure about ten feet high, ten feet wide, and forty feet long built by Mike Van Grevenbroek a few years earlier. The beauty of this particular enclosure was that it was built around a large acacia tree, so the bird had living branches for perching. The enclosure also had a man-made perch at one end, so the eagle could fly back and forth from tree to perch for exercise.

Saint Patrick was making very good progress by now and started to show his individuality. Each morning at breakfast, he'd greet me with a loud *jeeee! . . . jeeee!* and hop enthusiastically about the aviary. And such breakfasts he would devour! Although I still hadn't found any volunteer snakes, I did find an agreeable butcher in a meat market in Eilat who offered all manner of chicken heads, necks, and other parts that humans normally disdain. Saint Patrick dined on these contributions to eagle conservation with great relish. He loved them so much that I feared that he would become the most notorious chicken thief in all the Negev after his release.

As the weeks passed, I could see Saint Patrick's recovery progressing admirably. He was commonly seen flexing his muscles, sometimes arching his neck forward, and sometimes stretching one leg forward and exercising his powerful talons. On several occasions I watched in awe as he unfolded his enormous wings and spread them to their five-foot span. Even sitting quietly on a limb of the acacia tree in his aviary, Saint Patrick was the image of strength — erect, watchful, and with an air of extreme confidence. For two months we worked patiently with the ailing bird. Gradually, Nathan and I watched Saint Patrick's eyes turn from dull, half-closed mirrors of pain to bright yellow windows of fierceness. Daily he improved in strength, alertness, and coordination.

Although he became quite tame with me, I knew that once he recovered, Saint Patrick had to be released to his freedom in the desert skies. The day finally came. "That's it, friend," I told him, "you've malingered around here long enough. It's time you were kicked out and made to work for a living."

I entered the aviary one morning, fed him his breakfast, and just as he was finishing it, I tossed a large army blanket over him and scooped him up in my arms. He squirmed a bit, and pulled, and flexed those formidable talons, and *jeeee! . . . jeeee!*'d at me, but we went out the door together, nevertheless. The release ceremony was simple. I had one word for him, *"Shalom!"* I opened the blanket on the earth, and Saint Patrick leapt into the sky.

There are few sights in Nature as glorious as an eagle climbing into the heavens. And there are few delights that bring a wildlife worker greater joy and satisfaction than returning to Mother Nature one of her recovered children. When both of these events are brought together, the moment is sacred.

Patrick climbed on strong wings into the sky. The short-toed eagle has incredibly powerful wings. It's the largest bird in the world capable of hovering in one place — a maneuver that requires extraordinary amounts of strength and energy. Up he went, circling widely, his gleaming white underside standing out sharply against the electric blue sky. And I understood why Solomon said that the first thing too wonderful for his understanding was "the way of an eagle in the air" (Proverbs 30:19).

The recovery of this particular eagle was something of a miracle. The great majority of poisoned birds of prey — the raptors — die. Around the world, they have been killed off in the millions. In Israel, the major problem of secondary poisoning from agrictultural rodenticides has in recent years been brought under better control, and the number of poisoned eagles has proportionately declined. In some other countries, however, the problem is still very severe.

Secondary poisonings are only a small corner of a worldwide tragedy. A recent eight-year study of bald eagles that died in the United States, for example, found that only 10 percent of them died because of poisoning, another 12 percent died of natural causes such as pneumonia and arteriosclerosis, and another 21 percent died accidentally — landing on electrical high-tension lines, being hit by cars and trucks, or flying into buildings and windows. Some were killed because they landed on steel-jaw leghold traps set out with meat baits to catch other animals.

The biggest mortality factor in the United States, however, was classified as "direct persecution." In spite of the fact that killing bald eagles is a federal crime, a full 43 percent of the bald eagles — America's national symbol — were killed because people wanted them dead. Most were simply shot. The rest were killed either with poison baits or with traps set out especially for them. These included the notorious pole trap — a steel-jaw leghold trap set and baited atop a tall pole especially to attract birds of prey.

The American situation is mild compared to that of Europe, where millions of raptors have been slaughtered for decades. The main reason this slaughter doesn't continue on such a scale today is that there just aren't many birds of prey left. There can be little wonder that the skies of most of the world are now empty of these magnificent birds.

Most birds of prey have been killed because ignorant people consider them to be livestock thieves. But field studies have disproven most of the old claims and accented the positive benefit these birds have on human agriculture. For example, when ranchers find eagles feeding upon dead sheep, they often assume that the eagle killed their sheep. But field studies have proved that it's just about impossible for an eagle to kill a full-grown sheep (although they may take an occasional unprotected lamb). However, they will feed upon sheep that have died from other causes.

Modern field studies demonstrate that raptors generally have a positive benefit for farmers. A pair of kestrels — the smallest of predatory birds — can eat about four mice a day. This means these skillful falcons consume about 1,440 mice a year. And this number increases if the pair builds a nest and has young ones to feed.

"We're trying to encourage farmers to attract kestrels to their farms," I was told by Yossi Leshem, the director of the Israel Raptor Information Center. Yossi, an ardent conservationist, constantly travels the length of Israel, and often abroad, preaching the protection of raptors. "Farmers can do this simply by not harassing them, and they'll move in of their own accord. They can also be encouraged by putting up nesting boxes and taking other positive steps. Just look at the good these birds can do for farmers, and all without the use of costly and dangerous pesticides."

Yossi's message is getting through. There is a much greater appreciation of these inspiring birds in Israel today, and as a result, their populations have been showing a steady increase.

Yossi is something of an eagle himself — at least in his nesting habits. He lives atop Mount Gilo, south of Jerusalem, in the Judean Mountains. His perch is nearly a kilometer above sea level, windswept, and with a fantastic view. More important, he lives near the nest of the area's resident pair of golden eagles. Each year since 1978, these extraordinary birds have been nesting in the pine forest along the southern edge of Jerusalem.

When the eagles started to nest here, there was a threat of violence by some of the area's local farmers and shepherds, who had heard stories about eagles stealing infants from cribs and all sorts of other terrible things. They wanted to raid the eagles' nest and destroy it before the birds had an opportunity to cause damage.

But someone else was also watching the nest — Yossi Leshem. He organized a massive voluntary effort within the Society for the Protection of Nature in Israel. They threw a cordon of guards around the nest and physically protected it twenty-four hours a day, seven days a week, throughout the nesting and fledgling season.

The nesting began in early February, a month that brings wind, driving rains, and occasional snows to these Judean Mountains. It's a bitter season, yet the volunteer guards took their turns at duty and maintained an uninterrupted vigil for nearly half a year. There were scores of confrontations and incidents, but nobody got within a hundred yards of the nest, and the eagles successfully hatched and fledged two young eaglets.

The eagles nested in the branches of an enormous Jerusalem pine tree on the property of Cremisan Monastery, a sprawling tract of mountainside owned by the Salesian Brothers. Formerly known only for its fine wines, the monastery soon became known for fine wines and golden eagles. Cooperating with the Christian brothers, Yossi established a guard station, along with a telescope-equipped bird-watching hide. In this hide, a bird-watcher could sit, relax, and watch eagle nesting activity in relative comfort, without disturbing the nest in any way. Many thousands of Israelis visited the site through the nesting season, and each gained the privileged experience of having viewed one of the most endearing sights in Nature — the nesting of golden eagles.

Adult golden eagles normally mate for life, maintaining great fidelity to each other, their young, and their nests. If an intruder comes to threaten their nests, the eagles will mount an immediate and ferocious defense. They will fly directly at any intruder, even one ten times their size, in efforts to drive it away.

During the incubation period, the female sits patiently on her eggs, while the male is called to double duty — feeding himself and his mate. This calls for a lot of work in February, when the nesting starts and the short daylight hours mean he must use the light as effectively as possible. And there's no rest for him once the eggs hatch. If anything, the male must work even harder to bring food for the eaglets, as well. And all the while, the female stays by her nest, brooding the young and protecting them from any threat.

During one afternoon of the Mount Gilo eagle watch, Israeli bird lovers found a new clue to an ancient mystery. According to ancient tradition, the Greek playwright Aeschylus died "in the wheatlands of Gela," when an attacking eagle threw a tortoise against his head. For twenty-five centuries, not many people had thought much about this traditional version of the death of one of the heros of Marathon. Then, one day in springtime, guards at the Mount Gilo nest saw the big male rummaging around in the grasses on the hillside below. He had evidently found something to eat but was having difficulty with it. Moments later, the identity of the prey was revealed — a tortoise, which had withdrawn into its shell. Unable to pry the reptile out of the shell, the big eagle grasped it in his talons and climbed into the air. Higher and higher he soared, until he was several hundred feet above the bird-watchers.

The eagle then turned into the wind, hesitated a moment, and began to dive, straight and purposefully, like a dive-bomber. He released the tortoise in middive, and the hapless reptile plummeted to its death, crashing forcefully against a rounded rock.

The eagle descended, took the meat from the fractured shell, and returned to his nest to feed the eaglets. And today, Israeli bird-watchers suspect that some ancient eagle probably presumed poor Aeschylus's bald head was a round enough stone to help him open a recalcitrant tortoise's shell.

Month after month, the progress of the eagles' nesting drew many people to view them from the Society's hide. Frequently, ordinary people — postmen, garage mechanics, and teachers, who formerly had little or no involvement in Nature conservation — stopped by the hide after a day's work, just to take a few moments of pleasure in watching this great wonder. Indeed, the nesting behavior of golden eagles elsewhere is a sight that many devoted bird-watchers will travel great distances and endure great hardships to see — so to have it available within twenty minutes of the center of a modern city was extraordinary.

Physically protecting the nest was only part of Yossi's strategy. Meanwhile, the Society for the Protection of Nature launched an educational program aimed at the region's farmers. They printed notices in Arabic and Hebrew, persuaded many journalists to write stories, and even secured a few spots on Israeli national radio and television broadcasting systems. The Society preached the benefits of protecting birds of prey but also acknowledged that they do occasionally cause some problems. To deal with these problems, the Society initiated a reimbursement program. It agreed to repay farmers for agricultural losses caused by the eagles.

Since there was a twenty-four-hour guard at the nest, details of what the eagles were eating could be carefully recorded. Usually, the birds brought in wild animals, mostly tortoises but also hares and hyrax. Occasionally, the eagles would steal a chicken. There were no lambs taken, even though sheepherding is an important part of the region's economy.

The guard noted the time and type of prey that the eagles brought to their nest. If the prey was a chicken, it would be noted as a Jewish chicken or an Arab chicken. These are easy to distinguish, because Jewish kibbutzniks and moshavniks prefer to keep the pure white domestic chickens, while Arab farmers favor the more colorful varieties. The eagles didn't discriminate and returned to their nest with a modest number of both types.

When a farmer complained that an eagle had snitched a chicken, he'd have to report the time the bird was taken and what kind of chicken it was. If his complaint matched the records of the eagles' guard, the farmer would be reimbursed the going rate for chickens at that particular time. The whole process has cost less than a hundred dollars through the past half-dozen years, and for that slight price, Jerusalemites have had the honor of seeing golden eagles soaring right over the center of town.

Although many eagles remain in Israel throughout the year, the great majority of them are migrants. The golden eagles of Mount

Gilo are migrants, and it is my opinion that Saint Patrick was also a seasonal vagabond. I suspect that he picked up the snake that ate the mouse that ate the poison somewhere along his migration route, flew a bit more, got sick, and crashed near Eilat. When he recovered and was released, I expected he'd be off and find his way as a straggler a few months behind the migration. But instead, he surprised me and took up residence around Hai-Bar.

I also figured he'd become the biggest chicken thief in history, but I was wrong again. His instincts guided him back to a tastier diet of desert snakes. I think he liked snakes better because they don't have so many feathers, making them easier to swallow. Also, because of their shape, they can be eaten whole — no need to get messy and break the snake apart; it's designed to slip right down the gullet like one long piece of spaghetti. Saint Patrick prefers, as I presume all snake eagles do, to eat his meal head first, thereby getting the dangerous end of the snake out of the way before it can do much harm. On several occasions, I have seen Saint Patrick sitting on a treetop with the back half of a snake still drooping limply from his beak.

For a while after his release, I kept putting chicken parts on top of the aviary, just in case Saint Patrick had difficulty feeding himself. That was unnecessary, however, as the eagle needed no transition period in his regained freedom. But all those chicken heads and necks didn't go to waste, as they were enthusiastically consumed by mobs of desert ravens.

In the Hai-Bar area there certainly are enough snakes for Saint Patrick to chase, and the neighbors aren't too bad. Sometimes, visitors touring the reserve and the adjacent regions report a most extraordinary sight. They claim to have seen an eagle, with wings nearly five feet across, hovering in the air just like a hummingbird — but somewhat less gracefully. Saint Patrick, being a true short-toed eagle, lets his legs dangle loosely while he hovers. And he does this right over people's heads — a bit frightening to the uninitiated — while he sings out his familiar *jeeee! . . . jeeee!*

Buzzy

ISRAEL is a critical point of passage for birds of prey on migration, the keystone in the only land bridge connecting the enormous continents of Eurasia and Africa. Its importance in the migratory patterns of raptors and other soaring birds, such as storks and pelicans, is due to the natural phenomenon of thermals, the rising columns of hot air formed over a land mass. When the sun warms the land, heat intensity builds up on one place and must be released. Thermals cannot form over water because any build-up of heat on the surface of the seas results in evaporation. On the land, and particularly in desert areas, there is much less opportunity for evaporation. Thus the heat has but one direction for release — straight up. The warm air rises in a great column, up to fifty yards across and as high as six thousand feet, where it disperses in cooler regions of the troposphere.

Many songbirds can take off on seasonal migration at their appointed day and fly straight for several days without rest. They have evolved the capability of crossing large expanses of sea without needing to land. Raptors and other soaring birds, however, are much too heavy to make the migration of several thousand miles by active flight. They require the support of thermals, and they also need to land each evening and spend the night on terra firma. Their migration patterns, therefore, have evolved across the tiny land bridge of Israel, where these conditions are ideal.

For several years, Yossi Leshem has painstakingly documented the great migrations of birds of prey passing over Israel twice annually. His efforts represent the most comprehensive raptor survey to date. On a map, Yossi pinpointed sites to set up a chain of bird-watching posts stretching across the center of Israel, from the Mediterranean to the border with Jordan. Any eagle flying across Israel on a north-south route has to cross these posts, which are kept staffed with volunteers seven days a week throughout the migration season. And as the eagles, buzzards, or falcons fly across this chain of observers, they are counted and identified. Over the years, Yossi has compiled a tremendous wealth of information invaluable to conservationists and bird-watchers around the world. So extensive is his data that Yossi can tell you almost exactly when and where to go to see a particular type of eagle.

One link in the chain of observation posts is the Arab village of Kafr Kassem, about twenty kilometers northeast of Tel Aviv. Over the fields west of the village, much of the world's population of lesser spotted eagles passes by on their autumn migration to Africa. This occurs at the end of September, with such precise regularity that you could set your calendar by the event. Vast numbers of these majestic birds with their five-foot wing span pull together in funnel formation over this spot, providing observers with an excellent demonstration of how soaring birds exploit the updrafts of the thermals. The spectacle is one of the most thrilling in all Nature.

The birds arrive from the direction of Samaria, thirty or forty kilometers to the northeast, having spent the previous night roosting on the hilltops there. With the sunrise, the birds awaken, but remain for a while on the mountain fastness, waiting for the sun to begin creating thermals and for a slight sea breeze to start wafting in from the Mediterranean. When all conditions are right, the eagles take to the air and fly in the direction of Kafr Kassem.

Within an hour or so of take-off, the first few dozen eagles come swooping down from the mountains, pioneers leading the day's aerial exodus. They glide in a straight line until they encounter a thermal of rising warm air. Entering the thermal, the eagles bank and cut a tight circle, staying within the air column and being lifted high by it. An eagle entering a thermal at an elevation of a few hundred feet can simply soar in a tight circle for a few minutes, while the rising air lifts it for more than a mile above the earth until the thermal loses its strength. From here, the pioneer eagles depart from the dissipating thermal and glide along the southward migration route, gradually losing altitude while seeking out the next thermal to boost them back up into the skies with only a wingbeat or two.

The numbers of approaching eagles increases, first by the score and then by the hundreds. At times, more than a thousand eagles soar overhead, climbing upward in great swarms within the thermal and then gliding single-file out of the top. The migration of the greatest numbers of birds assumes a more purposeful pattern as the best thermals, discovered by the pioneer eagles, become known. The great wave of migrants proceeds from one to the other like children using the same series of stones to step across a stream.

The lesser spotted eagle is a particularly impressive flyer, not only because of its astonishing numbers — sometimes counted in the tens of thousands — but also because of the bird's flight characteristics. It appears to be sleeker than other types of eagles, and I suspect it actually flies faster as well.

The eagles' speed is especially noticeable when they emerge from the top of a thermal. The birds take a moment or two to orient themselves and, upon sighting the next thermal in the chain of migration, they make a few shallow pumps with their wings to accelerate. They then bow their wings, with the centers arched upward and the tips pointing down, and in this flexed posture they sail like arrows through the air.

Another locale where migration of eagles can be witnessed is Eilat, at the southern tip of Israel, where professional ornithologists have documented the passage of more than one million birds of prey through the spring migration — the greatest known concentration of raptors on earth. Once the birds pass over this land bridge, they disperse across the face of continents where it is very rare to see more than a few individual eagles in a day.

The reason for these migrations is still a mystery, although there is a growing body of circumstantial evidence suggesting why they occur. Many biologists believe that current migration patterns evolved during the most recent Ice Age. As the Eurasian winters became more severe, resident birds were forced to fly south during the harsh winters in search of food. But these birds were also strongly attached to their breeding grounds. Not only was there the instinctive attachment — or "imprinting" to the breeding grounds — but those breeding grounds also became abundantly productive in warm weather. This meant the birds could distribute their numbers over a much larger area and reap important benefits such as greater amounts of food, greater availability of nesting sites, and less competition than was encountered in more densely populated regions. These advantages made it well worth while for the birds to migrate the vast distances between summer breeding grounds and winter refuges.

Of all the millions of migrants that fly across Israel twice each year, one of the smallest walked into my life quite by accident. This was Buzzy, a lesser kestrel (*Falco naumanii*), who even in her plumpest days couldn't press hard enough on a scale to mark six ounces. I met her one day while walking down Ibn G'virol Street in the Rehavia neighborhood of Jerusalem, when I noticed her sitting on the roof of a parked car.

It is quite common for pigeons and sparrows and other urban birds to hop about car roofs and any other sort of man-made object. But it is extremely rare for a falcon to sit idly and let people walk within three or four feet. Something was amiss.

As I walked toward the kestrel, she appeared to have no fear at all, although when I got within two feet and reached out my hand, she began to back away. I quickly saw that she was in no shape to escape. She was very weak and sickly.

I took off my shirt, and tossing it over the small falcon, I scooped her up and brought her home. Her overgrown beak and poor appearance revealed that she was starving, had been kept captive and was maltreated during that captivity, and, as is so often true of sick birds, she was infested with lice.

The therapy was similar to that which had pulled Saint Patrick through. First, I gave her a light meal and then slipped her into a cardboard carton to rest in a dark, quiet corner. Once she was tended, I made a few telephone calls — to Yossi Leshem and to

Avinoam Luria at the Nature Reserves Authority. I alerted them that I had the little falcon, and, more importantly, I let them know that she obviously had been held captive. It is illegal to hold birds of prey captive in Israel without a special permit. Such permits are issued only to qualified biologists who have the technical competence to care for the birds and who also have a valid reason for keeping them. Avinoam, who is responsible for issuing all wildlife permits, told me that, at the time, nobody in the country had a license to keep a lesser kestrel. Whoever had held the bird held her illegally. And if one bird was held, it was possible that there could be others. Both Avinoam and Yossi would now be especially watchful for illegal bird keepers and dealers.

After the falcon had rested for six hours, I retrieved her for another meal, feeding her bits of chicken with a pair of tweezers. She was still very weak, and immediately after the meal, I popped her back into the box for a long night's rest. By next morning, she showed signs of improvement, although her condition remained really quite poor.

She was severely undernourished, so much so that her breast bone (carina) was protruding, and she looked very lean and frail. She was also suffering vitamin deficiency. Vitamin A deficiency was especially obvious, as her feet were nearly chalk white (they should have been yellow), and a flaky squamous membrane was encrusted around her cere, the upper part of her beak, where the nares, or nostril passages, are located. I also suspected vitamin B deficiency, as well as very low blood sugar, because of the tremors that ran through her body. It was obvious that she hadn't been feeding on her natural diet.

Her beak was grossly overgrown, the main reason I suspected that this falcon hadn't become sick from natural causes. A falcon's beak continues to grow through its lifetime. But in Nature, it is also continuously worn down as the bird eats all sorts of roughage, from crusty insects to tiny mouse bones. Falcons living in the wild never have the opportunity to get overgrown beaks. But those kept captive and fed only soft foods, such as hamburger, very frequently suffer from this problem.

All these symptoms pointed to a disease that is all too common around the world — human vanity. There are millions of domestic parakeets, canaries, and finches available in pet shops in nearly every country on earth. But some humans are not content with these. They must have unique birds. Often, they want parrots, which are amusing and colorful and are almost always stolen from nests in the tropical jungles of Latin America and Africa. Parrots are extremely difficult to breed in captivity. Instead, pet dealers find it much easier to take them captive from Nature. There has been such an epidemic of capturing these birds for the pet trade in recent years that several species today are on the verge of extinction. Fortunately, a number of responsible agencies have stepped in to stem this horrid trade. CITES, the endangered species treaty, has taken steps to control trade in many rare species of birds, and governments, such as that of the State of New York, have passed prohibitions against the import of all wild-caught birds. These are positive steps and should be encouraged and expanded.

Birds of prey are a special case, however. There's a great macho element in keeping a bird of prey — a flying predator. Falcons, hawks, and eagles have long been associated with knights and royalty. They have stood as the symbols of empire, from the days of ancient Assyria and Rome, up through scores of medieval monarchies, and even to this day, when the bird of prey is often depicted as the symbol of power and authority. The symbolic value in keeping such a bird as a "pet" is very compelling; it is a status- and ego-enhancing phenomenon. And it comes at the price of robbing birds from Nature.

Worse are the falconers. They not only keep birds of prey, but they also use them to hunt other animals — small birds, rabbits, and other game animals. Some falconers use their birds simply as mercenaries that kill on behalf of their keepers. Others, however, are part of an even more outrageous activity that is still quite popular in several countries of the Middle East — using falcons to hunt in combination with dogs.

In this latter practice, the falconer trains his bird to attack unnaturally large prey, usually gazelles. In particular, the falcon is trained to swoop down on a gazelle and gouge out its eyes. The blinded and panic-stricken gazelle is then easily run down by the falconer's saluki dogs and torn to pieces. This is considered "sport" by certain barbaric people and is still commonly practiced by various wealthy persons and the nobility of the Middle East.

All falconry is illegal in Israel, and it is extremely difficult to practice it. After all, it requires that the falconer take his bird out into the open and let it loose in order to hunt. In a country as small as Israel, this sight would be quickly noticed and very likely reported.

Thus, I was a bit skeptical that this was an Israeli bird — although it certainly was possible, it was not likely. A greater possibility was that she had been kept in Jordan, a mere twenty miles east of Jerusalem. This theory was supported by the climate. The prevailing wind in this region blows from west to east. When kestrels take to flight, they instinctively face into the wind, for this way they can hover or proceed forward at a very slow pace, while their sharp eyes scan the ground below for prey. If Buzzy had escaped or been released by a Jordanian falconer, she most likely would have turned westward, into the wind, and flown toward Israel.

I presumed that she had been stolen from her nest in Nature as a chick by an incompetent amateur — hence her fear, vitamin deficiency, and overgrown beak. Competent falconers, despite the obscenity of their "sport," generally know how to calm a bird and they provide basic nutrition. The poacher probably kept the kestrel for some months during a very important part of her life — through the fledgling period — so she missed out on learning and perfecting the elementary skills of flight and hunting for food. After some months, it's likely that the little kestrel either escaped or was simply released by the disappointed would-be falconer.

But by the time she gained freedom, she had little or no flight experience. Her flight feathers were battered from captivity, and she didn't know how to feed herself in Nature. Naturally, she couldn't survive, and after a few days, or perhaps even a week, of struggling, she had simply settled down on the automobile roof where I found her.

After a couple of days of complete rest and increasingly larger meals, the little falcon was transferred to a large cage I had built for her on our home's north-facing balcony, which looked out on a quiet garden. The cage gave her room to leap from one perch to another. It was also protected from direct sunlight, and the little light that did enter was subdued by two layers of camouflage netting.

There was much work to be done in rehabilitating this bird, and as I began to work with her, she acquired her new name. Buzzy seemed to me to be an appropriate mixture of Hebrew and English influences. In Hebrew, the word for falcon is *buz,* so Buzzy came quite naturally this way. But there is also an English term "buzzwig," which described very important people who wore large, bushy wigs. (People who saw the popular film *Amadeus* may recall Mozart's buzzwig.) Buzzy, of course, didn't wear a buzzwig, but once she had recovered enough, she quickly assumed the airs of an arrogant and pompous aristocrat — just the sort who ought to wear such a regal headcover.

Buzzy's lice problem was quickly resolved with a bit of powder. And when she was strong enough, I began to give her proper meals — an assortment of "homemade mice," as I called them. These were composed of bits of waste meat and gristle obtained from a local butcher shop to which I added a few drops of avian multivitamin, and a small quantity of finely crushed pet bird mineral supplement. There was a bit of crushed eggshell to help restore her calcium and strengthen her weakened bones. The whole business was then folded and bound together with tufts of hair volunteered by my shepherd dog, Whyah, to provide the bit of necessary roughage.

Buzzy relished this messy meal and grew stronger day by day. After a month or so, she had regained full strength, although she had to wait until her next molt, when she would grow new feathers, before she could even hope to try flying.

Meanwhile, I converted our west balcony into an aviary and fitted it out with perches, proper perching stumps and stones, water trays, and other amenities, and this became Buzzy's temporary home.

Besides tending Buzzy, I tried to work with her whenever there was an opportunity. Admittedly, I used a few of the falconer's more benign techniques to encourage her skills. For example, I prepared a jess for her — a short strap provided with a ring for attaching a leash — and took her out into our garden. I'd set her on a perch not more than two feet from the ground and then pull one of my homemade mice in front of her at the end of a string. I wanted her to pounce on the meal as practice for the day when I hoped to let her free to fend for herself. But all she did was stare at me with her buzzwig sneer.

Other times, I'd slip on a glove and then set Buzzy upon my gloved hand. This was a pastime she apparently appreciated. Next, the operation was expanded a bit to make her use her wings — I'd swiftly lower my gloved hand, thereby forcing her to stretch her wings and use them for balance. This, I hoped, was a technique that could gradually be expanded to a point where she would have to use her wings to fly.

But she wouldn't fly. Instead, as my gloved hand was lowered, she ran up my arm until we were literally eyeball to eyeball, and I had to face her glowering and imperious stare from an uncomfortably close range. It is disconcerting to be a full-grown man and be intimidated by a five-and-a-half-ounce bird.

After many weeks of effort, it became apparent that I was not the person to rehabilitate Buzzy. And after consulting with a number of experts, I sadly came to the conclusion that the bird would never be free to soar in the skies.

My next option lay at Tel Aviv University, where Professor Heinrich Mendelssohn kept a breeding colony of lesser kestrels. I drove Buzzy there one summer day and delivered her to the university's zoological compound, where she was kindly received in a good-sized aviary that she now shares with about a dozen other birds of her species. At least there she receives proper care and will contribute to the knowledge and conservation of this species.

Her life was saved, but not her freedom.

Celebrities

"CALL YOFFE, right away," were Judy's first words upon returning home from her work teaching art to youngsters at Eilat's cultural center. "He called here around noontime, and it sounded important."

I dialed Avraham at home and quickly learned the reason for his urgency. Hai-Bar was to be visited by the BBC. "A man named Andrew Neal will be coming tomorrow morning with a film crew. They work for David Attenborough — the naturalist who wrote *Life On Earth*. I want you to show them every courtesy. And make double sure that Bin-Nun doesn't demand an entry fee when they show up at the front gate!"

"*Beseder gamor*, Avraham," I replied, "very well. I'll do that and more. I'll even have the truck washed, and I'll wear a properly ironed uniform shirt. Should I carry an umbrella?"

"Umbrella?" Avraham asked. "An umbrella in the desert?"

"Of course! Don't the British carry them everywhere?" I asked.

"Mind your tongue about the British!" he cautioned. Avraham was something of a sentimentalist about the British, an incurable Anglophile. Back in the 1930s, he had served in the Night Watch patrols of General Orde Charles Wingate, during the British Mandatory Period, and after three years he served another six years in the British Army during the Second World War. It was British training and discipline that made him into a very competent soldier, and with this background he became an important field commander in the Israel Defense Forces, reaching the rank of major general before he retired to take charge of the Nature Reserves Authority.

"Blimey, Avraham!" I continued with my friendly badgering. "I'll show the blokes so much courtesy that they'll think they're 'ome at Picadilly! And I won't even mention the Profumo Scandal!" Lord Profumo was a British aristocrat who had gotten involved with a spy scandal some years earlier. His mistress, Christine Keeler, and her "associate," Mandy Rice-Davies, ducked out of sight. Mandy re-emerged some time later in, of all places, Eilat, where she opened "Mandy's" — a Chinese restaurant on the beach.

"Just behave as if your future employment depended upon it," Avraham threatened.

"Dread naught!" I agreed. "Cheerio!"

"Cheeriiiii, bah. *Shalom.*"

Andrew Neal showed up the next morning with his crew in a rented van, and immediately we struck up a fine relationship. David Attenborough's *Life on Earth* had been an outstanding success both as a book and as a television nature series, Neal told me, and now he was working on a follow-up project, *The Living Planet.* The sequel was broken up into twelve hourly sections, one about each type of ecosystem — the Arctic, tropical rain forests, mountains, seas, deserts, and so forth. Neal was one of four producers working on the series, and he had been assigned to do three of the hour-long segments. One of them happened to be about deserts.

They had already been working on the desert project for several months but needed to do a bit more. In particular, they needed some wildlife footage. Neal explained that they had leased light aircraft and spent weeks flying over the Sahara Desert looking for Sahara oryx and addax antelope to film, but without success. These species were critically endangered. Their populations were so small and scattered that it was unlikely that they could be found.

Yet the script described how species such as these have adapted to the harsh environment of the desert, and, while Attenborough narrated a description of an oryx's unique metabolism or an addax's extraordinary anatomy, it would be nice to have some footage of these animals shown. Hai-Bar was the best nature reserve in the world for the filming because the animals were all healthy and located within a convenient tract of natural habitat. Even Hai-Bar's natural vegetation is identical to the typical plants found scattered across the Sahara.

The team spent a day scouting around the reserve, looking for the best filming angles and planning the rest of their production. Before closing time, Neal took me to a site on the eastern side of the reserve. "We'd like to put our camera here," he said, pointing to a brush-shrouded dune. "And we'd like a herd of addax to move from over there to over here," he added, indicating a route of about two hundred yards running obliquely to the camera site. "We can get our camera to cooperate," he said. "Can you do the same thing with a whole herd of addax?"

"Why not?" I replied. "All I have to do is tell them they'll be celebrities! They'll be so flattered that they'll do anything you want. Just like Hollywood starlets!"

We went to work the next morning at an early hour to catch the warm colors of the sunrise in the desert. I quickly fed all the other animals — to keep them busy and out of the way for a while — and then, finding the herd of addax, I drove the tractor near them — near enough for them to see and smell several choice bales of well-cured alfalfa hay on the trailer. This stimulated their interest, and they began to walk toward the trailer. I responded by driving away from them slowly.

Gradually, I lured the entire herd for about a kilometer, until we were near the site where the BBC wanted them to begin their walk in front of the camera lenses. Here, I was met by my helper Nathan, who had Whiskey all saddled and ready to gallop.

As the addax closed in, we slung two bales of hay like saddlebags across Whiskey's back. Nathan mounted and galloped away quickly, right along the same route that the BBC wanted the addax to take. When he got out of camera range, he wheeled Whiskey around and came to a halt.

Meanwhile, I tossed a couple of handfuls of straw on the ground — mostly to insult the addax. A few of them walked up to the stuff and did little more than sniff it. Straw, when they had been shown alfalfa! They seemed disgusted after such a long walk.

I had them, so to say, "waiting in the wings." I looked over to Neal and he gave me a "thumbs-up" sign — his camera crew were prepared to film. I glanced over to Nathan, who was standing by just out of camera range. Seeing everyone in place, I raised my arm and then dropped it swiftly — my signal for Nathan to go into action.

He sliced open the binding cords on the alfalfa hay, and, letting it fall to the earth, he began tossing flakes of the hay into the air with a wild abandon most frequently seen in young children. After tossing forty kilograms of the best hay available hither and yon around the desert, just out of camera range, he bounded onto Whiskey and rode off into the sunrise.

The addax did not miss the spectacle. In unison, they spit out the inferior straw that had been offered and made a bee-line straight for the alfalfa. In fact, a few were so excited over this superior breakfast that they began a light gallop, which was contagious. In moments, the whole herd was thundering across the sand, right in front of the BBC cameras.

"Well, do we get a million-dollar contract from this screen test?" I inquired of the BBC crew, who were obviously pleased with the performance.

"I wish we could offer one," Neal replied. "It all came off astonishingly well. We have some excellent footage here. Instead of a multimillion dollar contract, can we invite you to dinner this evening?"

"Certainly!" I replied.

"There's a restaurant near our hotel which is supposed to be quite good," Neal told me. "Let's meet there at about seven. Perhaps you are familiar with it? It's called Mandy's."

Dinner was divine, and I agreed that on the following day I'd take the crew around to a few of the more spectacular landscapes in the region so they could make shots of desert scenery that might be useful for the film. We climbed up into *Biquat HaYare'ach* — the Valley of the Moon — with its stark panoramas and barren vistas. And we found our way into *Nahal Shlomo* — Solomon's Canyon — which until recently, had been the high point of the region's cinematographic history.

"How many rocks do you see here?" I asked Neal.

"Millions," he replied. "Millions at least. There's nothing here but rocks."

"Ah, but you work with the fantasy industry," I noted. "A rose may be a rose may be a rose, but is a rock a rock?"

Neal stared at me with a perplexed expression. "Come, follow me a bit," I said, and we hiked up through a field of boulders on the canyon's southern edge until we reached a particular oddly shaped specimen.

"Here, feel this one," I invited. Neal reached out and tapped the boulder. "It's made of fiberglass!" he exclaimed.

"Precisely," I replied. "Hollywood fiberglass! Gregory Peck came here to film *Billy Two-Hats,* a cowboy movie, and the script called for a gun battle in this canyon. Peck had to hide behind a boulder, but none of the millions here suited the director. So they sent back to Hollywood to have one made. People around here have a saying — if we could only export rocks, we'd all be millionaires — but now look what's happening. We're importing them. The whole world's turning to plastic."

But Neal assured me that the BBC would use only real, live addax when making a film about addax, and it would be unthinkable to glue styrofoam horns on dairy cattle to simulate them. "That might be something for Hollywood," he said, "but Hollywood is a long way from Whiteladies Road, Bristol."

We met again for dinner and a tour around Eilat. It's a small city, but it has a unique sparkle and an appealing character. It is very much a resort town, with dozens of hotels and tourist facilities. But, I told our visitors, Eilatis haven't let all the glitter influence them. Most agree that their town is *hutz l'aretz* — abroad — because it's so far from any other community in Israel. And anyone who has driven clear across the entire Negev Desert to reach Eilat can appreciate this appellation. Some just call the town *sof olam* — the end of the world. Yet the friendly, relaxed ambience of Eilat is pleasing even to the tourists. One's room might not be in perfect order, but in such an easy atmosphere, who cares?

Eilat is the only community that I know of that has a neighborhood known as *HaOnesh* (The Punishment) — because it is *sooooo* far from the center of town — at least eight blocks. One complex of apartment houses is affectionately known as "Sing Sing." Everyone is constantly threatening to leave Eilat and move to one of the civilized cities further north — just like Moses, who passed through here during the Exodus — but few actually do. The charms of the town and its inhabitants exert a powerful hold.

Eilat has a number of locally famous physicians. One of these celebrities is Dr. Reginald Morris, who seems more British than Sir Lawrence Olivier. Dr. Morris earns a comfortable living treating the ailments of tourists staying in the town's five-star hotels. But he has also earned a favorable reputation by providing free medical service to the Bedouin in the desert, tending their many sicknesses with tremendous compassion.

Dr. Morris whisks around town in a pure white, air-conditioned Buick with New Jersey license plates, although nobody in Eilat recalls this well-mannered physician ever having been any place remotely near New Jersey. Never mind, he has the car, and that's what counts. Another idiosyncrasy of his is an extraordinary insistence on being properly attired at all hours of every day. On the hottest day in July, when the thermometer is bulging around 120 degrees Fahrenheit, Dr. Morris is seen in all the suave aristocratic coolness of his starched collar, Regent Street suit, and pure silk tie — or should I say cravat?

Dr. Morris' lovely wife, Faye, is the honorary British consul in Eilat and represents Her Majesty's Government admirably in this picturesque town beside the Red Sea. When we first moved to Eilat, we had to live without a telephone for several months, and Faye, striving to keep up our spirits, made her weekly "telephone call" to us in person.

The Morrises have the largest private lawn in the entire Negev Desert. People stroll through their neighborhood just to peek through the hedges to see such a lovely expanse of green. Some people make a point of passing by at eleven at night, because that's when the Morrises have their nightly computerized thunderstorm; hidden sprinklers burst with showers for the brief irrigation of the lawn.

Friday night is a special night at the Morrises, for they regularly invite about six or eight guests — most of whom are tourists visiting the city, but a few of whom are selected locals who are invited twice or three times a year. "Yes, of course," Mrs. Morris is fond of saying, "we keep precisely the same menu every Friday night, but we insist on changing the guests."

Dr. Aviezer Rippin, the chief surgeon at Eilat Hospital, has adopted the unusual habit of strolling in the evening with a small bell. "Wouldn't a flashlight be more useful?" I once inquired. "Certainly," he responded, "but by no means as eccentric."

Eccentricity aside, Dr. Rippin has one of the most difficult jobs in town, for he is the one most frequently called on to tend severe injuries. He's a skilled emergency surgeon, so when I faced severe crises with animals, I usually thought of him first. His competent hands have been volunteered to save the lives of injured gazelles and wolves on several occasions.

Dr. Rippin is the closest Eilat has to offer to compare with the Hawkeye Pierce character of M*A*S*H. And, indeed, he is just as quick with a wisecrack, while expertly lacing a dozen sutures.

Of all the local celebrities, perhaps the best known is Rafi Nelson, proprietor and boss at Nelson's Village, an appealing holiday shantytown, which has recently become the focus of international attention.

Two decades ago, Rafi Nelson drifted to the south edge of town, down the coast a bit, to open an informal beach resort, where his clientele enjoyed nice sun, good sand, clean water, and occasional topless nymphs. To enhance the atmosphere, Rafi installed a golden calf on a nearby hillside — or at least it has a golden color — as evidence that not all the Children of Israel have as yet reached the Promised Land.

Nelson maintained an easy manner and was often found in varying states of relaxation. He became locally famous for his big black cowboy hat, bushy gray beard, and formidable necklace of many large shark's teeth. He wore sandals when important guests were expected, but otherwise he went barefoot. Cool beer was always available, and his guests became accustomed to sharing their bit of desert beach with a few chickens and perhaps a horse or a goat.

The most excitement ever to happen at Nelson's Village occurred one day when a crowd of people were having a jolly time, socializing on the sand, sharing wild schemes, and flirting with one another. Suddenly, Nelson suffered an attack of appendicitis. Fortunately, Dr. Rippin was one of the merrymakers at the beach that day, so a whole party drove off to the hospital, where the surgeon quickly scrubbed and changed, the patient was wheeled into the operating room, and the appendix was removed.

A few days later, everything was back to normal except for a new topic of conversation — Rafi Nelson's appendectomy scar.

Then catastrophe struck. Egypt and Israel signed a peace treaty — but they couldn't agree on where the border should be. Israel claimed the few hundred yards of sand known as Nelson's Village. Egypt claimed the same sandlot and called it Taba. And Rafi Nelson was rocketed to the front pages of the *Times* of London, the *New York Times*, the *Washington Post*, and all the other major newspapers of the world. People on every continent saw glimpses of Nelson's exotic hideaway, because all the major networks braved the chickens and goats and sleepy Eilatis and even the threat of a divine lightning bolt — which everyone agrees must eventually come to strike down the golden calf — just to document on their video cameras this vital intersection of the world's body politic.

Were the Camp David accords so fragile that they could break down over sovereignty of a miniscule sandpile supporting no more than a tumbledown beach house and a couple of palm trees? Were the superpowers really teetering on the edge of confrontation behind their Middle East client states in the great dispute over a remote, formerly quite open-air bar?

The diplomats fumed. They made claims and counterclaims. They had big meetings in Geneva, and they sent emissaries back and forth carrying "notes" from prime ministers. They thundered and wailed and everyone cried "foul!" Today, nearly a decade later, the great Taba controversy over a couple of hundred yards of sand has finally been resolved. After extensive diplomatic dickering, Israel and Egypt agreed to go to arbitration — and the process awarded the sandlot to Egypt, which must also pay Israel for the "improvements" added since 1967.

A visit to the disputed beach was an adventure of major

proportions when it lay between the Israeli and Egyptian border posts. One needed a passport to get to Nelson's Village!

One of the more humorous delights of the Village was taking a good pair of binoculars and studying the Egyptian border guards a hundred yards away. They were the offspring of a conservative society, and here, usually for the first time in their lives, they were exposed to the exposed. That is to say, this was the first time most of them had ever heard of, no less actually seen, a topless beach. They spent many hours scrutinizing the no-man's-land beach to make sure there were no infiltrations from Israel.

Not all of our celebrities are local. Eilat in general and Hai-Bar in particular have drawn a substantial number of well-known personalities, from New York's ever-popular Mayor Ed Koch, to the staff of U.S. television's "You Asked For It," who filmed a number of segments at Hai-Bar. As they and Andrew Neal will tell you, the real celebrities are the addax, the oryx, and the other residents of Hai-Bar. The famous and the near famous may pass through, but these eccentric natives remain the natural stars of the desert.

Humbaba

A LEOPARD shall watch over their cities: everyone who goeth out thence shall be torn to pieces" (Jeremiah 5:6).

The marauding spotted cat that stalked ancient Israel still exists. This elusive predator, uniquely adapted to a harsh existence in the desert mountains, is the awesome Judean Desert leopard — the rarest of the great cats. Only about twenty-four of them are known to exist.

To learn more about this exceptional feline and why the biblical prophets regarded it as the ultimate symbol of brutality, Israeli conservationists have been tracking it back into its lair. They have been penetrating the spectacular, forbidding landscapes of the mountainous Judean Desert.

Giora Ilani, a sinewy forty-nine-year-old zoologist and field researcher for the Israel Nature Reserves Authority, knows more about the Judean Desert leopard than anyone else. In 1974, after years of tracking these elusive cats through the rugged mountains of Judea, he became the first man to prove they survived, by photographing one. These first pictures finally convinced many skeptics that the great cat described in the Bible by the prophets Isaiah and Jeremiah, but not seen since 1890, was not extinct. Since that dramatic rediscovery, Giora has been the principal investigator in the Israeli effort to study this extraordinary predator in its desert habitat — and his remarkable findings are perhaps even more significant than the rediscovery of the Judean Desert leopard itself.

My work at Hai-Bar brought me into contact with Giora, and one day, not long after I started work at the reserve, he invited me to join him on one of his leopard-tracking expeditions. That was an offer I could not refuse. Not only should wildlife field-workers take every opportunity to swap notes on each other's projects, but besides that, a hike out into the desert mountains to study leopards was bound to be an exciting adventure.

Thus, I joined Giora for an excursion into Nahal Arugot, a favored habitat for the Judean Desert leopard. Nahal is a Hebrew word meaning "canyon," and this one happens to be located in the Judean Desert, about two hundred kilometers due north of Hai-Bar.

Giora and I organized our gear at the eastern end of this canyon. We shouldered our packs and silently gesturing upward, toward the west, Giora stepped out with a lithe, catlike gait, habitually precise about each footstep. He evidently had picked up a few characteristics of the leopards that he has been stalking for decades. I followed in his footsteps as quietly as possible.

We entered the austere canyon near its exit to the Dead Sea — 1,290 feet below sea level, the lowest point on earth. From here, all the world is uphill. Even California's Death Valley, at 282 feet below sea level, is more than a thousand feet closer to the stars. We gained elevation and lost sweat.

Gradually, the gray face of the Dead Sea faded behind us, and with a bend in the canyon, it disappeared completely. From here, this steep-walled canyon plunges westward into the jagged, sun-parched mountains, which rise thousands of feet into the bright desert sky. Surrounded by stark, towering cliffs, we kept to an ancient serpentine path hacked into the rock of the canyon's north wall. We trekked westward and upward. The sun was hot and the air parched.

After a brief rest and a sip of water, we pushed on another three kilometers along the rugged trail and then stopped once again just before a sharp bend. Giora slipped the pack from his back and began digging into its tangle of aluminum tubes, wires, and electrical gadgets. In minutes, he assembled a radio antenna and plugged it into a small receiver. "We're tuned into Humbaba's frequency," he said, flicking a small switch. "Let's hope she's in the area today."

Humbaba — named for the great spotted monster of the ancient Sumerian *Gilgamesh Epic* — is a Judean Desert leopard. Like her namesake, who guarded an enchanted forest four thousand years ago, Humbaba is mistress of her own magical oasis, Nahal Arugot's slender thread of vegetation thriving in the midst of a barren desert. The greenery is gathered around a little brook that springs from a desert mountain and then tumbles down along the canyon's sandy floor. The verdant thickets clustered along the brook are the ecological foundation of the entire region.

Unlike the snow leopards and clouded leopards, which zoologists classify as separate species, the Judean Desert leopard is a race of true leopard — *Panthera pardus* — a species that is distributed across nearly all of Africa and most of southern Asia.

True leopards are generally considered to be the most adaptable of the great cats. They manage to survive in places that would present hopeless difficulties for tigers, lions, or cheetahs. Leopards can be found near urban centers such as Nairobi, in the densest growths of tropical jungles, out in open grasslands, and, of course, in desert mountains. They don't have the speed of a cheetah, nor can they claim the brute force of a lion. Instead, they rely on their wits. They're smart, and, pound for pound, they're the scrappiest of the big cats.

A couple of dozen races of true leopard have been identified and range from some of the big maulers of central Africa, which can weigh in at 200 pounds, to the fly-weight Arabian leopard, which, at fifty pounds, is the pygmy of the species. The Judean Desert leopard, at about ninety pounds, is on the light side of the middleweights.

Until Giora's study began, there had never been a scientific field survey of the Judean Desert leopard. In fact, even today we are not precisely sure what race of leopard this is, because it hasn't yet been described in scientific literature. The closest known relative is the Sinai leopard — *Panthera pardus jarvisi* — but that cat's scientific description was made only from a museum collection of a few bones, two skulls, and a skin, in 1932. The resources used for defining that subspecies are surely very slender and very suspect. But just because the scientists don't have a proper Latin name for our big cat doesn't mean we dare ignore it. This big feline is very important, even if it may have something of a scientific identity crisis.

Adapting to its desert mountain habitat has made the Judean Desert leopard a unique cat. Compared to other leopards, the Israeli race appears to be proportionately shorter and better muscled — nearly a hundred pounds of spotted spring steel slung between four short legs. This reflects the Judean Desert leopard's mostly vertical habitat. There really is little place to use long running legs. Instead, short legs and extra-strong muscles give an advantage in climbing up and down the face of desert cliffs.

The Judean Desert leopard is a bit paler than most of its cousins and blends better with the desert landscape. Put a bright yellow jungle leopard in this habitat and you could spot it five miles away. The Israeli cat has proportionately larger paws and thus has better traction climbing up and down steep rocks. It has also made a few useful adaptations that aren't obvious in a physical examination. For example, it can get along indefinitely without drinking water — just as long as there are ample ibex, hyrax, and other prey available.

But the Judean Desert leopard also retains many characteristics shared by other members of this Eastern Hemisphere species. It has a typical rosette pattern on its coat and commonly walks with its shoulders raised a bit higher than its backbone, giving it a fluid, slinky action. And like other leopards, the Israeli cat has a white-tipped tail, which it carries in a slightly raised position. If anything, this tail is a bit larger than average and perhaps serves as a useful balance when climbing through precarious places.

All of these adaptations served the Judean Desert leopard very well for thousands of years in its desolate mountain habitat. It fit in perfectly with the dynamics and rhythms of life in the desert. It even managed to coexist with humanity for many centuries. Indeed, within three miles of Nahal Arugot's mouth, the remains of a five thousand-year-old Chalcolithic period community can be seen. This is where people stepped out of the Stone Age. The name of the settlement is *Ein Gedi* — the Spring of the Kid.

Actually, the "gedi" in the name *Ein Gedi* means the kid of an ibex and not that of a domestic goat. Ibex are quite common in these mountains and are one of the most important prey species for the leopard. The kid of the ibex in particular is especially favored leopard prey.

It seems certain that the prophet Isaiah knew this when he composed his beautiful prophecy of the peaceable kingdom, for in it, the leopard does not lie down with just any creature. Isaiah's prophecy has the leopard reclining beside the kid of an ibex, ". . . and the leopard shall lie down with the kid" (Isaiah 11:6).

The Judean Desert leopard is also the creature that Jeremiah saw and mentioned in another famous biblical passage, when he asked if the leopard could change his spots (Jeremiah 13:23). There are several other biblical references to leopards, and generally they're used as symbols for violent revenge. Even though the mighty Judean lion, and the ponderous brown bear roamed ancient Israel, the prophets knew that the Judean Desert leopard was the most feared predator of all. That's because a typical leopard attack is a bloody tooth-and-claw brawl. No other predator confronts its victim with such rampaging fury. No other predator is so brutal.

The Judean Desert leopard survived in its lair throughout the biblical period and for another eighteen centuries without much difficulty. The armies of Rome, Byzantium, and Islam swept through the region — and the leopard survived. The Crusaders ruled for two centuries, and then Saladin, the Mamelukes, and the Ottoman Turks.

Disaster came only when firearms were introduced. In the open terrain of the desert, a leopard can be seen a mile away. With a rifle — even an old-fashioned flintlock — it's possible to sit on one side of a canyon and pick off a leopard stalking the opposite wall. Through the nineteenth century, the Judean Desert leopard population plummeted. By 1890, the animal had vanished. It was presumed extinct.

There were occasional reports of leopards in the Judean Desert earlier this century — but they were all unconfirmed. Bedouin shepherds reported terrifying stories of spotted monsters prowling the edges of their camps and occasionally preying on their goats and sheep. Army patrols would catch glimpses of some large creatures marauding in the night.

Before 1967, Nahal Arugot was dangerous territory — it lay just a few miles on the Israeli side of the border with Jordan. Back in those days, the rugged canyons were favored regions for terrorist infiltrations, and the army discouraged wildlife biologists from romping around in there. But after the Six Day War in 1967, the Nahal Arugot area became secure, and Giora Ilani went to work. Before long, he was picking up evidence of the great cat's presence — urine marks here, footprints there, trees used by the feline as big scratching posts. He spent seven years collecting a mountain of circumstantial evidence, never once having actually seen the leopard. But he was persuaded that the Judean Desert leopard survived, even if most of the world's experts remained doubtful.

The break came in December 1974. Kibbutzniks from Ein Gedi discovered the remains of a freshly killed ibex and alerted Giora. He inspected the kill and was sure it was the work of a leopard. He was also aware of the leopard's well-known habit of returning to the kill to feed day after day.

Giora set up a blind in the rocks above the kill, prefocused a camera, set up a flash unit, and settled down for the evening's watch. As expected, the leopard showed up. Lights flashed. Shutters clicked. And Giora had all the evidence he needed.

From then on, Giora Ilani has been the Judean Desert leopard's constant companion. Indeed, he has been tagging along with them so much through the past decade that they've come to take his presence for granted and don't show any concern when they see him climbing about the rocks and cliffs in their habitat.

Giora, on the other hand, is very concerned about the leopards. Year by year, he has documented their recovery. Whereas ten years ago there were perhaps a half dozen leopards stalking Israel's deserts, today there are at least two dozen — a fourfold increase.

The reason for this increase is certainly strong conservation policies. Many Israeli conservationists consider the survival and recovery of the Judean Desert leopard to be a very important indicator of their overall conservation success. This is because the leopard is the top-level predator, the peak of the region's ecological pyramid. In order for the leopard to survive, an entire, functioning ecological infrastructure must support it. For the leopard to exist, there must be a vigorous population of prey animals — ibex, hyrax, and other herbivores, to supply it with food. For the prey species to exist, there must be ample amounts of suitable natural vegetation to support them. And there must be reliable supplies of unpolluted water. For the entire ecological fabric to function properly there must be effective conservation programs and protection measures. Thus, when one knows that leopards survive in Nature, one also knows quite a bit about the quality of the natural environment they inhabit.

For many countries that have large land areas, there's enough room to absorb both pollution and wildlife in separate regions. But little Israel is only the size of New Jersey, and simple natural resources, such as fresh water and good soil, are very scarce. There's no room for pollution or poor management of resources. Everything must be disciplined as strictly as possible.

Because human activities such as industry, agriculture, and housing are carefully managed, Israel has achieved the position of being able to set aside a very large percentage of its national territory for nature conservation. About 20 percent of the land area is protected as nature reserves. National forests occupy another 12 percent. National parks, regional conservation zones, and a uniquely military concept, *shetah esh bli esh* (firing zones without firing) cover yet another 20 percent of land area. From some perspectives, the military zones are among the best for conservation, because their use is strictly controlled and open only for radio communication exercises, training hikes, and other army activities that don't disturb Nature. The general public is excluded — along with the general public's litter and other disturbances that sometimes affect wildlife in more accessible areas.

Nahal Arugot is part of the Judean Desert nature reserves complex — a patchwork of nature reserves drawn together into a comprehensive system. Through the past decade, Giora has identified it as one of the most important leopard habitats in Israel, and this is where some of his remarkable discoveries have been made.

One of the reasons he has made his discoveries here is that he has been able to catch a few leopards in the region with big box traps. Once the cats are caught, radio collars are strapped on and then they're released again. So with the big felines transmitting loud and clear, it's usually easy to find them again with a directional receiver.

And that's precisely what happened on the day we climbed up into Nahal Arugot together. The instant Giora switched on his receiver it started to pop and crackle excitedly. "She's near," he told me, "very near."

We peeked around the bend in the canyon. I half expected to see a pair of bright amber eyes peeking right back at me. No such luck. All we could see was kilometer after kilometer of perpendicular stone. If Nahal Arugot was ever flattened out, I think it would probably cover half of Texas.

Giora explained that these canyon walls tend to confuse the radio signals the big cats transmit. Radio waves can bounce off opposite walls, double back on themselves, and create amplified echos that appear to be coming from the wrong direction. With experience and a bit of luck, he said, one develops a knack for using the electronic gadgetry.

Giora also assured me that one develops a knack for hiking around this plumb perpendicular neighborhood. And it's an enormous neighborhood indeed. While the average African leopard claims a territory of about twenty-five square kilometers, his Israeli counterpart requires a two hundred and fifty-square kilometer living room. This means that the average Israeli wildlife biologist gets a bit more exercise trying to find the feline. And since just about all of that living space is in regions inaccessible to jeeps and Land Rovers, the Israeli wildlife biologist tends to wear out hiking shoes at a faster rate than his African counterparts.

We moved ahead, further into Nahal Arugot, scanning the canyon walls for Humbaba. Moving along the trail, Giora explained that the Israeli leopards require so much room because of the nature of the desert they inhabit. One square kilometer of the Israeli desert can barely produce one-tenth the vegetation found in more humid climates, like that of the Serengeti Plains of East Africa. Thus, it can support only one-tenth the population of grazing and browsing animals. With prey populations so small, the leopard must adjust itself by inhabiting a range ten times the size of its African cousins'.

The trail bent downward a bit and skimmed the edge of the vegetation area on the floor of the canyon. I could hear a brook gurgling away in the thickets somewhere, but we didn't enter. Passing a Euphrates poplar tree, Giora pointed out that this particular tree had been used as a scratching post by several leopards — its bark was tattered and gouged by long, deep clawings. He explained that this tree is part of the reason why leopard experts around the world are reconsidering what they thought was "normal" behavior for the leopard.

For centuries, people interested in leopards agreed that the big cat was a notorious loner that would go into a rage if any other leopard entered its territory. Popular presumptions said that adult leopards only got together for a very brief romance and then went their separate ways.

But the poplar tree was obviously used by several leopards, and that meant their territories had to overlap. They had to coexist in the same area to be using the same scratching post. Giora doesn't like to use the term *territory* because, to a wildlife biologist, territory defines a region from which a particular leopard will evict all others — and that wasn't the case here. So he says they have overlapping "ranges."

After climbing around through the cliffs for more than a decade, Giora believes that each Judean Desert leopard has a "home range," which may overlap with the home range of other leopards. The area of overlapping range Giora calls a "core area."

Judean Desert leopards tolerate each other in the core area, Giora explained. "This doesn't mean they socialize," he added. "Generally, they simply avoid each other in the core area and let each other pass through without conflict."

A bit farther along the path, we came across a shallow scratching in the sand. It was only about two or three inches deep and about a foot and a half across. I bent down to take a good sniff. Leopard, for sure.

Giora explained that these trapezoid-shaped scratch marks are the most common "calling cards" that the Judean Desert leopard leaves

Caligula, the Nubian ibex.

General Avraham Yoffe, feeding lunch to an orphaned gazelle, Zvika.

Nathan Minkovski gets a kiss from orphan ibex kid J.R.

Saleh Makladay, Druze manager of Hai-Bar Carmel, with mountain gazelle Zvika.

Judy and Joe with a few friends in the ibex enclosure.

Nathan Minkovski, clipping an overgrown hoof of a Nubian ibex.

Joe, Claudius the
ibex, and a bale of
hay.

Joe on Lightning,
his donkey, standing
next to Lightning's
lunch.

Scimitar-horned oryx. Note that although the herd has a broad desert to roam, they prefer to walk single file on a well-worn path.

Napoleon, the scimitar-horned oryx.

Scimitar-horned oryx
and her calf.

Infant scimitar-
horned oryx.

Mountain gazelle.

Saint Patrick,
the short-toed eagle.

Moshele (*left*) and Danny Dishon, addax antelope, jousting.

Two young addax antelope, resting in the shade of a salt bush.

Addax antelope Sarah (*center*), Haim (*left*), and Leah.

Addax antelope Sarah.

Bin-Nun the ostrich.

Ostriches Bonnie
and Clyde.

Bonnie the ostrich.

African wild ass
foal Avraham.

African wild ass
with foal.

African wild ass
at Hai-Bar.

African wild asses.

Cinderella the "unicorn" (*left*) with other white oryx antelope.

Can you spot the unicorn?

White oryx antelope.

Onagers in Israel's
Arava Valley,
with the biblical
Mountains of Edom
beyond.

Two onagers take a
morning drink.

Three onagers.

Four onagers.

Onagers on the run.

in its habitat. To announce its presence, the leopard scratches out a shallow hole and then sprays urine into it. Unlike its cousin the housecat, the leopard leaves its urine uncovered. This way the odor is a bit stronger and is easily identified even by the relatively insensitive nose of a human.

All the while, Giora's radio receiver was crackling away like a swamp full of insects on a summer's night. Humbaba was around, and she certainly must have sensed our presence. But she just wasn't up to revealing her whereabouts.

We pressed on to what Giora calls "the information center." This area of about an acre in size, some three hundred yards up from the canyon floor, was the hub of the core area, and every leopard in the region stopped by here once in a while to leave a calling card. A faint scent of leopard urine continuously lingers, and one encounters many scratch marks. It was the strongest evidence that Giora had developed to confirm that the Judean Desert leopards share habitat, that they tolerate each other in a communal living space.

We moved through an extraordinary clutter of enormous boulders and reed thickets. The sounds from the radio receiver increased in volume and intensity. The thing sounded like a Geiger counter sitting on top of an atomic bomb. No question about it, Humbaba had to be very close by. Moving on parallel paths about forty or fifty yards apart, we ascended a steep slope of loose rock. We climbed until we reached the face of a sheer cliff, which shot straight up for several hundred feet. If she were up there, we would have surely seen her.

We swung back down toward the information center and probed through the reed thickets. There was a clearing just about ten yards away from where we had been standing a while before, and there we found some provocative evidence. When we had been standing in this area earlier, Humbaba had been right there with us — just a few short strides away, beyond a growth of reeds. We found her fresh footprints; just to make sure we got her message, she had dug out a shallow pit and filled it with urine. It was so fresh that it hadn't been completely absorbed by the sand.

We leopard stalkers had been stalked by the leopard!

Humbaba played her own game of "cat and mouse" with us, and

search as we might, the great feline wouldn't reveal herself. We scouted around the area a while longer in a fruitless search for more clues. But fate decreed that we weren't to see the leopard that day. So while we still had enough daylight, we packed it in for the day and made our way slowly back toward camp. Perhaps we would have better luck the next day.

Over supper, Giora told me more about the Judean Desert leopard and what makes it unique. This cat sets its business hours according to the thermometer. In the winter, when the temperature rarely gets much warmer than 75 degrees Fahrenheit in these parts, the leopard prowls about at almost any hour of the day. But in summer, when temperatures push up past the 110-degree mark nearly every day, the leopard restricts its activity to the cooler morning and evening hours.

The Judean Desert leopard prefers ibex and hyrax as prey but will grab anything that moves if the opportunity presents itself. A few years earlier, Giora had spent a memorable hour watching Shlomzion, another Judean Desert leopard living in this region, dining on termites during the stage in which the termites have wings and flit about in their nuptial flights. Shlomzion sat back on her haunches and swatted tiny termites out of the air with her massive paws and then ate each little delicacy she successfully grabbed.

On another occasion, she was after more substantial prey — hyrax — the little rabbit-sized coney. Usually, the leopard makes a conventional attack, springing from ambush or carefully stalking its prey. But on this occasion, Giora recorded a new hunting tactic. The big cat evidently heard hyrax chattering on the opposite side of a large boulder. Carefully and quietly, she climbed the back of the boulder, and without actually seeing what was on the other side, she sprang over the top with claws extended and mouth open.

Hyrax bolted in all directions, and the leopard came up with a miss. Undaunted, however, she tried the tactic again, by another rock — and missed again. And then a third time and a third miss. And then a fourth time and bingo — lunch. A 25 percent success rate isn't too bad for a predator only recently specializing in blind flying leaps over great boulders into a tribe of panic-stricken hyrax.

On our second day of leopard tracking, we woke up at about

three in the morning, grabbed a quick snack, and were back on the trail while stars still filled the sky. We had just about reached the information center when the sky lightened and the radio receiver began crackling away again.

After the disappointment of the previous day, I didn't expect any miraculous appearances on this expedition. Nonetheless, as we got near the information center and light began to bathe the canyon, we saw Humbaba stretched out on top of a large boulder — just like the Queen of Sheba on her divan. Despite the dull grayness of the dawn light, her coat appeared a bright gold. Squarely in the middle of the information center, she surveyed the canyon floor below, casually yawning, now and then flicking the tip of her tail to and fro in the morning haze. She was certainly aware of our presence, but she paid no heed to us at all.

Moving quickly along the path, we skirted below her and pushed deeper into the canyon. Then we crossed to the other side and climbed the facing wall. About five or six hundred feet up we found a comfortable rock and perched ourselves at that convenient lookout post. Humbaba was in plain view directly across the canyon.

She was still reclining and acting quite indifferent to the world. But every few moments, she inspected the region around a small fissure in a nearby cliff with her stern gaze. There must be something of great interest in there, we thought.

An hour passed, and the sun peeped up from behind the bibilical Mountains of Moab. Still, Humbaba rested and kept watch on the cleft in the rocks. A while later, she stood and surveyed the landscape. We could see that her breasts were distended — a certain sign that she had cubs.

Humbaba turned and entered the small cavern she had been so concerned about all morning. Ten minutes later, she re-emerged and stretched.

We were pretty sure she was keeping her cubs in that little cave — and we decided to leave today's record as "pretty sure." It would be easy to confirm whether Humbaba had cubs, but this would involve violating an important principle of good wildlife conservation — never intrude into a wild animal's den unless it is absolutely necessary. Humans snooping around a den tend to upset the animals living there. Most wildlife, including leopards, will move their cubs to a new den if they learn that the location of their original lair has been discovered. Usually, the new den is not as good as the old one — perhaps it is more exposed or subject to more intense noontime heat or some other factor that originally made it the number-two choice. Moving young animals to a new den involves a certain risk — and we didn't want to force Humbaba to take that risk. Since there was no pressing need to confirm the existence of cubs, we decided to let well enough alone.

(A later expedition, in which I did not participate, confirmed that Humbaba was indeed nursing two healthy cubs, which were, by then, old enough to follow their mother for short expeditions out into the canyon.)

As the heat of the day began to sear the canyon, Humbaba slipped back into the crevice. We were quite sure she wouldn't come back out again until the day cooled down toward evening.

Meanwhile, we were starting to sizzle like a pair of sunny-side up chicken-fruit on a hot skillet. We took the cue from Humbaba. It was time to move to a shadier environment.

As we left Nahal Arugot, Giora told me he was positive that at least twenty-four Judean Desert leopards live in Israel today. They range in the mountainous areas, just about twenty kilometers southeast of Jerusalem, all the way down to Eilat, on the northern tip of the Red Sea. There have also been reports of leopards in the north of the country, in the Upper Galilee district. Even with all the agriculture, military movements, terrorist infiltrations, and other human activity along the border with Lebanon, Giora believes the leopard may still stalk that region. If so, it would be the southern limit of a different race of leopard, the Anatolian leopard (*Panthera pardus tulliana*), a somewhat larger cat, not adapted to the desert but perfectly at home in the oak and pine forest of better-watered parts of the Middle East.

"There are some skeptics who think the Anatolian leopard couldn't possibly exist up in the Galilee," Giora acknowledged. "But when you get to know the leopard and how flexible and adaptable they are, it makes you reluctant to believe that they've been exterminated."

If the Anatolian leopard — which ranges up into eastern Turkey — does survive in the Galilee, it can be counted as another biblical cat that still inhabits the Holy Land. For this is the giant leopard that Solomon referred to when he wrote, "Look from the top of Amana, from the top of Shenir and Hermon . . . from the mountains of the leopards" (Song of Songs 4:8).

The Great
Camel Stampede

SPRINGTIME is the most active season at Hai-Bar.
There's a great rush to accomplish as much work as
possible before the torturous heat of summer makes each job many
times more difficult. Springtime is a season for mending fences,
repairing watering sites, and keeping a close watch on increases in
Nature's inventory. Springtime is the main season of birth-giving at
Hai-Bar. Nature carefully arranges for the great multitude of calves
and colts and kids to arrive when the desert blossoms with rich
vegetation and the thermometer avoids extremes. This is the season
when well-fed dams can produce their best milk, the season of least
stress and most abundance in the desert.

Springtime also means extra hours at a nature reserve to keep up
with the many special needs of all the newborns. This ibex gave
birth to triplets but will nurse only two. The odd one is out, and
if it is to survive, it must be hand-reared. That antelope has a sickly
infant with diarrhea. In the wild, it would be dead in a day or two,
but, here, we strive to save all we can. So the youngster and his
mom must be caught and temporarily kept in a pen, where proper
medicines can be administered daily until the calf is recovered.
There are thousands of little chores that fill the days of springtime.
They're pleasant chores, rewarding but also exhausting.

One of the most important springtime chores at Hai-Bar is
wolf-proofing. Dozens of desert wolves live in the wild just outside

the reserve fence. They are smart, organized, and extremely sensitive. In the springtime, those wolves know very well that there are many young, defenseless animals inside the reserve, so they do precisely what their instincts tell them to do — try to get into the reserve and prey upon the newborns.

In Nature, predators such as wolves usually kill a significant number of youngsters each year. This is part of the dynamics of the wild. Alert, fleet-footed infants get a head start on their less sensitive and more awkward brothers and sisters. Those that are best prepared to escape a wolf attack have the greatest likelihood of survival. Thus, for example, because of wolves, young gazelles are extremely alert and nimble animals, for only such youngsters can survive. If the wolves were eliminated from the environment, less alert, less nimble gazelles would tend to have a better survival ability, and the lovely gazelles of the desert would gradually become quite a different sort of creature.

I firmly believe that wolves are an important part of Nature and ought to be protected in their own natural habitats. I also firmly believe that wolves have no role in Hai-Bar and that every effort must be made to keep them outside the reserve. Hai-Bar is a special refuge for endangered animals, and the life of each one of these animals is important to the future of their species. Special efforts must be made in this situation to step beyond the natural course of life in the wild and give the endangered animal special attention to help it survive. This means hand-rearing orphans, providing special medicines to the sickly, and *keeping the wolves outside the reserve!*

This last aim is more easily stated than accomplished. Wolves are very inventive animals, and when they hear a potential meal bleating only a short distance beyond the fence, they make every effort to get in. My job was to make every effort to keep them out. There were two keys to the Hai-Bar defense against wolves. The first was the design and construction of the fence, and the second was patrols, patrols, and more patrols. The best fences in the world won't keep a persistent wolf out unless they are frequently patrolled.

Our fence design incorporated several strategies. The main part of the fence was a vertical wire mesh, which was too small for the

wolves to squeeze through. This part extended upward about seven
feet and downward about one foot into the earth. On the top part,
another three feet of fencing jutted out at a forty-five-degree angle
from the vertical fence, thus creating an overhang. This upper
fencing was left rather slack, so if a wolf did climb up the vertical
part, he also had to climb back over the loose-slung overhanging
mesh. At the base of the fence, another four feet of wire mesh was
buried parallel to the surface at a depth of about six inches. If a wolf
tried to dig under the fence, he would get as far as the buried part
and, perhaps, become discouraged.

Despite all these intricate precautions, occasionally wolves did
get into the reserve and cause some damage before they were
eventually captured, and booted back outside where they belonged.

Wolves, being incredibly smart, fear humans. And a simple
human presence along the fence tended to dampen their enthusiasm
for getting through. This human presence was enhanced in several
ways. For example, all through the birthing season, I had a
standing order at every barber shop in Eilat to save all the day's
sweepings. Great bales of human hair were collected and spread on
the ground at key areas along the fence. Hair retains human scent
for a long time, and this freely donated contribution spread along
the fence left a lingering scent that wolves preferred to avoid. Hair,
being organic and biodegradable, eventually decomposes, and so an
added bonus to this tactic was that it avoided littering the desert.

There are many other schemes for deterring scheming wolves —
portable radios, trip wires, even lion excrement carried down (in a
tightly sealed container!) from the safari park in Ramat Gan near
Tel Aviv. I tried them all. But the most effective protection of all,
I learned, is a physical human presence. Wolves won't approach a
fence actively patrolled by a human.

This only confirms the adage that the best way to protect sheep
is to hire a shepherd. And so, all through the year, I insisted upon
daily patrols of the fence, and through the birthing season, extra
patrols were added at night.

I did much of this patrol work myself, and actually I rather
enjoyed it. The hike around the main breeding area was about
twelve kilometers — about two or three hours, depending on my

vigor and the number of distractions I encountered along the way. It was a very pleasant walk. Usually, I'd pack a small kit bag with a flashlight, canteen, and other items I might find useful along the way. Then I'd strap on an old revolver — its main function was to signal for help in an emergency, as two shots in the air this close to the border would surely bring a squad of Israeli soldiers very quickly — and then I'd be off. Out the gate, I'd hike south two kilometers along the western fence. This area is quite dense with thorny acacia trees and is home for a pair of little owls. It runs parallel to the main Arava highway, and, during the night patrols, the traffic, with its noise and bright headlights, was quite distracting. In fact, traffic was usually heaviest in the evening hours, because many drivers preferred to make their long, cross-desert hauls during these cooler hours, rather than during the heat of the day.

At the southwestern corner, I'd turn away from the road and follow the south fence eastward for another two kilometers, cutting first across some knee-deep brush, and some loose sandy areas, and then to the broad, flat desert. At the end of this leg of the fence, the desert continued eastward, flat as a billiard table, without a single blade of grass growing. The border with Jordan lay a couple of hundred yards out there.

This border had been quiet for years, and, although Israel and Jordan were technically in a state of war, a de facto peace reigned. Walking along this sector, it was easy to see the Jordanian highway, which comes up from the port of Aqaba. And the lights from a small Jordanian village glistened along the highway just a few kilometers to the north. Often, I'd come across one of the Israeli army patrols that moved up and down the border all through the night. They had not encountered any infiltrating terrorists for quite a few years in this sector, although wolf packs had become an increasingly common phenomenon.

The Hai-Bar fence ran north, parallel to the border, for four kilometers, moving across the flat hard surface of the desert floor and then into some rough terrain of sand dunes. The dune area in particular was quite lively at night, with many desert rodents scampering about and occasionally a desert fox prowling after them.

At the end of this fence section, the reserve abutted the date palm plantations of Kibbutz Yotvata, and the walk across the northern flank was usually accompanied by the music of a desert wind rustling the palm fronds. A last stretch of two kilometers ran south along the west fence, and by the time I reached this point, I was but a few steps away from my favorite haystack, a waiting bedroll, and perhaps a half hour of stargazing before slumber carried me off to other worlds.

The desert has a unique character at night, a softness and tranquility that are very rare on this earth. And sometimes, I was treated to a special concert of the wolves howling in the darkness — just to let me know that they were behaving themselves outside the reserve.

On one such nighttime stroll, a fine spring evening with stars so bright that I could see distinct shapes at a very good distance, I was walking along the eastern fence just about a kilometer north of the southeast corner. It was a still evening, no breeze at all, and my last diary entry had been made about forty-five minutes before — "wolves heard howling to the east." But now all was quiet, and I was nearly halfway through my night patrol.

My first warning was a dull thud followed by a familiar hiss. *Fump . . . sssssssssssssssssssssssssssssss . . . pah!* And the heavens were alight. Something had tripped a parachute flare out along the border; the device rocketed skyward, and at the peak of its trajectory, a very brilliant light was ignited. The flare then slowly glided earthward, hanging from its small parachute and illuminating the face of the desert below.

The glare was so bright that I had to shade my eyes while looking back across the desert. But I couldn't see what had tripped the flare. *Fump . . . fump, fump . . . fump . . . fump, fump, fump . . . SSSSSSSSSSSSS!* In seconds, dozens of flares were rocketing skyward, burning with a brilliance not seen since the bicentennial display over New York harbor. Without bothering to look much closer, I decided what had set off all those flares — it must have been the entire Jordanian Arab Legion. They must be attacking right here, right now, and here I was standing like an idiot on the border, just hanging around and waiting to become the first casualty of Middle

East War number eighty-two. The only thing between me and the route away from the border and toward safety was a formidable fence, which I had helped to build and keep in good repair.

Dangling on the fence, trying to swing myself over, I heard more flare's rocketing aloft. Alarms were being sounded at the Israeli army base near Yotvata. I heard the cough of heavy diesel engines starting and then the clanking of tracked vehicles. This had to be the opening round of World War Three! Somehow, I lurched over the fence and crashed to the ground on the opposite side. I bolted to my feet and ran westward.

The reserve was in bedlam. Panicky antelope, ostriches, and onagers were stampeding this way and that, running in terror from the fires in the skies. About half a kilometer from the reserve work house, I found an addax antelope calf, less than a month old, stumbling around with a broken leg. It had apparently been trampled in one of the stampedes.

Scooping the young animal up into my arms, I continued toward the house. Within moments, I heard helicopters coming from the south. Ours or theirs? What kind of sound does an Israeli helicopter make? Or an Arab helicopter? I ducked beneath an acacia tree for safety.

Sitting there with an injured antelope calf in my arms, trying to catch my breath, a puzzling thought crossed my mind. Amidst the pandemonium of flares and helicopters, alarms, tracked vehicles moving everywhere, not a single shot had been fired! Why wasn't anybody shooting? What kind of war was this?

I gathered up the injured calf and began trudging back toward the work house, fully perplexed about the course of events. By the time I got there, a squad of Israeli soldiers was waiting for me.

"What do you know about herding camels?" a sergeant demanded.

"Not a damned thing," I replied with perfect honesty. "Why are you having a war on such a lovely spring night?"

"We're not having a war tonight," the sergeant snapped back. "We're having a camel roundup."

The sergeant explained that something across the border in Jordan had caused a herd of about three dozen camels to stampede into the night. They had galloped due west and crashed through the border like a . . . like a herd of stampeding camels.

Crossing the border, the camels must have set off a few hidden trip-flares. This made them panic even more, and they ran in all directions in the darkness, resulting, of course, in more flares being tripped, until the entire border was glowing like Methuselah's birthday cake.

The camels had also set off every alert alarm south of Beer Sheva, and half the Israeli army was poised to repel the intruders.

"So, you gonna help us round up all those camels?" the sergeant asked with a tone of politeness mastered only by sergeants.

"Maybe later," I replied. "I've got a little calf here with a broken leg."

The sergeant shuffled off with the rest of his squad, somewhat uncertain as to what to do. I had my own work cut out for me and went right to it. With the calf wrapped in a heavy jacket so it couldn't move, I set about preparing a little emergency clinic in the work house. Plaster bandage set to soak in a bucket of water, wads of cotton out and ready, and all of the other items — scissors, antiseptics, iodine — lined up and ready for use.

By the glow of a gas lamp, I carried the frightened calf to the sink for a good cleaning with Cetavlon soap. This done, I was able to get a better estimate of the damage, and, on close inspection, it seemed we were not dealing with a major catastrophe after all. The leg was broken all right, but it was only a simple fracture of the metatarsus. I could feel the two parts of the broken bone and set them back in place without any problem. The frightened calf was a willing patient and made no effort to complicate my work.

I wrapped an extra thickness of cotton around the broken leg before making the plaster cast. This cotton would compress as the infant grew over the next couple of weeks, thus giving room for expansion within the supporting structure of the cast. Soon enough, the cast was in place, and the little calf was set into a dark box with some comfortable hay bedding. There was nothing more to do until morning.

Back outside, I noticed that the war was quieting down. The flares had fallen from the skies and the stars had reassumed their proper locations in the firmament. There were some soldiers down to the south trying to gather errant camels in the darkness. Their task was futile, but they accepted it in good spirit. They developed a sort of picnic attitude about their work, but after another half hour or so, they too gave up. Camel herding in the desert is best accomplished in daylight.

I was nervous about what other damage had been done in the reserve during the panic, but it would have been foolish to go looking in the darkness. Just as a security measure, however, I climbed on our tractor and drove a quick patrol around the fence to make sure that none of the stampeding animals had crashed into it. The patrol revealed that everything was intact, so I put all my tools away, climbed to the top of the haystack, and had hardly contemplated half a dozen stars before sleep carried me away.

I awoke about a half hour before sunrise the following morning to find the army sergeant from the night before approaching the nature reserve with his squad and eleven camels. "Can we put these in the reserve?" he called out. "This is all we could catch during the night, and there's still another twenty-three camels scattered around the desert."

I thought for a moment and then decided against taking the camels. I had no idea of their health, and for all I knew they could be carrying any number of ghastly parasites and diseases. If I let the camels in, I'd be risking the health of all the other animals in the reserve. As an alternative, I suggested, why not herd them into Biqat Timna, a box canyon just a few kilometers south. I would donate a few bales of hay to ensure that the camels would be fed, but it was best to impose some sort of quarantine until their health status was determined.

After chucking four bales of hay into the back of an army truck, I said good-by to the sergeant and went right to work. The most immediate problem was the antelope calf. A check proved her to be quite well and able to hobble around on her new cast. But she was surely hungry, so we had to go look for mama.

I slipped a light harness around the infant and set her in the cab of our pickup truck. Next, some stout lasso rope and a large transport box were loaded into the back of the truck, and we were off. Touring the reserve as I looked for the addax antelope herd, I found the damage to be slight. One watering area had been pretty well smashed in a stampede and some brush was flattened out, but there was nothing that couldn't be repaired.

I sighted the addax herd in the dunes at the northeast corner of the reserve and saw that they were slowly drifting westward. I moved about a half kilometer in front of them and stopped the truck in a large, open area. The herd would drift this way in about ten minutes or so.

With the back of the truck facing the approaching animals, I lowered the tailgate and set out a ramp. I then opened the big transport box and unraveled the lasso. Next, I carried the calf out and tethered her to the back bumper with about three meters of light rope. And then I sat down to wait. As the antelopes wandered into sight, the young calf began bleating for its mother. Her mother heard her and came running to her daughter at full gallop. Their reunion was joyful, accompanied by much sniffing and a few licks. In moments, the tethered calf was nursing. It had been a long while between meals.

When I saw that the calf was just about satisfied, I flipped a lasso over one of the dam's spiral horns. The rope slipped down, and I pulled it snug as it rested at the base of the horn. The other end of the lasso was already secured to a steel frame piece on the truck. With the mother safely captured and pulling with all her might against the rope, I snatched up the calf and set her into the truck bed. Now it was simply a matter of fishing the mother aboard.

This technique involves keeping steady pressure on the capture rope and, every time the antelope relaxes, pulling in a few more inches and tying them off. Gradually, the mother was brought closer and closer to the truck, up the ramp, and into the transport box. With gates closed and both animals secure, we drove back to the work area, where mother and daughter were released into their own paddock. This way, I could keep a close watch on the calf's broken leg, and the youngster could stay with her mother until she was healed enough for both to be released.

My helper Nathan showed up for work as I was tossing some

extra bedding into the paddock. "You've had a busy morning!" he observed. "And a busy night!" I replied.

We came to name the little calf Terpsichore, after the ancient Greek muse of dance, because of her spritely frolicking, despite a relatively large and heavy leg cast. And her dam, appropriately, was named Mnemosyne — the mother of all the Muses.

Young animals usually heal quickly, and Terpsichore was no exception. Within a few weeks, she was in fine shape, and we set her free with her mother. The pair rejoined the addax herd and are still among them to this day.

The camels presented a different sort of problem. Once all thirty-four of them were rounded up and herded into Biqat Timna, nobody could figure out what to do with them. Nobody wanted them. Eventually the authorities decided to send them right back where they came from. Squads of soldiers opened a hole in Israeli defenses, and all the trip-wires, flares, and fences were cleared away. A great camel drive herded the animals eastward to the border, and with a great shout and holler, nearly three dozen stray camels were shooed back across no-man's-land into Jordan.

Salim

L ET'S GO visit Salim," Mike Van Grevenbroek suggested one evening. So we gathered three boxes of fresh vegetables, loaded them into the back of Mike's Peugeot station wagon, and drove off to a rendezvous in the Sinai.

We were four — Mike, Judy, Dan Barber, and myself. Dan was a young volunteer from New Mexico who was working at Hai-Bar for a few months to get a taste of a different desert and different wildlife. We rolled south out of Eilat and into the twilight along the Red Sea coastal road. After twenty kilometers, darkness had engulfed the desert and we turned west along a bumpy gravel road. Within a half hour, we reached the end of that road. "And now we walk!" Mike announced.

Shouldering the boxes of vegetables, we trekked westward across a rugged gravel plain laced by numerous small ravines and studded with rocks and boulders. The desert night air was clear, and, even though the moon had not yet risen, there was adequate light from the stars alone, as we followed a narrow goat path toward our destination. Eventually, we saw a slight glimmer in the distance — a small campfire out in the desert.

Coming closer to the camp, Mike hailed, "Salim! *Habibi!*" and a middle-aged Bedouin came to greet us. We were all introduced and ushered into Salim's one-room stone house — the only permanent dwelling in this part of the desert. A fire was kindled on the sand floor inside the house, and a pot of sweet red Bedouin tea was set over it to brew. Outside, Salim's several wives and daughters went to work cutting up the boxes of vegetables and baking a number of large Bedouin-style pita breads in the ancient ovens near the edge of the camp. The fragrance of the food filled the night air.

Meanwhile, we sat inside the house with Salim's elder son, a nephew, and a cousin. Judy was the only woman there, and she was feeling a bit uncomfortable in this traditionally masculine circle. Salim passed a stone carving of an ibex to Mike, who admired it and passed it on to me. "Salim's a stonecutter by trade," Mike explained, "and his main work is shaping stone bowls and grinding wheels used to make flour. He became quite skillful at this trade and eventually began carving stone figurines during his spare time. They're quite good. In fact, some people from the Smithsonian Institution in Washington came here and acquired several of them as examples of primitive Bedouin folk art." Salim passed one for me to inspect — a rather overweight gazelle. "A Bedouin image of ideal beauty!" Mike joked.

I saw that on his right hand, Salim had but a thumb and two fingers. "Before 1967," Mike explained, "the Egyptian army was in the habit of taxing the Bedouins simply by confiscating a few sheep or goats whenever they chose. One day they came here, but Salim is a stonecutter and didn't keep animals. So they went to his brother and demanded some animals, but his brother denied having any. The soldiers searched the region and discovered a small flock belonging to Salim's brother. As punishment for lying to the soldiers, they shot and killed him on the spot and took all the animals. They also grabbed Salim and cut off three of the fingers of his right hand, simply for being the brother of a liar."

The feast was prepared. About half of the vegetables we had brought were cut up, sprinkled with herbs and olive oil, and set in a large bowl in the center of the floor. Large pieces of freshly baked pita were distributed, and we shared a common meal by taking pieces of pita bread and using them to scoop up bits of salad from the bowl. All the women and girls, save Judy, ate outside.

The night progressed with tales of the desert and of wandering Bedouin. Salim presented Dan with a newly made Bedouin dagger, which he had fashioned during the past week. Donkeys brayed in the distance.

Fresh tea was constantly served to anyone who drained a cup. Those who had had enough were careful to leave a small pool of tea in the bottom of the glass cup as a sign that no more was desired. Mike produced a new pack of American cigarettes, and passed it around. Most people took one cigarette to smoke then and two or three more to slip into the folds of their robes for enjoyment later on. We sat on old mattresses spread on the floor, and the conversation went on for hours.

The night lingered with a sleepy enchantment. Certainly there were all the exotic flavors of a Bedouin camp, just as one might expect to have found in the *Tales of the Arabian Nights*. But there was also the frustratingly slow pace of conversation and ceremony. There were moments of talk followed by complete silence, broken only by the occasional sputter and crackling of the small fire.

At a late hour, there was a yawn or two to signal that it was time to go home. Good-byes were said, and we turned for our hike back to the car. The moon was up and the desert clearly illuminated. We found our way back to Eilat.

I met Salim many times after that, always journeying out into the desert to find him. Once, Mike had received a dozen chickens in exchange for helping a farmer up north. "Let's give them to Salim!" he said. And we were off again, into the Sinai, with a car full of clucking chickens. We lugged the flock from the end of the road out across the gravel plain to Salim's stone house, where we were received with great enthusiasm. Now, we thought, Salim could have a continuous supply of eggs and an occasional chicken dinner. But this was not to be.

On the next morning, Salim went to check his chickens and found only eleven of them. There were also a few scattered feathers in the little pen he had set up, a few drops of blood, and the tracks of a caracal.

The caracal is one of the most beautiful of cats. It's a lean, long-legged desert-dweller, which grows quite a bit larger than the average house cat. Some weigh as much as thirty pounds or more. They are probably best described as elegant. They have a sandy brown color and the tips of their ears have long, tassel-like tufts of black hair.

It's not difficult to track these animals, because they have unique footprints — typical cat feet, but more delicate and well protected with lots of fur. The track tends to be indistinct, even on ground that leaves a good impression.

That night, Salim brought all his chickens into the house save one — his bait. This lone chicken was set in a wire crate that was surrounded by many snares. And Salim spent the entire night on top of his stone house, keeping watch on the bait chicken and his snares.

Before dawn, the caracal returned, looking for another chicken dinner. But instead, as it approached the bait chicken, it stepped into one of Salim's snares and was caught. The cat put up a furious fight, but Salim sprang from his roof and ran straight toward the raging caracal. He flung an old burlap bag over the snarling cat, scooped it up, and tossed it into a stout wire cage he had ready.

With the marauding caracal safely captured, Salim went into his house to sleep among his chickens. Sometime the next morning, he arose and went out to look at his captive. Salim had anger in his heart and fully intended to kill the predator that had killed his chickens. But when he looked at the beautiful cat lying in the cage, Salim decided to put off the fatal blow for a day. Instead, he studied the cat and decided to make a stone carving of its image.

Salim became mesmerized by the cat. He stared into its golden eyes and studied its svelte anatomy. The caracal was unlike other predators in the desert. The leopards are brawlers and menacing. They maul their prey and live up to their reputation for being bloody and savage. The caracal, however, is more refined. It stalks quietly and keeps track of its prey until the precise moment. There is a quick pounce, and in a second or two, the prey lies limp at its feet. There is no extended fight.

The caracal is also a loner, unlike the packs of desert wolves or hyena that stalk the night. The caracal is among the most enigmatic of species in a most enigmatic family. It is the most mysterious of cats.

Salim sat and watched that caracal for three days, trying to find
the courage to kill the animal that had stolen food from his family.
But he couldn't do it. And after three days, Salim finally surrendered. He released the long-legged cat into the desert. The next
morning, there were only ten chickens.

Salim's love-hate relationship with the caracal continued for a few
months. Often, at evening, the cat would come calling and spring
up into a low limb of an acacia tree growing near Salim's stone
house in the desert. There it reclined, staring at Salim, and Salim
would perch himself on a boulder and stare right back. They would
gaze at each other for hours.

Occasionally, at odd intervals, Salim would take one of his
well-guarded chickens as dinner for his family. And occasionally,
also at odd intervals, the caracal would slip through Salim's
ingenious defenses and snatch yet another chicken for itself.

But even after all the chickens were gone, that caracal kept
coming back, leaping up to its perch on the acacia tree and staring
at the Bedouin stone cutter who couldn't kill it.

Years passed, and from time to time I visited Salim and his
family; eventually he presented me with a few of his carvings. Each
of the primitive chunks of chiseled stone — a well-fed stone viper,
a veiled, almond-eyed Bedouin girl — has something of his heart
and his feelings and his soul in it.

One day, Salim disappeared with his whole tribe. The police had
learned that a Bedouin youth from a neighboring tribe had come
calling on a young woman in Salim's tribe. The youth's intentions
appeared more lascivious than the girl's brother would tolerate.
Knives flashed, and the courting youth from the neighboring tribe
died. His tribe, many times larger than Salim's, vowed a blood
feud. To save his people from the ancient Bedouin eye-for-an-eye
and life-for-a-life code of the desert, Salim simply packed all his
belongings, gathered the tribe's animals together, and wandered off
into the emptiness of the Sinai Desert.

We had occasional contact with him. Salim's regards were
sometimes carried to us by a soldier from an Israeli army patrol that
had stumbled across the tribe's encampment in some lost valley or
windswept plain. Then, in late 1981, Salim returned. His tribe was

camped in a new site, on the western edge of the Valley of the Moon, about an hour's drive from Eilat. I visited him several times there. His years of running in the desert had taken a terrible toll. He was lean, and his face was deeply creased. His eyes were still clear and penetrating, but now they were also filled with pain.

Peace had been made with the dead boy's tribe, Salim said. Through intermediaries, Salim's people had surrendered their lands and the stone house and nearly everything else they owned as payment to the aggrieved tribe.

Although there was peace with the neighboring tribe, larger political events were sweeping about them. The Camp David accords had provided for the return of the Sinai to Egypt, and Egyptian soldiers would soon be back, confiscating whatever they pleased.

"Maybe not," I tried to assure the Bedouin, and I introduced him to a detachment of the Multinational Force and Observers (MFO) — the United Nations' units in Sinai that were to enforce the peace treaty between Israel and Egypt. The unit turned out to be a detachment of U.S. paratroopers, and they were pleased to meet this desert nomad.

Somehow, the tribe had acquired a thirty-year-old truck and started a little business lugging cargo around. If the American paratroopers wanted a ton of stones to fill a gully, Salim's tribe would pitch in and do the job. The truck was also useful for gathering all the tribe's belongings together, for from time to time they were offered work at different places around Sinai; when there was work, the entire tribe would show up and camp nearby until the job was done.

March 1982. There were just a few days left before the last bit of Sinai was to be returned to Egypt. Mike and I visited Salim as he camped along the edge of the Valley of the Moon, not far from the now abandoned Etzion Air Base. It was meant to be a good-bye of sorts, but it turned out that Salim needed a favor. "A fan belt for the truck," he said. "You can bring one from Eilat. We can no longer cross the border into Israel, and the nearest place for us to get a new fan belt is at El Arish. Three days, and a hard journey."

I returned on the last day of Israeli occupation of Sinai to deliver the fan belt. My son, Joe, and I drove up to the Bedouin camp on that warm, sunny afternoon in the Hai-Bar Renault-4. I felt that it would be a sad occasion, but once we arrived, the atmosphere became cheerful. Steamy sweet coffee was brewed. "This is American coffee!" I remarked with the first sip. "Ah! It comes from American paratroopers!" Salim replied. "We are friendly now. I have started to carve stones again for the first time in years. We keep our camp on the hillside, but within sight of the Americans. I do not think the Egyptians will bother us when the Americans will be able to see what is happening."

The afternoon was festive and light. One of the young men started playing a spirited tune on his oud — a traditional Bedouin lute. Another started beating a rhythm on two small drums, and yet a third started dancing barefoot in the sand, all the time spinning the new fan belt around his fingers and wrists.

During the festivities, Salim confided in me that one of the rival tribe's toughest leaders was in an Israeli jail, so life would be even more bearable for his little group. "Auto theft," he whispered.

It appeared that a few of the more larcenous Bedouin of the Sinai had struck upon an ingenious scheme for making their fortunes. Once the Camp David accords had been signed, and the whole world knew that Sinai would be returned to Egypt, a conspiracy of car thieves developed in Israel. Car theft is relatively rare in Israel, mainly because in such a small land it is nearly impossible to get a stolen car out of the country. But the transfer of Sinai opened a new possibility.

Cars were stolen in Israeli cities and quickly driven to Sinai, which still was under Israeli occupation and had a completely open border with Israel. In Sinai, the thieves would sell the cars very cheaply to Bedouin middlemen. The Bedouin would then take the cars to a remote site and simply bury them. If they waited for a year or so, the place that was formerly Israeli-occupied would be Egyptian. The cars could then be dug out of the sand, driven to Cairo or Alexandria, and sold on the black market. There would be no need to smuggle the vehicles across a border. Instead, the border would move across the vehicles.

Everything worked quite well for the thieves, except for a few foul-ups that landed some of them in jail. Israeli army patrols were particularly active during the final phases of the withdrawal, and all the surveillance equipment they were using started to pick up the hot cars being spirited across the sands.

"You know, these Israelis have machines that can tell if the Egyptians are moving trucks and jeeps around the desert," Salim said. "You think the same machines can't see a stolen car?" The Bedouin chuckled and stretched.

We parted as friends on that last day as did my son and his son. We said our good-bye, climbed into the car, and started to drive back toward Eilat. In less than one kilometer, the little Renault's engine blew out. Oil splashed on the road, and all was quiet. There were some eight kilometers to go before we crossed into Israel proper, and another fifteen kilometers down through the mountains to Eilat. I knew that if I left the car there and simply hiked home, the next morning it would be in a foreign country and virtually impossible to reclaim. Not only that, it was Israeli government property, and there would be hell to pay if I left it behind.

"How are you at steering?" I asked my seven-year-old son. "Love it!" was his response. And so I got out and started to push that little Renault across the flat face of the Valley of the Moon. While pushing, I realized that a steady west wind was blowing. Why not put it to good use? We opened the doors of the light car and they acted like small sails, catching the breeze and pushing the Renault along at a modest walking speed; so we continued for about an hour until an Israeli army patrol caught up with us. They had a special route to follow, but they said they could at least push us the remaining four kilometers to the border. *"Bevakasha,* Please do!" I replied, and thus we were literally driven out of the Sinai.

From the border to Eilat, the road is nearly all downhill, dropping nearly a kilometer in elevation from the eastern end of the Valley of the Moon to the sea-level elevations of Eilat. Joe got to steer while I pushed up the few modest inclines along the route, but the whole descent took no more than an hour. We rolled the car into the marine pollution control station, and there it rested.

That was the last time we went to Sinai and the last time we saw Salim and his family. It is possible to enter Sinai now, and some

Israelis do. But the peace with Egypt is not a warm peace, not an inviting peace. And it is sometimes marred by tragedy. Israelis recall all too clearly the terrible events of Ras Burkra, in 1985, when seven Israeli tourists in Sinai were shot to death by a deranged Egyptian soldier. Some were killed outright. Some died because the other Egyptian soldiers at the scene refused to let the wounded be evacuated to medical help so they bled to death. Despite the formal peace treaty, anti-Israeli sentiment runs high in Egypt. It is published in the daily newspapers and weekly magazines and broadcast on radio and television. It is felt in the polite decline of an invitation I extended to an Egyptian colleague involved in conservation to visit Israel. "I would like very much to visit your country," he told me at a conservation congress in Europe recently, "but I'm afraid it might be misunderstood at home. These are not good days for Egyptians to be too friendly with Israelis."

Salim is still up at the far end of the Valley of the Moon, according to the soldiers from the U.N. who visit Eilat for their free evenings. And perhaps when the winds of peace blow over this part of the Middle East, it will be possible to visit with him again.

The Druze

I DON'T LIKE HUNTING. Thus, I feel very comfortable in Israel, where less than one person in a thousand holds a hunting license — and where even this minuscule one-tenth-of-one-percent average is in decline.

In Israel, a high proportion of the hunters come from the Druze who live on the peaks of Mount Carmel, Mount Meron, and the Golan Heights. The Druze are a very noble people who broke away from Islam about ten centuries ago; consequently, they were considered heretics by Muslim rulers in the Middle East. Their communities were scattered through what today is Israel, Lebanon, and Syria, and because of frequent persecutions, they developed two very effective defenses.

First, the Druze faith went underground. Even today, its basic tenets and dogmas are known to only a few initiated members of their community. Most Druze are aware only of various traditions and customs, the outward practices of their faith, while its substantive matter remains a well-guarded secret.

The second defense that the Druze adopted to protect themselves from persecution was a powerful warrior ethic. The Druze became the Spartans of the Levant, and, more often than not, imperial rulers found it more convenient to tolerate them than to try to dominate them in their mountain strongholds. It simply was never worth the tremendous effort that would have been required to conquer these few, but intensely independent, villages.

In Israel, the Druze community has an extraordinary amount of autonomy, and there rarely has been any serious friction between the Israeli government and these mountain villagers. Because Israel has never hinted at any enmity toward the Druze, and indeed they have been given full rights of citizenship without having any Jewish customs, ethics, or religious doctrine imposed upon them, they have responded by being among Israel's most loyal citizens. Many Druze soldiers and officers in the Israel Defense Forces have distinguished themselves time and again in battle.

Early in the days of the State of Israel, the parliament (Knesset) passed a law that requires every Jewish citizen be drafted into the I.D.F. at age eighteen. Young men serve three years of active duty and then serve at least one month of reserve duty a year until they reach age fifty-five. Young women serve two years of active service and then have monthly reserve each year until they're thirty-five (unless motherhood intervenes). This is a heavy burden of military service, and the legislators agreed that it should rest squarely on Jewish shoulders. All others holding Israeli citizenship — the Christian and Muslim Arabs, Druze, Baha'is, Samaritans, and others — were to be exempt from military conscription.

The Druze, however, did not agree. They conducted a community meeting, and when the sense of their villages was determined, they petitioned the Israeli government. If they were to accept full citizenship, they insisted, their own young people should bear a full share of the defense burden by being conscripted into the military. The petition was granted. Today, many Druze are members of crack paratrooper and assault units of the I.D.F., and there are also quite a few memorials to Druze soldiers who have fallen in defense of Israel.

Israel's Jewish population, therefore, has a special appreciation for the Druze and are extremely reluctant to criticise any of their traditions — even the tradition of hunting.

Druze hunting is, to a very large extent, an autumn ritual. Usually, the older men of the village are the hunters. They are still very sensitive to centuries of persecution, when secrecy and vigorous defense were their best protection. The tiny Druze communities survived many centuries of hostility because they were skilled in the use of weapons and tactics, and an echo of this warrior ethic is seen in Druze hunting practices today.

Traditionally, the older men gather in an evening and make plans for the next morning's hunt — who will pair with whom, what fields they will hunt, how the game should be shared. Early the next morning they gather at a prearranged location, with each hunter wearing a distinctive uniform — baggy pants and high leather boots, a heavy woolen jacket with a bandolier of cartridges slung over a shoulder, a carefully wrapped turban, and the traditional enormous, meticulously tended handlebar moustache. Each is armed with an aged shotgun.

They strut off, conducting the hunt something like a military operation. By the end of the day they may have shot two or three partridges and a hare, each of which is properly cleaned and presented to a widow or some other needy person in the village. The hunters remain together through the evening for much socializing and storytelling.

Druze hunters are in no way like typical European or American hunters. Hunting is not "sport" to them. Instead, it is a cooperative effort to bring some meat to a needy village — or so they say. But there seems to be a deeper motive in the ancient Druze ethic, hunting as free men, armed, upon their own lands.

The Druze, incidentally, do not drink alcohol — not a drop — and they're much too modest to swap lewd jokes and stories, as is the custom among hunters elsewhere on this planet.

Although the hunting ethic is strongly retained by the older generation, many of the younger Druze are not inclined to follow this tradition. They serve their periods of conscription in the I.D.F., and they are keenly aware that the defense of their mountain villages is intimately tied to the greater defense of Israel. Shooting a hare on an autumn morning has little to do with preparing to face Syrian tanks on the Golan.

One Druze villager who exemplifies this shift in traditional views is Saleh Makladay, the curator of Hai-Bar Carmel, the wildlife restoration facility located in the oak and pine forests that crown the higher reaches of Mount Carmel. Here, various species of forest animals, such as fallow deer, mouflon, and wild goats, are being bred and restored to wild areas.

In this work, Saleh is entrusted with the day-to-day care of the Mesopotamian fallow deer (*Dama mesopotamica*) one of the rarest animals on earth. Once, this elegant species thrived in the forested areas of the Fertile Crescent, and browsed on tender shoots and acorns from the Land of Israel clear up to ancient Persia. In the Hebrew version of the Bible, it is known as *yachmur*.

As with so many other species, the introduction of modern high-power, rapid-fire, highly accurate firearms into the Middle East meant catastrophe. Through the past century, the species was ruthlessly exterminated throughout nearly all of its range, including Israel. A decade ago, the last population still surviving in the wild found refuge in the dense swamps around the Shatt al-Arab — the wetland border between Iraq and Iran.

This last refuge has been a war zone for eight recent years and subjected to devastating barrages of artillery, automatic weapons, bombings, and even poison-gas attacks. Most conservationists think there's little likelihood of any wild fallow deer still surviving in the no-man's-land of the Gulf War.

Besides these, a few captive populations of Mesopotamian fallow deer have survived. One is a small herd of the Baron von Opel Zoo in West Germany, and another is at a former hunting reserve of the former royal family of Iran.

The brother of the late shah, Prince Abdoulrezza, was the family's most avid hunter, and it is widely agreed that he had one of the largest trophy collections in the world. In his palace there was a great hall with scores, perhaps hundreds, of the most impressive animal heads from all around the world — so many animals, all shot down during the most magnificent days of their existence.

To me, trophy hunting is one of the most odious aspects of the blood sport. Hunting itself is reprehensible, a nasty butchery. But trophy hunting goes beyond this and works against the best interests of Nature. Under the normal dynamics of Nature, the best, or most "fit" animals most often survive. The biggest and the strongest are the most capable of holding their ground and parenting the coming generations. But it is these best animals —

the ones with the largest horns, or most perfectly proportioned physique — that trophy hunters consciously select for killing. Given a herd of antelope, for example, it is extremely unlikely that a trophy hunter will take aim at a weak, crippled, or lagging animal — the one that Nature usually provides to natural predators. Instead, he'll shoot at the best specimen — precisely the animal that Nature intended to survive and assume a leadership position in the herd. Thus, the trophy hunter disrupts the normal dynamics of Nature, even to the point of undermining a key mechanism of those dynamics — the phenomenon known as "natural selection."

Prince Abdoulrezza was what I term an "unnatural selector." He was fabulously wealthy and could indulge in any whim or caprice. He even made a visit to Israel once and shot the only ibex I know of that was killed with the collaboration — albeit extremely reluctant collaboration — of conservation authorities. From an ethical point of view, the killing of the great male ibex was a harsh tragedy. But from a conservation point of view, there were important benefits. There were also a few political concerns.

At that time, back in the 1970s, Israel found Iranian friendship very useful. Iran was a major source of oil for Israel — indeed, the only state in the oil-soaked Middle East that would sell oil to Israel. Iran was also militarily strong and had a centuries-old adversarial relationship with Iraq — and this constrained Iraq to keep most of its army home every time there was an Arab war against Israel. Other political considerations also figured into the relationships between Iran and Israel.

In addition there were conservation considerations. Israeli conservationists wanted a few Mesopotamian fallow deer for restoration to their ancient habitats on Mount Carmel and in the Galilee. The prince knew this, and could charge a very dear price for them. He kept the world's finest population of these deer in a special shooting reserve in northern Iran, and from time to time he would go hunting there and kill one of the rarest animals on earth.

In the late 1970s, Israel managed to acquire a few surplus males from the Baron von Opel Zoo in West Germany. Thus the start of a fallow deer reintroduction program was at hand. The Iranian prince indicated that he was willing to supply a few females from his private reserve, which would be forthcoming if Israel could pamper his passion for hunting and let him shoot a trophy male ibex.

The prince was wined and dined and taken to a site in the Israeli desert where an ibex could be found. Unbeknownst to the prince, there was only one ibex in that area — an aged male with enormous horns. The ibex had been sedated with an injection and thus would not feel the full impact of the terrible blow intended for him.

The prince raised his expensive hunting rifle and peered through its fine telescope. His shot rang out, the ibex fell dead, and the prince had yet another trophy head for his palace. He also had a debt to Israeli wildlife conservation, and Israel fully intended to collect.

Then, catastrophe. In late 1978, civil unrest rocked Iran. The shah abdicated, and the prince fled to Paris, where his family's aged enemy, the Ayatollah Khoumeini, was nearing the end of his own exile. At the end of November, Avraham Yoffe received a telephone call from Teheran — if Israel wanted those Mesopotamian fallow deer females, someone had better come and collect them in a hurry. It would soon be too late.

Yoffe dispatched Mike Van Grevenbroek, then curator of Hai-Bar, to the Iranian capital, and from there, Mike set off for the prince's private shooting reserve. He live-captured four beautiful females, loaded them into shipping crates, and brought them back to Teheran in a rented truck. Entering the city, he found it in utter chaos. There were many factions vying for power in the streets. The royal family had gone, and most of the power structure had collapsed. Aboulhasse Bani-Sadr was trying to restore order, but the forces of change were too great for him. There was anarchy and an outburst of Muslim religious fundamentalists were calling for the return of Khoumeini.

Mike's driver abandoned the truck and its deer at the edge of the city, so Mike took over the vehicle and drove it to the Israeli embassy, which had fortified itself against street attacks and was preparing for immediate evacuation. The situation was perilous, and at a time when there was a great danger to life and limb, more than a few thought it curious that someone would be so insistent about bringing a small herd of deer along.

Nevertheless, Mike persevered. The rare deer were brought behind the Israeli compound's barbed wire. Mike fed them by making a number of expeditions to Teheran's city parks, where he collected sacks of acorns. He was then notified that one more flight to Israel would be permitted by airport authorities — for the evacuation of the Israeli embassy personnel — and after that, Israelis would be persona non grata in Iran.

But what of the deer? They could not be left in an evacuated embassy compound. They were much too rare and too important to wildlife conservation programs in Israel. Mike resolved the problem with one of the oldest techniques of human politics. He bribed every Iranian who crossed his path. He paid baksheesh to get fuel for the truck so it could be driven to the airport. He obtained some irregular export documents that showed the animals to be destined for Europe. He paid hefty tips to airport administrators, customs officials, and security officers — and bit by bit, the doors and streets and security fences were opened for him and his truckload of Mesopotamian fallow deer.

It rained in Teheran on the eighth of December 1978. Stormy blasts and low-hanging clouds obscured the last El Al jet as it taxied along the tarmac at Teheran. Israeli embassy officials hurriedly boarded the aircraft, and four precious wooden crates were carefully lifted into the cargo hold. In late afternoon, just before dark, the pilot opened the throttles and the El Al jet lunged skyward into the cloudy darkness.

Three hours later, the jet landed at Israel's Ben-Gurion International Airport, where Avraham Yoffe was waiting. His eyes welled, and he burst into tears of joy. He embraced Mike and then peeked into the wooden crates. Another species had been rescued for Israel's modern ark.

The fallow deer — large, yet elegant creatures, with reddish brown color and long, svelte necks — were brought to paddocks at Hai-Bar Carmel, where Saleh was already tending the males brought from the German zoo. The careful process of introducing the males to the females and establishing a social structure for the newly composed herd was started.

Before long, the deer got on very well indeed. They formed a cohesive herd that fitted well with Mount Carmel's oak and pine forest habitat. Despite the lush vegetation, the deer seemed to glide through the forest with hardly a sound in their fluid, rhythmic gait. They seemed very much "at home" in these forests, and, indeed, they were in the home of their ancestors.

From the first day, Saleh took charge of the Mesopotamian fallow deer's care. Every day, he ensured that they had proper food and water — for although the vegetation is lush, our program sought to stimulate the birth rate of this very endangered species, and that meant supplementing natural foods with high-nutrition feeds vital for peak reproductive success.

Saleh also began studying the deer closely, watching for sores and parasites, or the slightest irregularity. He became devoted to the animals and constantly devised new techniques to protect them and encourage improvements in their lives. There is a certain danger in this sort of work because, in autumn, during the rutting season, the big bucks can be particularly aggressive. Once, in 1984, Saleh got caught in the antlers of an attacking buck, who lifted him from the ground and threw him forcefully through the air. He was fortunate to escape with only a broken arm. Yet despite the injury, Saleh's devotion to his deer never wavered.

And the deer understood this. They soon learned that Saleh worked for their interest and that he would not harm them. As an expression of their trust, Saleh had only to stand in a clearing and whistle his peculiar melody, and the deer emerged from the forests in twos and threes, responding to his call.

Today, there are nearly fifty deer. Their paddocks have been enlarged several times in recent years, and now they inhabit a couple of square kilometers of forest atop the biblical mountain. Within the next few years — once the population is a bit larger — an experiment will be made and a few deer will be released into unprotected forests in Israel. If the experiment works, a full restoration effort will be made to return the Mesopotamian fallow deer to appropriate wilderness areas of Israel.

Meanwhile, however, another type of experiment is underway. Saleh's devotion to his animals has become infectious and is spreading throughout his family and throughout the Druze villages.

Youths come to help him after school. They stack hay and clean yards. They bring their friends to see and appreciate the pretty forest creatures that now inhabit the Druze mountain of Israel. It is unlikely that the traditional hunting ethic will find much support among these youths as they grow to maturity.

One episode that reveals the protective sentiments of the younger Druze is the story of an illiterate boy named Mustapha, who spent much of his time wandering the deep forests of Mount Carmel.

One afternoon, a couple of years ago, Mustapha was rambling through his verdant haunts when he saw a man with a rifle. The Druze boy concealed himself and followed the armed man. It soon became apparent that the man was hunting wild animals and that he was stalking a mountain gazelle.

Mustapha continued, following after the hunter and watching his every move. Within an hour, the hunter had worked himself within range of the gazelle; he slowly lifted his weapon and shot the protected animal. Retrieving the dead gazelle, he cut it open and eviscerated it, then carried the meaty carcass back to a car parked along a quiet forest road.

Mustapha watched as the hunter loaded the carcass into the car trunk. The poacher then opened the door, climbed in, and prepared to drive away. For a moment, the Druze boy didn't know what to do. He was enraged that someone would shoot a gazelle — but the man was armed and shouldn't be confronted. The Druze youth then saw what he could do. On the edge of the road there were bits of broken glass. He picked up the sharpest piece he could find and cut the car license plate number into the flesh of his left arm.

The poacher drove away, and Mustapha, with his bleeding arm wrapped in his shirt, ran to a police station. He told the desk sergeant that a poacher had killed a gazelle in the mountain forest and showed him the number of the poacher's automobile cut into his arm.

The police identified the owner of the car and supplied the information to nature wardens, who paid the man an evening visit. They found gazelle meat freshly wrapped and packed into his freezer. The man was arrested immediately and carted off to jail. At the trial, Mustapha positively identified the poacher who was convicted and sentenced to prison.

Mustapha will carry scars on his left arm for the rest of his life. But no scars are more honored in his Druze village on the mountaintop. Other boys on Mount Carmel now have one of their own as a heroic protector of animals — even to the point of trailing dangerously close to an armed criminal, even to the point of cutting into his own flesh to see that justice was done.

It is unlikely that Mustapha, or any of his village friends, will lift weapons against animals as they grow up — even during legal hunting season against legal game. And thus the old hunting traditions of the Israeli Druze will fade gradually, without any outside pressure forcing the issue.

Sue-Ellen

SHORTLY AFTER SUNRISE on a fresh spring morning, a truckload of reserve soldiers and kibbutzniks came roaring in through the north gate of the Hai-Bar reserve, lights on, horn blaring, in a cloud of dust so imposing that it would have made the Lone Ranger's horse envious.

Screeching to a halt beside the haystack where I was working, my excited visitors called out *"Bo mahair! Bo mahair!—* Come quickly! Come quickly! *Yesh ze'ev katan b'chud tile b'gvul!* There's a little wolf caught in the barbed wire on the border!"

Quickly, I gathered my emergency equipment, tossed it into the Peugeot pickup, and followed the truckload of soldiers and kibbutzniks out of the reserve. Racing through the north gate, we cut due east, toward the border with Jordan, and bounced down an old dirt road at a speed that approached recklessness.

As we neared the border, we slowed a bit and turned north, skirting the eastern edge of Kibbutz Yotvata's date-palm groves. Off to our right, only barbed-wire entanglements separated us from the Hashemite Kingdom of Jordan — and in those entanglements, we found our little *ze'ev.* Actually, I soon learned she was a *ze'eva,* a female wolf. She was properly known as a desert wolf, or scientifically as *Canis lupus palipes,* a race of true wolf that is specially adapted for life in the desert. This is the creature known to the prophets Jeremiah, Habakkuk, and Ezekiel, and the race of wolf that Isaiah knew and pictured in his vision of the peaceable kingdom, where "the wolf shall dwell with the lamb" (Isaiah 11:6).

We rolled to a halt, and before approaching the poor creature, we made a little reconnaissance of the area. As anxious as I was to help the suffering animal, it didn't seem wise to rush out into the border area between two countries that had been in a state of war for more than three decades. It was a mere technicality, perhaps, but we needed to check around a bit, as it would be somewhat embarrassing if we bumped into an Arab Legion patrol and got ourselves involved in an international incident. But all looked quiet, and with a few lookouts posted, we prepared to rescue the little wolf.

First, I could see that the wolf was only a cub, no more than seven or eight weeks old. It was all entangled in spirals of concertina wire, a particularly nasty type of barbed wire that is spread across the ground in loose, springy coils. It has a razor edge with many sharp little barbs, and its spring-steel design ensures that it snaps back and forth with only a little prodding. It is very effective in blocking the paths of terrorists who attempt infiltration at night-time, but it is also sadly injurious to any wildlife that blunders into it.

The little wolf was caught up in the wire, and cut badly by it. I could see that she had some terrible wounds, and since she knew we were watching her, she struggled to get free — but that only made her wounds worse. Immediately, I called to everyone to hide behind the truck, out of the wolf's sight and downwind far enough to be out of her scent. The less threat we posed to her, the less she would struggle against the wire and injure herself further. I adjusted the truck's rearview mirrors so I could keep an eye on her while I prepared my rescue equipment.

Digging the lightest syringe-darts out of my supply box, I prepared three small doses of ketamine for the rescue. Each dose was loaded into an individual dart. A light canula needle was set on the front end of each dart, a moderate air charge in the back end, and a soft tail stabilizer attached to the rear.

Ketamine is a very good immobilizing drug for many carnivores, including the wolf, but is generally unsuited for most other wild animals if used only by itself. It's a derivative of phencyclidine hydrochloride and usually considered to be a rather safe drug. It has two other attributes that were very important in this situation. First, it comes in a strong veterinary concentration — 100 milligrams of ketamine per milliliter of solution — and this means I'd only need a few drops to put the cub to sleep. Second, it's fast-acting, and starts taking effect within about three minutes of injection. This meant we could rescue the animal relatively quickly.

It should be noted that this same drug, in more dilute concentrations, is often used by surgeons during operations on humans. It's highly regarded as an effective, safe anesthetic. Also, because it has been used so frequently, all the adverse effects of ketamine have been very well documented, so remedial action can be taken. For example, on very rare occasions it can produce convulsions, but the wildlife worker knows that when it does it can be quickly neutralized by administering diazepam.

With two of the prepared darts in my jacket pocket as spares, I set the third into my blowpipe. A little diversionary tactic appeared useful for drawing the cub's attention from me while I worked, so I persuaded a group of four soldiers to move straight back from the truck, slip into the date-palm grove, and then move northward a bit under the cover of its foliage. They re-emerged in the open about fifty yards north of our position and casually wandered into the wolf's view. They spoke to each other in soft tones, ignoring the wolf all the time, and moving nonchalantly away from her at a slow, easy pace. Of course, they held the cub's attention, and she watched them with very keen interest. But since they didn't seem to threaten her, or even notice her, she didn't struggle. Instead, she simply lay still in the wire and focused all her senses on them.

Meanwhile, I circled toward the south with my blowpipe and darts. The slight northerly breeze kept me downwind from the cub, thus keeping my scent out of her nose and covering the sound of my footsteps. I managed to move within twenty yards of the animal without being noticed, and, foolishly, decided to try a long shot. I aimed and gave the dart a good puff of air. It sailed out the opposite side of the blowpipe, arched through the air, and landed uselessly on the other side of the barbed wire, startling the cub and giving away my presence.

My only option now was to load another dart quickly and move up as fast as possible for a very close shot. Actually, the cub behaved very well. Instead of struggling to free herself, she simply twisted around as much as she could, laid back her ears, showed her tiny teeth, and prepared to defend herself from where she was. I moved up to within three yards and leaned across the wire to get a clear shot at her rump. The dart flew and hit its target properly, injecting the full dose in a fraction of a second. Just as this was done, the cub stretched over and snapped the plastic dart in her jaws. But the drug was already injected, so the best thing for me to do was retreat and leave the animal alone for a few minutes, while the drug knocked her out.

Back behind the truck, the kibbutzniks said they had been surveying the area and had pieced together what had apparently happened. They had spotted the tracks of one large wolf, plus four or five smaller ones, all coming down in a parallel direction from the north. They speculated that a few hours earlier, when the first gray light of dawn dimly silhouetted the Mountains of Edom to the east, a mother wolf had taken this year's litter out for one of their first runs in the desert. It looked as if they had been moving along the edge of the date palm grove when something startled them — perhaps an army patrol scouting along the border in the early morning twilight.

The mother wolf and most of the cubs ran into the date palms for concealment. But at least one of the wolf cubs ran in the wrong direction and barreled straight into a coil of concertina wire. She became entangled in the barbs, and the more she struggled, the more she suffered.

The cub now appeared unconscious on the wire. I gave her another couple of minutes to ensure that she was in deep slumber before moving out to help her. The kibbutzniks piled several layers of extra-heavy-weight plastic mesh bags — the kind used to protect ripening dates on the trees from being excessively damaged by birds and bats — on the concertina wire next to the unconscious wolf. Next, I laid several heavy blankets above the mesh bags to give an extra layer of protection. We then climbed onto the mesh bag–blanket sandwich and moved in close enough to reach the wolf cub.

Working as a team, we snipped the wire carefully and extricated the drugged cub in only a few minutes.

We moved her into the shade of the date palms and assessed the extent of the damage. She was very badly cut up by the wire, including one particularly nasty gash across her abdomen from which part of her viscera had begun to ooze. Despite the severe wounds, the bleeding wasn't very bad. Simple gauze bandaging served to retard the slight bleeding and to protect the wounds.

One of the soldiers fashioned a makeshift muzzle and slipped it gently over her mouth. The cub was sleeping peacefully, but if she woke up at an awkward moment while we were driving back to Eilat for proper medical attention, she could cause a tremendous amount of damage with those sharp puppy teeth, so it was best to make certain that they were properly secured. We also made a crude collar and leash and slipped it over her head.

The wounded animal was wrapped in a couple of blankets and then slipped into one of the plastic mesh date sacks. Two kibbutzniks carried the unconscious cub to the seat of the pickup truck, while I prepared a couple of syringes with more ketamine — just in case she started to revive during our half-hour trip south. She did indeed start to move a bit on the seat next to me as we were driving down the main highway about fifteen kilometers from Eilat. But back to sleep she slipped, after I pulled to the side of the road and injected a follow-up dose.

My first stop in Eilat was the home of my friend and neighbor Dr. Aviezer Rippin, the chief surgeon of Eilat Hospital — nothing but the best for this club. Aviezer is a fine physician with plenty of experience repairing mangled bodies. Formerly, his clientele had been almost exclusively human, but ever since I had moved next door, he had been prodded into expanding his sphere of professional interest. Never before had he operated on a wolf cub.

Fortunately, he was home, having just returned from a shift at the hospital, still dressed in his surgeon's greens. I told him the situation, and we immediately went to work setting up an operating theater next door — in my kitchen.

As we carried the little wolf in for the repair job, our small house was also sheltering two orphaned ibex kids, a large shepherd dog, a few stray cats, and a recuperating golden eagle. Judy took charge and quickly sorted out the confusion — dogs to the front yard, ibex to the back yard, eagle to the bedroom, and stray cats to the neighbors. The table on which I had eaten breakfast just a few hours before was then scrubbed down with disinfectant and became our operating table.

We slipped the cub out of the mesh sack and blankets and set her down on the table, tying each of her legs gently, but securely, to a corner. Aviezer went to work; it was a very difficult job. First, he had to get rid of all the bits of barbed wire that were still twisted in the folds of her skin. When we had cut her free from the entanglements on the border, we had not had the time, nor the skill, to attempt the removal of all the bits of wire. I feared that in trying to remove all the pieces of wire, we might actually cause further injury to the suffering animal.

Skillfully, the surgeon snipped away the wire, and then cleaned the patient while I served as his nurse-assistant. "Actually," he cracked, "we've got nicer nurses at the hospital. And you know, I did work on a wolf once before, but he was the two-legged kind. He was a beach bum who pinched a lady soldier in the wrong place down at Rafi Nelson's beach village. She didn't like being pinched. No, she didn't like it at all."

"Forceps!" he interjected. And I handed him the instrument.

"Yes," he continued. "She did not like being pinched by this two-legged wolf. And so she sent him to the hospital, and I had to go there and put all his pieces back together again. I even worked on Rafi Nelson himself, you know. Appendectomy!"

Aviezer shaved a broad area around the abdominal wound with the same twin-edged razor I had shaved with that morning. Then, he began cleaning the protruding viscera before tucking it back into the open cavity.

At just about that time, my son Joe came tramping in, home from school. "What's Buba doing on the roof?" he asked.

Buba on the roof! She was one of the two infant ibex we were hand-raising that spring. When last seen, she was being ushered into the back yard with J.R., the other ibex kid. Somehow, they must have found a way to leap the ten feet to the roof. The trouble was, our roof was connected to the neighbors' and theirs to the next house. You could walk more than a hundred yards from roof to roof. And you could jump down nearly any place. All I needed was two infant ibex wandering around Eilat.

"Sorry, Aviezer," I said. "I hope this will only take a minute. I'd better round up those ibex before they get very far." Judy stood in for me at the operating table, while I went out the back door after the ibex. The last thing I heard was Joe asking Aviezer, "What are you doing?"

The ibex were prancing around the Eilat rooftops like Santa Claus's reindeer, and we made ourselves a merry chase hither and yon. It was obvious that the mischievous ibex wanted me to chase them in a mirthful game of tag.

There was only one thing they liked better than playing, and that was eating. So back down to the house I clambered and quickly poured some milk into a baby bottle. Back on the roof, I had only to cry "gweeeee," wave the bottle of milk in the air, and my two adventuring kids came bounding back to me. I scooped them up, carried them down to the back yard, and put Joe in charge of their lunch.

Returning to the kitchen, I found Aviezer suturing the wolf's abdominal wound closed with lengths of black silk thread. After the other, smaller, wounds were tended with stitches here and there on her legs, flanks, back, and neck, the poor wolf club looked like a rag doll or a hand-sewn patchwork quilt. Next came doses of antibiotics to ward off infections and a number of powders, ointments, and salves to protect the wounds and help them to heal. It was then only a matter of time until we would learn the young animal's fate. We put her into a small transport cage in a darkened room and let her rest after the operation.

As we were doing this, Sue-Ellen Ben Zvi stopped by with her youngsters, bearing a very important item that I didn't have available — a properly manufactured muzzle. Judy had seen the contraption we had on the poor cub's face, and as we worked at the kitchen table, she made a few telephone calls to find a more appropriate alternative. With the muzzle, the cub could be left alone without any worry about her chewing at her wounds and perhaps pulling out the stitches that Aviezer had gone to such trouble to put in.

Before long, half the town knew we were harboring a wolf, and a steady stream of youngsters came to the door asking for a peek. "Wait a few days," we told them all. "The little cub was badly injured and must rest now. But when she has recovered, you'll surely be invited to see her."

The wolf cub's wounds started to heal, and within a few days, she was obviously headed toward recovery. Nevertheless, I had to keep her for a while. After such trauma there was a great risk of infection, and she needed daily antibiotics. It would be at least a week and a half until the stitches could be taken out. Though at first she didn't like me at all, those passing weeks witnessed the development of a friendship between the wolf cub and me.

I had to spend a lot of time with the cub because of a conflict between her medical and her nutritional needs. For medical purposes, she neded to be muzzled so she couldn't pull her stitches out. For nutritional purposes, I had to remove the muzzle every few hours so she could eat and drink. Putting a muzzle on and off a wild wolf cub, however, isn't the easiest or safest job in the world, and during this delicate procedure, repeated eight or nine times a day, we got to know each other very well.

The first time I took the muzzle off was when she had recovered from the ketamine after her operation. I wanted to give her the opportunity to drink. I found, however, that she was also hungry, and she went straight for the closest food available — my fingers. She didn't get very much, though — just a slight nick. I resolved the situation by tossing a heavy blanket over the cub and holding her still underneath it. Slowly, I worked the blanket back until only the tip of her snout protruded, and from there, gradually slipped back the muzzle. A new technique for letting her get an occasional drink or meal had to be developed.

The system that eventually evolved was for me to slip a leash on the cub and then loosen the muzzle to a point where it could be pulled free with a simple tug of a gloved hand. Meanwhile, I had wrapped myself from the waist down in a heavy blanket — just in case the patient took a liking to my ankles or some other edibles uphill from my toes. Once the muzzle was slipped off, I'd stand as erect as a British soldier and lead the cub around on her leash to do whatever business might be at hand — a drink of water, perhaps a bit of dried dog food mushed with raw egg and milk, followed by a stroll around the yard to explore her new world. I'd do this only in our secluded back yard, for I felt rather foolish — a grown man, director of a major nature reserve, wearing a horse-blanket skirt while walking a little puppy. But, let me assure you, a wild wolf cub has incredibly sharp teeth and astonishingly quick reflexes, and she was not particularly fond of being held captive.

The healing went well, and with the daily antibiotics, the threat of infection was gradually diminished. The cub was somewhat playful but still enough of a wild carnivore to command respect. We played rough-and-tumble games, which she enjoyed with tremendous enthusiasm, but any time we did this, I made sure I wore an old, very heavy winter coat with the arms wound with extra strips of blanket. She was at a stage where her playfulness could be deadly for any domestic animal smaller than a donkey. Although she was sporting, she played hard, and she had an aggressive nature, which is quite natural for young, wild-born wolves.

I named her Sue-Ellen, after Sue-Ellen Ben-Zvi, the benefactor who had brought us the puppy muzzle on the day of the operation. This useful item was not Sue-Ellen's first contribution to Hai-Bar — indeed, she had performed a tremendous amount of volunteer work at the reserve and earned a great deal of respect for her simple, quiet labors.

Sue-Ellen Ben-Zvi had arrived at the reserve side gate one morning, driving her battered 1969 Buick, and said she wanted to work as a volunteer among the animals. "What does this housewife type want to do out in the desert?" I wondered, but if she was volunteering, I surely could find something for her to do.

It was a few weeks before the beginning of the ibex birthing season, and one of my priorities was to tighten security around the nursery yard where I had herded all the pregnant does. My big concern was the little foxes, which were already quite numerous in the reserve. If they could penetrate the ibex yard fence, they could easily prey upon the newborn kids.

Although the mesh of the fencing around the ibex nursery was too tight for foxes to squeeze through, I was concerned that they would try to burrow under the fence. I wanted simply to bury more fencing around the existing fence, to discourage burrowing — but there was a matter of finances involved. Five hundred meters of close-mesh fence buried around the ibex nursery would cost more money than the finance administrators in Jerusalem were able to invest at that time. So the next alternative was simply building a carpet of heavy stones for that entire length — stones so heavy that they couldn't be pushed away by a fox wanting to burrow at the base of the fence.

Sue-Ellen Ben-Zvi took a wheelbarrow and a pair of work gloves and started moving a half kilometer of ten- to twenty-pound stones — thousands of them — to build a continuous protective barrier that would foil the intentions of any fox planning to dig under the fence. Not a single fox broke in that year, and our ibex infants remained safe from all predators. Added together, Sue-Ellen Ben-Zvi's ounces of prevention weighed several tons — all done by hand solely for love of Nature and wild animals. When that job was done, she put her hand to other projects — from helping to rescue an enormous male ibex caught in a fence to preparing a properly equipped cage for our young wolf cub.

All this volunteer work was well appreciated and a valuable contribution to the Hai-Bar project. Since we didn't have any proper certificates of appreciation, plaques, or other tokens of thanks, the most appropriate way of expressing gratitude was to name one of our animals for this dedicated volunteer.

Of course, there was another Sue-Ellen known in Eilat at that time — Sue-Ellen Ewing — the character in the "Dallas" television series. "Dallas" was extremely popular in the southern Negev. Nobody would dare schedule a social event, fire drill, or anything else during the weekly hour allotted to the show by the Israeli Television Authority. "Dallas" was one of our few direct links to American culture, and thanks to the series, everyone north of the Saudi border knew that the average American earns about six or seven million dollars a year, uses a helicopter when traffic is too thick for the Mercedes, and has nearly as much oil as the people living south of the Saudi border. Of course, the Eilatis realized that there's also a human dimension to the American personality and that Americans carry tremendous psychological burdens and spend a lot of time crying into their martinis and/or swimming pools.

Sue-Ellen Ewing, wife of the notorious J.R., had eyes that appeared to be on the brink of tears even at the happiest hours. Our little wolf had such eyes. They were bright, yellow-green orbs, and you knew upon looking into them that their melancholy could reduce a block of Nubian sandstone to a pool of melted butter.

Any way we looked at her, our little wolf cub was destined to be called Sue-Ellen. So why defy destiny? We called her Sue-Ellen.

We got along quite well through the healing period. She never trusted me, and I never trusted her. But we were somewhat tolerant, even friendly, with each other most of the time. The glaring exception to our pact was the daily dose of antibiotics. Sue-Ellen didn't like the hypodermic needle, and she'd put up a furious defense trying to avoid it. There was more hellfire and brimstone for that quarter hour each day than was rained down upon Sodom and Gomorrah, but, like it or not, she did get her proper dosage. The potential for infection was too great after she was cut open by the rusty barbed wire.

There was one sad aspect of our relationship. It was clear from the start that Sue-Ellen would never be released free back into Nature. Despite all the heartwarming animal stories, such as that of the endearing lioness Elsa of *Born Free,* it is almost impossible to release carnivores that have become accustomed to humans. They simply don't survive. Indeed, Elsa the lion was herself dead within a few weeks after being freed. The price paid for her restoration was simply too great by most conservation standards.

Sue-Ellen had been pulled out of the learning cycle of her life at a crucial time, when her mother was teaching her the arts of survival in the wild. If we released her back into the desert, who would teach her? Would she be accepted back into her pack? Or rejected and driven away? It seemed unlikely that she would find her way back to her litter and even more unlikely that they'd accept her and help her make up all the education she had missed. Also, during her weeks of recovery she lost her fear of humans, and as a consequence, she could become something of a nuisance. She'd probably find her way to some kibbutz or army base in the desert and then try to live on the periphery, snitching garbage from the back door of the kitchen or maybe raiding a chicken house.

A release into Nature meant disaster, so I had to find the most humane and useful captive situation for her. By the end of the third week, the stitches had been long out, the danger of infection safely passed, and the cub appeared completely recovered. She was staying in a roomy enclosure at Hai-Bar, where she had plenty of space to exercise and even play with a few toys contributed by generous youngsters. Meanwhile, I conducted a permanent-housing search for little Sue-Ellen. And good fortune found us just the proper situation. She became a teacher.

Tel Aviv University had just opened a new facility for zoological studies at its campus in Ramat Aviv. Professor Heinrich Mendelssohn ran the modern, clean, private zoo. It was a closed institution, not open to the general public, and this meant much less likelihood of vandalism or harassment. Sue-Ellen would be tended by zoology students who had keen interests in Israel's native wildlife and who would also spend many hours keeping her company. Most important, perhaps, she would contribute to the education of these students and assist in creating Israel's next generation of conservationists and Nature lovers.

The university's zoological garden received the young wolf with much enthusiasm, since at that time Sue-Ellen was the only animal of her kind in captivity in Israel. The desert wolf was exterminated throughout nearly all of its range in the Middle East, and just a fragmentary population survived in Israel. The Nature Reserves Authority had declared the animal completely protected and was keen on trying to help it recover its lost numbers through a program of strict legal protection and a number of hands-on projects to stimulate population growth.

The desert wolf is unique. One of the extraordinary characteristics of this race can be seen in its very large feet. Although the desert wolf is relatively small, growing to perhaps fifty or sixty pounds, it has feet as large as those found on other wolves nearly twice its weight. These relatively large feet give the wolf tremendous support and produce a snowshoe effect when it walks across the soft sand of the deserts. Thus, while many other animals tend to sink into the sand when they encounter it, Sue-Ellen and her relatives are swift and agile in this type of habitat.

The vast majority of Israel's several hundred wolves are roaming free in Nature, running in packs numbering from three to twenty-two animals — although the large number might represent a group in which two or three packs joined together for a brief period. They inhabit many of the arid parts of the country, and favor the Negev Desert, the Judean Desert, and the barren shores of the Dead Sea.

Although wolves in general have a reputation for being ferocious predators, they are not as aggressive as many popular writers have suggested. Mostly, wolves dine on rodents, hares, and rock hyrax. They often eat carrion and only rarely will they try to bring down larger animals such as ibex or gazelles. Indeed, an alert gazelle can easily outrun a wolf — sand or no sand — and an alert ibex will leap into a rocky cliff face with such agility that a wolf, or any other predator for that matter, has little prospect of pursuing it.

There are no documented cases of wolves attacking humans save, perhaps, in fairy tales such as Little Red Riding Hood and Peter and the Wolf. A pack of wolves living free in Nature will go to extraordinary lengths to avoid contact with humans, because these intelligent canids know that humans are their most relentless enemy.

In Israel, wolves are completely protected. Israeli conservationists are well aware that wolves play a vital role in the ecology of the Land and that without them there would be serious disruptions. Wolves are the "sanitation men" of the desert and consume the carcasses of many animals that die in the wilderness; in this way, they prevent putrefaction and its related diseases from getting into the environment. Wolves are also among the best mousers and have a ravenous appetite for rodents. This tends to keep the rodent population in check, and this, in turn, is beneficial for the plants of the desert. It must be remembered that a desert environment is very difficult for a plant, and only the hardiest survive. One of the most problematic phases of plant life here is reproduction, because there is so little water available for a plant to sprout. Thus, many desert plants tend to produce a great abundance of seeds and distribute them very widely, thereby increasing the prospect that one of them will blow into that vital microclimate, a temporary pool or muddy ravine where it can sprout. If there is a population explosion of rodents, however, many more of these seeds will be eaten; therefore, the likelihood of their finding places to sprout will be reduced.

Wolves perform many other functions in Nature. For example, they are opportunistic and will attack weak and sickly gazelles. If the wolves are alert enough, they will weed out sick animals at the earliest opportunity — when the first symptoms become noticeable — and thereby prevent sickness from spreading through a herd. A gazelle suffering foot-and-mouth disease, for instance, will be lame and will salivate. It will be feverish and have a reduced awareness of its surroundings. Wolves will notice this and will select this gazelle because it will be the easiest to attack. Thus, in preying on such sickly gazelles, the wolves help to prevent the infected animals from communicating their diseases to the rest of the herd.

Like wolves around the world, Israel's desert wolves are generally crepuscular — that is, they are active in the early morning and evening hours and tend to sleep through the middle of the day and middle of the night. But because they're totally protected in Israel, they can be seen at any time of day, particularly in the winter, when heavy clouds hang over the desert for days at a time. I've seen wolves many times during the midday hours, including a few times during the midsummer, although this is quite rare. Wolves, like most animals of the desert, prefer to rest in the shade during the hottest hours.

Desert wolves are very social animals and live in family-grouped packs led by an "alpha" male and an "alpha" female. Contrary to persistent popular reports in several publications, desert wolves can howl with good volume and energy. They can commonly be heard at night in various parts of the desert where they tend to congregate and socialize. I decided to explore this phenomenon a bit one evening by making a little experiment. There is a commercial recording of wolves howling on the Canadian tundra, and I took a copy of it to Hai-Bar and played it at full volume on a portable tape cassette player one evening. To my delight, after about eight or ten minutes the desert wolves west of the reserve began to howl back to the recording. Perhaps it was the Canadian accent on the recording, but after about a half hour of howling, the desert wolves became curious about who was calling to them, so they trotted over toward Hai-Bar to investigate. In the light of the nearly full moon, I counted eighteen wolves together headed toward the reserve.

Anxious that they not come too close, and perhaps a bit concerned about becoming the first wolf casualty on record, I flipped the tape over and offered them Antonio Vivaldi's oboe concerto as a delicate warning that something other than their Canadian cousins existed beyond the Hai-Bar fence. They took it all in good spirits, hung around for a few minutes — perhaps to listen to the music — and then padded off as a pack into the desert night.

The following year, a young male wolf was rescued in the Northern Negev. In a situation similar to Sue-Ellen's, he lost his fear of people and appeared to be a bad risk for release back into Nature, so he, too, was brought to Tel Aviv University. He became good friends with Sue-Ellen, and two years later, they became parents. Two of the cubs were retained by the University so zoology students could study them, learn their behavior, and understand the species' vital role in the ecology of the desert.

The other two cubs were sent back to Hai-Bar, where a large enclosure was built for them. These cubs have been with humans since the day Sue-Ellen gave birth to them at the university and therefore are quite tame, with none of their mother's feisty independence. Visitors touring Hai-Bar can see these frolicking youngsters at the newly built predator compound at the southern end of the reserve.

By breeding these wolves in captivity, Israeli conservationists hope to create a nucleus population that can be offered to Arab countries in the Middle East once peace has been brought back to the region. Many of these countries have had their wolf populations totally exterminated, and the only hope of restoring the animal to its appropriate place in Nature would be via a long and difficult — but not impossible — reintroduction program.

I visit Sue-Ellen from time to time, when I drop by the university. She has a relatively happy life — companionship with much activity — although she'll never be as tame as a wolf born in captivity. She remembers me well enough, but in an unusual way. If I am with a group of people, she will approach to within a few yards and then stare at me. I do not know what thought processes go on in her mind, other than simple recognition and interest. She reserves all signs of affection — tail wagging, licking, playing and such — for the wolves of her own family. But for humans, there is only the penetrating stare of her golden eyes.

Bonnie and Clyde

BONNIE AND CLYDE are Israeli criminals. They're also unclean, stupid, cruel, mournful, and the inheritors of pagan ruins — at least that's what the Bible has to say about their species.

Bonnie and Clyde are ostriches, and their specialty is larceny. The biggest thieves of the desert, they have a passion for the most heartless sort of stealing. Surely, the prophet Jeremiah was well aware of this tendency when he used them as the symbol of cruelty: "The daughter of my people has become cruel, like the ostriches in the wilderness. . . ." (Lamentations 4:3).

A shameful sample of this avian ill will was demonstrated near noontime on a day in early summer. I had just picked up a quarter ton of freshly cut alfalfa at Kibbutz Yotvatah and was driving back through the Hai-Bar reserve to spread the nutritious delicacy among the animals, when I noticed Sarah, an addax antelope, and her young calf Chaim, not far from the edge of the road. Little Chaim, whose Hebrew name means "life," was one of the most energetic and endearing youngsters of the season.

By now, Chaim had started on solid foods and was following his mother's lead, nibbling on the succulent salt bushes and tender acacia twigs of the desert reserve. I decided to try him with a little alfalfa.

This day's alfalfa load was especially good. I had collected it from the harvesting tractor no more than fifteen minutes after it had been cut. The alfalfa was cool, moist, and fragrant, with thousands of tiny flowers scattered through it. Indeed, just this precise moment, when the delicate flowers have blossomed on the alfalfa plant, is the best possible time, in terms of both taste and nutrition, to harvest it.

Carefully, I selected a handful of the chopped alfalfa from the back of the pickup truck, making sure to include an extra abundance of the tasty bluish purple flowers. I set this salad on the ground about ten yards upwind from little Chaim, and then slowly backed away to watch.

The sensitive youngster caught scent of the alfalfa almost immediately. He stared at it and then looked back toward mother Sarah. She seemed to approve, and the antelope calf cautiously advanced toward the inviting snack, pausing every few steps to look back toward mother for continued approval. The calf reached the alfalfa, nudged it gently with his nose, licked it lightly, and then looked back to Sarah for final approval.

At just this moment I heard the steady thump-thump-thump-thump-thump-thump of sprinting ostriches. Bonnie and Clyde were attacking. I turned and saw them running straight toward the little calf, but I was too far away to do anything but yell.

My screaming caused Bonnie to pull up to a halt. But Clyde charged right by, booted the little calf aside, and gobbled up all the alfalfa himself. I dashed toward little Chaim to see if he had been injured by the ostrich's kick, but the calf managed to jump to his feet in an instant and ran bleating back toward Sarah. Sarah, meanwhile, had already lowered her long spiral, sharp-pointed horns to attack Clyde — the addax is one of the most protective mothers in the desert and doesn't tolerate any threat to her calf.

Sharp-eyed Clyde, having gulped down the handful of alfalfa, saw Sarah advance and easily jumped aside — ostriches are incredibly fast runners and can easily outdistance almost any four-legged animal. Preoccupied by the present drama, I hadn't been paying much attention to Bonnie. She was using the spectacle as a diversion, and while I was busy with Chaim, Sarah, and Clyde, Bonnie was busy elsewhere. She casually sauntered up to the pickup truck and poked her long-necked head through the open window to see what edibles might be found therein. She spotted my canvas bag and flipping it open with a snap of her beak, she helped herself to my lunch.

By the time I noticed her, my orange was gently gliding down her throat. She didn't bother removing the peel or breaking the fruit open into parts. Instead, she swallowed it whole with a single gulp. The sight made me think of an olive gradually slipping down the length of an elastic soda straw.

I knew my sandwich had been immediately beneath the orange in my canvas bag, and that would be the next to go if I didn't act quickly to deter that filching fowl. I let out another scream and leapt toward Bonnie. She nonchalantly backed away. As I was involved with chasing Bonnie, Clyde doubled back around the opposite side of the truck and nabbed the sandwich, which, of course, he swallowed with a single gulp — wrapper and all.

By now, little Chaim was safely back with Sarah, and, since my lunch was gone, Bonnie and Clyde had taken to raiding the alfalfa in the back of the truck. There was little else to do but barge my way into the back of the truck too, gather up a big armload of chopped alfalfa, and toss it out across the desert floor.

Jumping back into the truck, I shooed the ostriches away. Chased from one meal, they immediately went to the next and attacked the alfalfa I had tossed on the ground. Meanwhile, I slipped down into the cab, started the engine, and made my getaway.

I nibbled on the alfalfa flowers myself for lunch, and little Chaim got his first taste of this delicious salad a few days later, when no ostriches were lurking about.

It's obvious why the prophets called the great bird *ya'en,* which is derived from *ya'an,* meaning greedy.

The ostrich's greed can be its undoing, and on one occasion Joe and I used the big bird's gluttony in a scheme to catch a whole flock of them. It was getting near the breeding season, a time when the male ostrich gets downright dangerous, so I wanted to close them away in safe quarters for a while.

In the breeding season, the male ostrich's neck turns bright red, and a change in his body chemistry makes him very aggressive. A few statistics show how formidable an angry male ostrich can really be. I made some measurements on one of these birds, an ornery fellow I called Archie Bunker. He was intolerant, hostile, avaricious, and everything else the Bible says ostriches are supposed to be. He was also precisely eight feet three-and-a-half inches tall, and weighed three hundred and seventy-two pounds. It might also be added that Archie was drugged and sleeping like a baby when these measurements were made.

Besides these impressive bodily dimensions, the ostrich's anatomy contributes another intimidating element. The joint about halfway up his leg is an ankle, not a knee. This means it bends — and kicks! — straight forward. Only a demented person or a candidate for suicide would walk in front of a male ostrich in breeding season. On one occasion, Archie actually killed a horse with a single kick. Another time, a different male — "Bin-Nun" — gave the reserve's little Renault-4 a swift kick. He put the car up on two wheels and poked a hole clear through its steel door with the nail of his big toe. These birds can get plain nasty, and breeding season is the time of year to round them up and put them in a safe place for a few months until they settle back to normal.

I had a lovely, romantic hideaway for Bonnie and Clyde, which I intended them to share with three other females — ostriches are communal nesters, and several hens contribute to a single nest. It was a spacious enclosure of about fifty thousand square feet. It had a nice sandy surface, with several good sites for nesting, and there were also a few shady areas, constantly available fresh drinking water, and a good variety of natural vegetation — a veritable ostrich paradise. Most important, it was completely surrounded by a nine-foot chain-link hurricane fence, which would protect any chicks from the foxes that lurk about Hai-Bar; the fence would also protect the rest of the universe from the deranged aggressions of Clyde during the more frantic days of the breeding season.

The single remaining problem was to persuade Bonnie and Clyde that, for the benefit of all concerned, it would be better if they spent a few months in the little resort I had prepared for them. But no amount of persuasion seemed to work. The pair of avians had an entire nature reserve to roam and could wander for kilometers in any direction to make the worst sorts of mischief. They weren't prepared to surrender this freedom for free room and board at the poshest ostrich enclosure this side of the Red Sea.

My first effort involved setting a large pile of sweet alfalfa in the enclosure and leaving the gate invitingly open. But all this accomplished was to fill the place with four antelopes, three wild asses, a half dozen ibex, and a stray gazelle. Bonnie and Clyde stood outside, looking longingly at the alfalfa, but refusing to enter.

The following Saturday, Joe joined me as my six-year-old-helper for a day. After sharing the morning rounds, we drove out of the reserve to visit the nearby Israel Defense Forces military base. I had an arrangement with the base cook, and once a week, I'd drive by and pick up all his stale bread for the animals.

Army bread around the world has a reputation for being pretty terrible, but Israeli army bread is even worse. The Israeli army traces its ancestry all the way back to David, the shepherd boy who killed the mighty Goliath by slinging a single stone at him. Israeli troops claim this account is not precisely accurate. What David did, they say, was scale a slice of Israeli army bread at the Philistine giant. It not only killed him, it also frightened the entire Philistine army into disorganized retreat. The Jews had a new secret weapon! Another axiom notes that during an emergency, it is safer to take shelter behind a case of bread than behind sandbags. Despite, or perhaps because of, these bizarre characteristics, ostriches love Israeli army bread.

The cook offered us thirty loaves of old bread, each marked with the ironic name "Angel" — we suspected that this had little to do with its heavenly lightness. My helper suggested the cherubic name was printed as a warning — eat a slice and be prepared to try negotiating your way through the Pearly Gates.

We loaded up the bread, thanked the cook, and schemed. Back in the reserve, we transferred thirty loaves from the pickup truck to the little Renault-4 — the one with the door punctured by an ostrich toe. It was an aged machine, near the end of a long, hard life in the desert. It wasn't very fast or powerful, and it frequently broke down because of hard use and age, but it was precisely what we

needed. The little Renault-4 could easily be driven through the gate
of the ostrich enclosure. Also, it had a back hatch that could be
removed — a vital element in our plan.

Leaving the enclosure gate open, and emptying about a dozen
loaves of sliced army bread on the back floor of the Renault, we
drove around the reserve until we found our mischievous ostriches.
With our quarry sighted, Joe jumped to his action station by the
rear hatch. I slowly drove in close to the big birds. Joe flipped out
a single slice of bread.

Thump-thump-thump-thump-thump — Bonnie got there first
and gobbled the goody down. I began driving away in first gear,
and after about fifty yards or so, Joe heaved out another slice of
bread from the back hatch. Thump-thump-thump-thump-thump-
thump — Bonnie got it again.

Then Joe stood up in the back of the Renault, and, leaning out
the hatch, in plain sight of both Bonnie and Clyde, he ate a piece
of stale army bread himself — the ultimate sacrifice on the part of
the child for the success of our mission. He also held up more bread,
flashing a half dozen slices like a winning poker hand.

This, of course, infuriated Clyde, who quite naturally attacked.
Bonnie followed in quick pursuit. Joe ducked back into the safety
of the car. The ride across the desert was fast and bumpy. A few
extra bumps were added by the ostriches, who, because they could
run faster than we could drive, gave the little Renault a few boots
along the way.

About two hundred yards from the enclosure, Joe scaled out three
or four pieces of bread, Frisbee-style, and this diverted the ostriches
away from us for a few moments. Then, I made a deliberate beeline
for the enclosure gate. Joe flipped out another slice of bread every
twenty or thirty yards along the way.

Bonnie and Clyde charged every piece of bread as it blew from the
back of the Renault. They ran furiously, with their necks stretched
out horizontally. Often, the big birds collided in their rush to
snatch the individual slices of bread as they bounded crazily across
the desert floor. The pace was maddening.

We scooted through the gate, trailing a chain of bread slices, like
Hansel and Gretel into the gingerbread house. And once inside, Joe

started tossing out slices of army bread as fast as he could while I drove in tight circles.

The greedy ostriches charged in right behind us, snapping up bread slices in blind fury. Indeed, their fury was so blind that they didn't even notice that they were in the enclosure.

Joe heaved out another loaf of bread for good measure before I raced the little Renault to the gate and used the vehicle to block the only exit. Next, I swung the large gate shut and secured and locked it — our two marauding ostriches safely within. All Creation was protected from catastrophe for another ostrich breeding season.

One task remained. I wanted to gather in three more ostriches to enlarge the flock of females. Having several females is important for a number of reasons, the most obvious being to protect a lone female from the single object of a crazy male's affections. If this happened, she'd soon be exhausted and would have little energy for the important duties of nesting. Also, there's a good biological reason for ostriches to nest with a harem flock. This reason is the ostrich egg, which is the biggest living single cell presently known to exist on earth. The ostrich egg is a marvelous structure that weighs about three pounds and measures about six inches in length. It has a tough outer shell, which is strong enough to support the incubating parent birds throughout the nesting season.

The ostrich egg is so large and complex that it takes a hen two days to make one. Thus, if a hen wanted to fill her nest with sixteen or eighteen eggs, it would take more than a month to do it alone — and this would leave her in a very difficult quandary. If she started incubating right from the start, some chicks would be hatched a month before the others, and what would she do then? Would she continue to incubate the unhatched eggs? Or would she simply abandon them and spend her time brooding her hatched chicks?

A breeding harem includes one dominant hen, which has the right to incubate eggs and brood chicks, and several subdominant hens, which simply contribute an egg to the nest every second day and otherwise keep a respectful distance from it. The activity of the subdominant hens is sometimes called altruistic behavior by ethologists and has sparked many debates over the reasons why animals contribute something for the good of the flock of the species as a whole, while deriving no apparent individual benefit to themselves.

With four females in the enclosure, I could count on about twenty eggs in ten days, and this was just about right. The birds would spend a week and a half adding eggs to the nest, and the dominant hen would then begin incubating. Since the incubation process wouldn't start until all the eggs were in the nest, they'd all hatch at about the same time. Everything would work according to Mother Nature's clock.

Rounding up the three subdominant females wasn't a very difficult task at all. Job was observing as a naturalist and not as a male chauvinist when he penned his famous description of the ostrich: "Because God hath deprived *her* of wisdom, neither hath He imparted to *her* understanding" (Job 39:17). The subdominant hens in particular are both docile and stupid, having none of the fury of a breeding male, nor any of the tenacity of the dominant female.

I have a special tool for catching these hens. I made it by cutting legs off jeans — thus creating shorts for warm weather, plus some nice sleeves. One end of each sleeve is sewn closed so it can be slipped over an ostrich's head without sliding down its neck. A small hole is then cut a few inches below the closed end, thus permitting a place for the bird's beak to protrude so it can breathe.

The sleeve is rolled up, just as one would roll up a sock before sliding it onto a foot. Then, it's only a matter of driving out into the reserve with a bit of alfalfa in the back of the pickup truck, parking near the ostrich enclosure, and waiting for the hens to come to me — and this is what happened.

I sat in the chopped alfalfa and waited for the ostriches to begin feeding. As one hen started pecking at the greenery, I just reached over, grabbed her by the back of the head, slipped the sleeve over her head, and released her. The blindfolded bird stepped back a couple of paces and stood still. An ostrich doesn't have the sense to bend its head toward the ground and let the sleeve drop off.

When I had three subdominant hens standing around with sacks over their heads, it was simply a task of grabbing them by the upper beak and leading them into the enclosure. This was easily done because the ostrich, being a bird, has no teeth, so the beak can be grabbed without injuring it. Also, the ostrich has a long but rather weak neck. When the beak is grabbed, the head can be pulled down to waist level and the bird simply towed along like a pull-toy. If one remembers to keep the head held down — say to about three feet from the ground — a female ostrich can be led rather easily and safely. The bird doesn't kick when its head is held in this position, presumably for fear of kicking itself in the head.

Before the hens could be put into the enclosure, however, another diversion was required. I knew that as soon as I opened the gate, Bonnie and Clyde would try barging out. They knew that they were confined, and they didn't like it one bit. But this was not a very difficult obstacle at all. It only required hiking down to the far end of the enclosure and heaving a few loaves of old army bread over the fence. While Bonnie and Clyde were preoccupied with this dubious banquet, I quickly ushered the three subdominant hens into their new home.

As expected, Nature took its own course through the breeding season, and I had little to do but bring an extra ration of alfalfa each day, make sure the watering system was functioning properly, and keep up with a few other housekeeping chores around the enclosure. The breeding season provided an excellent opportunity to study the ostriches and reconsider what the Biblical writers had to say about them. The observations of Job, one of the finest naturalists of the ancient world, are the most important. Besides his previously noted comment on ostrich intelligence, he also forecast the modern debate between evolution and creationism with a single question. Addressing the Almighty, Job asked: "Gavest thou . . . wings and feathers unto the ostrich?" (Job 39:13). The implications of questioning why ostriches have wings and feathers are very great indeed, for today we realize that the ancestors of the ostrich did have the capability of flight, but that the ancestral bird adopted land-living habits and its wings became useless appendages, which, over the generations, evolved to little more than feathered fans. More than two dozen centuries ago, Job was asking questions that are still hotly debated.

Job was also perplexed by the ostrich nest, which is no more than a cavity dug in the sandy earth. It's about a yard across and a foot deep. Job observed that the ostrich "leaveth her eggs in the earth, and warmeth them in dust, And forgetteth that the foot may crush them or the wild beast may break them" (Job 39:14–15). One might ask where else a three-hundred-and-fifty-pound flightless bird might nest. The ostrich has little choice as to where she must build her nest. I've seen only one case of an ostrich egg being crushed underfoot — and that was on purpose. One breeding season, Archie Bunker took it upon himself to kick open all the eggs in a nest and indulge himself in what must have been one of the biggest omelets in history.

Normally, however, the ostrich eggs are pretty durable and support the weight of the incubating adult without problem. Usually, the dominant hen and the male share the incubating work. The female, with her mottled, greyish brown color, sits above the eggs through the daylight hours, and on hot days her work involves keeping the eggs from cooking in the desert sun. Quite often, through the course of a hot day, Bonnie would stand over the eggs and fan them with her wings. She'd also turn all her eggs over each day — otherwise, the embryos inside the eggs would tend to settle toward the bottom of the shell, and this would interfere with the proper development of the chick inside.

The male takes his turn over the eggs at nighttime. His black feathers are excellent camouflage, so he is well hidden atop the eggs from sunset to sunrise. And if a predator does happen to wander near the nest, the male can put up a vigorous fight to protect the eggs — thus it's better to have him on duty at night, when most of the desert's predators are lurking about.

Job also noticed that when the ostrich "lifteth up herself on high, she scorneth the horse and his rider" (Job 39:18). We already know that the ostrich can scorn the Renault-4 and its driver, for indeed this bird is a very fast runner.

The breeding season is also the time of year when one can listen to the ostriches. The prophet Micah was familiar with the sad-sounding call and wrote: "I will make a lamentation like the jackals, and mourning like the ostriches" (Micah 1:8). It's the male who does all the mourning, as females are usually quiet in this species. The male's call sounds something like *who, whoo,*

whooooooooooo . . . who, whoo, whooooooooooo. This might sound sorrow-
ful to some, but actually he's announcing his passions and is trying
to encourage several of the neighborhood's females to pay him a
visit.

The ostrich can make one other sound, a loud hissing, which
usually means that he's upset and ready to attack. A memorable
experience involving this hissing occurred one evening shortly after
some eggs hatched. A fox was lurking in the bush not far from the
chicks, probably calculating how he might acquire one for supper.

The chicks were still in the enclosure, so there was little danger.
I decided to sit back and watch quietly through my binoculars.
Back and forth the fox prowled along the fence until it became
obvious that he couldn't get around it, so he tried to go under it.
He started burrowing, but I knew this would also be a dead
end — when building the enclosure we made sure that the chain-
link fence extended a full yard into the earth to prevent predators
from tunnelling under.

When the fox was well into the earth, and only his tail showed
above his excavation site, both Bonnie and Clyde got to their feet
and strolled over toward the fence. There wasn't much they could
do to the fox either, but somehow they seemed to have agreed that
the bushy-tailed fellow ought to get a good scare. As they
approached the fence, both birds opened their wings to make their
bodies appear twice their normal size. They lowered their snakelike
necks and started pounding the earth with their feet, hissing all the
while like a basketful of cobras. The fox peered up from his
tunneling, saw this terrifying sight, and vanished in a flash.

As a matter of practice, each morning during the nesting season
I checked around the reserve's interior fences just to make sure they
were all secure; I also checked for tracks — keeping an eye on what
predators might be in the area. From that evening forward through
the rest of the season, there were no fox tracks around the ostrich
enclosure fence.

The ostrich and its eggs also have to contend with another
predator, and this particular creature is the only one ever to cause
any damage to the Hai-Bar ostriches. It's the Egyptian vulture;
many ornithologists agree that it's one of the most intelligent birds

in the world. The Egyptian vulture, for example, is the only bird known to use tools. The tools in this case are sharp rock — similar to the type people used during the Stone Age. The vulture uses rocks by throwing them at ostrich eggs left unguarded in a nest, a very effective means of breaking eggs open so they can be eaten. Egyptian vulture raids on ostrich nests usually occur during the week or so after the laying starts and before the incubation begins. Once the incubation starts there is always an adult at the nest, and the vulture has no opportunity to attack.

Hai-Bar's ostriches are wild North African types known to science as *Struthio camelus camelus*. The ostrich that inhabited Israel during the biblical period is today extinct. It is said to have been a bit smaller than the present type and to have had very luxurious feathers. In fact, there are records of some having been captured and used as part of the stock introduced to domestication in South Africa during the last century.

The reason for the extinction of the Israeli ostrich is pure and simple — it was exterminated by greedy humans. Through much of history, the ostrich was highly valued for its beautiful feathers, soft leather, and meat, for which people traveled great distances to catch and kill these greatest of living birds. Ironically, the Jews living in Israel generally left the birds alone, even though they were so easily available. The reason for this is that Jewish law has branded the ostrich unclean, or not conforming to the laws of kosher.

Mass exploitation of the Israeli ostrich started about eight hundred years ago, during the Crusades. Ostrich feathers were highly valued as adornments for European knights. Exploitation continued through the nineteenth century, when fashionable ladies found ostrich feathers appealing for their wardrobes — particularly their outlandish Victorian hats. The introduction of modern firearms into the Middle East during World War I was the death knell, and the few survivors were quickly killed off. The race is now generally regarded as being extinct.

There are, however, occasional reports from the Bedouin that some ostriches survive in very remote parts of the desert on the Arabian peninsula. Perhaps there is hope for recovering them some day.

Meanwhile, however, the ecological niche for the ostrich still exists in Israeli deserts, and thus the North African ostrich has been included in the Hai-Bar program. When they are numerous enough at Hai-Bar, flocks of them will be distributed through appropriate habitat areas in the Negev Desert.

No account of the Hai-Bar ostriches would be complete without relating an incident in which an elderly woman had the misfortune to encounter Clyde on one of his more larcenous days. The woman came as a tourist in a rented car, one summer afternoon, and took delight in making a round through the reserve to see all the animals. She saw everything distinctly until she saw Clyde. He boldly strutted up to her car and stared intently at her for a few moments. She stared right back. He stepped closer and stared more intently. She continued staring back. He took yet another step closer — and then snapped the eyeglasses from her face. Naturally, he swallowed them whole.

While the woman fumed at this avian highwayman, Bonnie stuck her head in the opposite window, and, as might be expected, stole her lunch.

Cinderella

CINDERELLA was ornery one morning. I tried to be nice to her, but she just stomped around and snorted something I couldn't understand.

"C'mon, princess," I pleaded. "Look here! I've brought your favorite breakfast." I fluffed up an armful of well-cured, sweet-smelling alfalfa hay and set it in her feeding crib.

But she just snorted again and showed me her horns, which were nearly as long as yardsticks and sharper than barbecue skewers. When she waved them around, it meant she wanted to be left alone. Unicorns can get like that sometimes.

Job knew all about this problem: "Will the unicorn be willing to serve thee, or abide by thy crib?" (Job 39:9). Cinderella wouldn't abide by her own crib, even when I served her.

After depositing the alfalfa, I respectfully backed away. That's another bit of applied ethology I learned from Job: Never turn your back on a temperamental unicorn. "Wilt thou trust him, because his strength is great?" (Job 39:11).

Job included the unicorn in his detailed observations of the ostrich, the crocodile, the wild ass, the ibex, and many other animals of biblical Israel. Recent decades have brought more weapons into the Middle East, and native wildlife has suffered sorely — unicorns included.

In an iconoclastic, scientific age, not many people call these antelopes "unicorns" anymore, although that's the name they go by in several translations of the Bible, including the ever-popular King James version.

We biologists insist on calling them *Oryx leucoryx,* a name that is useless except when you're talking to other biologists, or when you're really hard up for a few points at a scrabble match. An oryx is a type of antelope that inhabits deserts, and leucoryx simply means white (leuco) oryx.

Commonly, they're called white oryx — except by politicians. Many people call them Arabian oryx, but this never sat well with my boss, Avraham Yoffe, the quintessential Israeli nationalist. "Anybody who calls them Arabian oryx will be fired on the spot!" he bellowed one day. "We shall not call them by the name of the people who have presided over their near extinction!"

One day, in a fit of inspiration, Avraham proposed, "Let's call them *biblical* oryx!" I groaned. "Why not?" he questioned. "It is an accepted taxonomic practice to give an animal its first descriptive name, and the first known description of this animal is in the Bible. Yes, we'll call them biblical oryx. And anybody who doesn't like it can appeal the matter to the prime minister!" The prime minister at that time was Yitzhak Rabin, who also happened to be Avraham's brother-in-law. There was no escape. We called them biblical oryx whenever Avraham was within earshot. Otherwise, we called them *re'em,* which is the Hebrew name that Job knew them by. And when I was all alone, I called them unicorns.

Cinderella, the dominant female in a female-led herd, was my favorite unicorn.

The term *unicorn* originated in remote antiquity, but it only came into general popularity at the time of the Crusaders. Those pompous European knights who came to save the Holy Land for Christianity had a certain gift for exaggeration. Reading their journals, we encounter incredible natural barriers — impenetrable forests, endless deserts, formidable mountain ranges, and rampaging rivers. Intrepidly, those valiant knights conquered them all! It all makes mighty impressive reading for anybody who has never visited the Land of Israel.

But when one arrives here and gets a fair estimation of the lay of the land, one also becomes keenly aware of the Crusader's capacity for magnifying and embroidering reality. Israel, for example, is no larger than New Jersey. And while Nature often shines her finest here, natural extremes are by no means quite as impressive as the Crusaders would have us believe. The River Jordan, for example, is the greatest river in the Land, but at its rampaging worst, it's barely more than twenty yards across. In most places, it's hardly knee-deep.

Crusader sensationalism made the unicorn something a bit more than it really is. The white oryx is a smallish antelope, standing about a yard high at the shoulders and weighing about 140 pounds. Exposed to the desert sun, its hair can become bright white, except for a few chocolate-to-black markings on its face, legs, and tail. It's a lithe animal, with an extremely graceful canter, a sort of straight-legged stride.

It has two horns, for certain — although they are closely spaced and very straight. From a distance, they can appear as one, particularly in profile. When an oryx flees a potential predator — whether wolf or Crusader — it generally sets a zigzag course. This way it can keep a sharp eye on its pursuer. Thus, the hunter sees this antelope in an oblique profile most of the time, and from this perspective it can appear to have but one horn. Furthermore, males occasionally lose a horn when fighting, and so there are a few one-horned oryxes running around the Land of Israel to help encourage the legend.

It is unlikely that the crusading knights ever got very close to these antelopes. Just imagine Sir Gawaine of Bumbleshire, all dressed up in the most fashionable of chivalrous attire and seated upon a large charger — a great horse of tremendous power but not much speed, particularly when ankle-deep in desert sand. Horse and rider were burdened with armor, shields, lances, swords, maces, banners, helmets, and other assorted hardware, which, as a unit, must have been somewhat akin to an inverted stewpot that simmered nicely under a 120-degree desert sun.

Most likely, the white antelopes simply cantered away from the knights, seeming, with their unique and lovely strutting gait, to float over the desert floor.

Like frustrated fishermen describing the "one that got away," the Crusaders embellished their descriptions of the elusive creatures. Unicorns developed fantastic dimensions and ferocity and were feared as the most dangerous critters of the wilderness, unless, of course, you happened to be a young maiden. Every Crusader knew that unicorns had a soft spot for young maidens and became very docile in their presence. Even the great Leonardo da Vinci, reporting a Crusader tale, notes that unicorns will curl up in a young maiden's lap and go to sleep — and that's the only way they can be captured!

In any event, by the end of the Crusades, all Europe had heard about the great white untamable beast with one horn. And a few centuries later, when the scholars of King James's court got around to translating the Bible into English, they didn't call the Hebrew re'em an oryx. Nope, they knew precisely what it was. They had eyewitness accounts from the flower of European chivalry. They had the most reliable testimony available to confirm that this critter was indeed the unicorn.

The white oryx hasn't been as successful in avoiding twentieth century poachers as it was in dodging Crusaders. The introduction of modern firearms into the region was the main culprit in the mass extermination of this species.

At the turn of the century, the white oryx ranged over more than a million square kilometers of the Middle East, from Israel clear across to the Arabian Sea. The arrival of modern firearms brought the first wave of killings, and the animal's own behavior contributed to its rapid extermination. Typically, the white oryx simply avoids predators whenever possible. When it feels threatened, it will attempt to flee by running its zigzag course into the desert. But when it realizes the predator is closing in and the attack is deadly serious, the oryx will turn and stand at bay. Rather than expend all its energy trying to evade a predator, it will halt, lower its incredibly sharp horns, and meet its pursuer head-on.

This tactic is pretty successful when used against the oryx's most common natural predator — the desert wolf. But it's absolutely useless when used against human hunters. Indeed, an oryx standing at bay is a much easier target than one that is running away.

At the turn of the century, most of the firearms in the Middle East were relatively primitive. They were single-shot weapons, very heavy and not very accurate. World War I changed all that, however. The conflict brought Colonel T. E. Lawrence — the fabled Lawrence of Arabia — into the region. His assignment was to foment a revolt among the desert tribesmen and throw off the yoke of Ottoman oppression — or so it was put. Instigating a Bedouin revolt, the British thought, would force the Ottoman Turks and their German allies to drain some troops away from other fronts in order to suppress the rebellion, and that would possibly relieve some of the pressure on the British Army in the trenches of France.

The revolt in the desert didn't amount to much. A few railroad trains in a remote part of the Ottoman Empire were derailed and sacked. Lawrence's main achievement was the capture of Aqaba on the Red Sea — but this was little more than a few palm trees on a sleepy coast defended by about a hundred second-rate Turkish soldiers who were unfit for duty on a real battlefront.

Hollywood has made a glorious spectacle of this romantic epic. I can still close my closes and see Peter O'Toole admiring himself in his flowing Bedouin robes and kaffiya, while the smoking wreck of a Turkish supply train crackles behind him.

The film doesn't mention, however, that Colonel Lawrence acquired sixty thousand nearly new Lee-Enfield rifles for his revolutionaries. That was more than a dozen weapons for every man he could put under arms! Very few of those rifles were actually used against the Turks. Instead, they were distributed among the Bedouin tribes throughout the region and used for hunting. Wildlife biologists can date local extinctions from the time those highly accurate, rapid-fire, long-range, high-power British rifles arrived in the Middle East.

Within a decade, all the white oryx in what is now Israel, Jordan, Sinai, and Syria were exterminated. The native race of wild ass was also shot into extinction at this time, as were the last populations of native roe and fallow deer. The native race of ostrich was shot into oblivion during the second decade after the arrival of those rifles. There were many local exterminations of gazelles, ibex, and birds of prey. The bloodbath was devastating — the worst destruction suffered by wildlife during the entire history of the Middle East.

There remained two populations of white oryx in Nature. The smaller survived around the Great Nafud Desert in northern Saudi Arabia, and the larger was concentrated in the vast Rub al'Khali — the Empty Quarter — of southern Saudi Arabia and adjacent areas of Oman. The northern population was obliterated first. Shortly after World War II, four-wheel drive jeeps became available on the Arabian peninsula, and hunters used them to pursue their oryx trophies into previously inaccessible regions of the Nafud. By about 1952, this population was extinct.

The big oil boom that started about that time brought all manner of new exploration vehicles to Saudi Arabia — aircraft, helicopters, all-terrain vehicles — which carried geologists even into the depths of the Rub al'Khali in search of oil. Here, they also found the last refuges of the white oryx.

Those were the days of cheap oil, when Arab princes let major oil conglomerates pump oil from their land for a nearly token payment. To humor the princes (and keep the prices low), oil companies lavished gifts on the Arab royalty, and one of the most popular gifts was to use modern vehicles to take them on hunting safaris into the most remote parts of the desert. Returning with the head of a white oryx was considered to be the ultimate victory.

The region inhabited by the white oryx continued to shrink, until only a small remnant survived in the sultanate of Oman along the southern fringe of Rub al'Khali. The Omanis were relatively protective of these animals, but they weren't sophisticated enough to deal with the tremendous poaching, particularly the raiding parties that came from Qatar and the United Arab Emirates. The oryx herds dwindled further.

Conservationists around the world sounded alarms about the imminent extinction of an extraordinarily beautiful antelope, a living link to Scripture, which was just about ready to pass into oblivion because of unrelenting hunting.

Then, in 1963, Britain's Fauna Preservation Society mounted a last-minute rescue operation. They appointed Major Ian Grimwood, then chief wildlife warden of Kenya, to lead a team into the

Protectorate of Aden and live-capture some of the last surviving white oryx for safe keeping.

The team searched Aden (the present South Yemen) without finding a single white oryx. So they sneaked across the border into Oman and after an intensive search, returned with three white oryx antelope, which formed the nucleus of a "World Herd."

"I can admit to the poaching involved now!" Grimwood recently told me. Indeed, it did violate Oman's conservation laws, but from our perspective of twenty-twenty hindsight, it was a saving grace for the species, because in the wild, the hunters maintained their relentless pressure.

Dr. Lee Talbot, the former director of the U.S. President's Council on Environmental Quality, studied the hunting syndrome of Arabia while it was happening and observed: "When automobiles and high-powered rifles came in, the oryx stood little chance. . . . Members of the (Saudi) royal family received most of the oil royalties from the foreign oil companies, and they did the greatest damage to wildlife. . . . Between January and April 1955, in a royal goodwill tour around northern Saudi Arabia, the retinue numbered 482 cars at one point. Hunting was part of this excursion, and this vast army of vehicles spread out, crossing the desert and shooting everything. As a result of the incredible blood lust of the past twenty years, virtually all the abundant wildlife of Arabia has been extirpated."

Dr. Hartmut Jungius, director of nature conservation for the World Wildlife Fund, confirms the cause: ". . . the oryx was exterminated as a result of direct human persecution, not because of environmental changes. It was not traditional tribal hunting on camelback with spears or rifles, but four-wheeled-drive vehicles and automatic weapons that caused its destruction."

Dr. James Dolan, of the San Diego Zoological Society, who maintains the studbook, or official international records for the species, also cites modern firearms as the chief cause of the animal's destruction. But he also points to folklore and superstition. Dr. Dolan said: "Among the Arabic people it is believed that eating the meat of an oryx can cause a bullet to be expelled from the body, and it is a sign of manhood to kill an oryx."

There are numerous other records of the species' extermination, but perhaps the most poignant is that written by David Henderson, a wildlife biologist working in Oman in 1973. Ranging the Omani desert, he came across the remains of what appears to have been the last white oryx in Nature. It had apparently been killed by poachers from Abu Dhabi, in the United Arab Emirates, who had chased it across the desert in their automobiles. "Its pursuers had left it where it had fallen," Henderson wrote. "We saw no human footprints. It was as nauseating and spleen-bursting a sight as I've probably seen: the world's rarest antelope run to exhaustion, killed, and abandoned. Even now I find it difficult to convert my thoughts into words."

And with that, there were no more sightings of these magnificent animals in the desert. Once master of a million square kilometers, once a biblical symbol of fierce independence, once an inspiration to prophets and saints and balladeers — the "unicorn" was annihilated in sheer blood lust of hunting.

Fortunately for the species, the Grimwood expedition rescued three, and another six white oryx antelopes were already held in captivity in zoos and were provided to the World Herd — it was a tenuous genetic base, but there was no alternative. The future of the species rested on the survival of these animals.

In addition, there were another nine oryx held captive by Saudi King Faisal in a royal zoo at Riyadh, although these were not made available to the World Herd effort.

But it was from this private stock of the Saudi king that Israel obtained its first white oryx for the Hai-Bar program.

For years, Avraham Yoffe had made every effort to obtain some white oryx from the World Herd for Hai-Bar. He demonstrated that Israel wanted to make a serious effort to reintroduce the animal to a protected existence in properly managed and patrolled nature reserves. He met all the criteria except one: Israel was Israel. The Jewish state just couldn't get hold of these animals of Arab origin. Yoffe wheedled and cajoled the zoos that participated in the World Herd program; he insisted and pleaded, thundered and bullied. But without success.

At about the same time, King Faisal developed a taste for

collecting animals. But rather than take an interest in his own native wildlife, the monarch was more inclined toward the exotic. At one point, he wanted a pair of orangutans for his private collection, and he made inquiries about how he might obtain them. None of these endangered primates were openly available. But a European animal dealer did manage to obtain a pair of them from a source of dubious legitimacy. The Saudi king could have them, not for a money payment, but rather in exchange for a pair of white oryx. Faisal agreed.

The white oryx made a circuitous journey from Riyadh, stopping for a while in Naples, where the cow gave birth to a male calf in a quarantine station. Eventually, the animals ended up on the far side of the globe, in the Los Angeles Zoo.

The president of the Greater Los Angeles Zoological Association at that time was Mrs. Reese H. Taylor, and, by good fortune, she was a friend of Avraham Yoffe's. By May 1978, the oryx herd had grown nicely, and Mrs. Taylor called Avraham to ask if he'd be interested in four pairs.

Avraham immediately set in motion all the activities necessary to obtain the white oryx. Since they were endangered antelope protected by both the U.S. Endangered Species Act and the endangered species treaty (CITES — Convention on International Trade in Endangered Species of Wild Fauna and Flora), there was a tremendous amount of paperwork to perform, including publishing the proposed export in the U.S. *Federal Register* and waiting sixty days to learn if anyone objected to the transfer.

Avraham sent Mike Van Grevenbroek, then curator of Hai-Bar, to Los Angeles when the export was finally approved, and Mike crated the eight white oryx and loaded them aboard a World Airways cargo jet for a free flight to Kennedy Airport in New York. I met the shipment there.

"Want a peek?" was Mike's greeting when we met on the tarmac outside the El Al cargo terminal. "Such an utterly unnecessary question!" was my reply, and I hurried straight for the crates, without bothering with the customary handshake and social platitudes.

I peered into the darkness of a crate through the ventilation holes cut about four feet from the ground. I could see only parts of each animal — broad white flanks, well-muscled shoulders. Most were comfortably lying on a bed of fresh straw. All of them wore yard-long sections of garden hose slipped over their sharp horns to protect them during the transport operation. I could not see them in their statuesque glory, but I was thrilled nevertheless. I simply knew they were the finest animals to walk upon the earth, and I was highly honored just to be part of this historic moment in conservation.

"Come, look at this one!" Mike invited. We circled around the crates to one standing on the far side of the group. Mike lifted the sliding door a couple of inches, and lying flat on the pavement and looking up along a flashlight beam, we stared at the belly of a female white oryx. "Well, what do you think?" Mike asked.

"I think this may be a herd of nine white oryx before too long," I replied. "And this will be the first white oryx born in Israel this century. You've got to take special care of this one!"

"I take special care of them all!" Mike protested. "Be sure to have a box of cigars ready for distribution in a few months," I responded.

"I'll give you a cigar," Mike countered, "but you've got to bring along a bottle of duty-free Scotch. What a celebration it will be!" It was a moment of enchantment. All our hopes and a decade of persistent efforts, had finally borne fruit. The white oryx, our *re'em,* our unicorns, were returning home to the land of their ancestors after a terribly close brush with total extinction.

Gil Jonas, of the Holy Land Conservation Fund, which also helped with this effort, joined us to look at the animals and make a few publicity photos. "Ah! This is the crowning glory!" he exclaimed, "a real feather in the cap!"

"A feather in the cap, and a fly in the ointment!" Mike snapped back. "I've just learned that there's a little hitch. El Al's late."

"Well, that's to be expected," I volunteered. "Isn't that what El Al means — Every Landing, Always Late? No doubt they'll cite security precautions as their excuse!"

But security was not the reason for the delay. When the big 747 Jumbo rolled up to the terminal, we learned that one of the engines required tuning before the long flight to Israel. But that was a small problem. The bigger problem involved eels.

The cargo jet had just arrived from Amsterdam, where it had

delivered a number of enormous vats filled with live eels — twelve tons of the slithery creatures, all told. But one of the vats hadn't been in perfect shape, and in midflight, it had ruptured. Thousands of live eels wriggled, writhed, and squirmed across the cargo deck at an altitude of thirty-seven-thousand feet. By the time the aircraft landed in Holland, the whole cargo compartment was in chaos. Administrators agreed to a quick clean-up in Amsterdam, and then dispatching the jet to New York, where other perishable cargo was destined. Then, in New York, a proper clean-up could be done before the 747 was turned around for its return flight to Israel.

We climbed up into the big plane just as the clean-up crews were preparing for work. The stench was nearly overpowering. "This may take some time," Mike noted. "We can't load the animals until the plane is cleaned and aired out. Those oryx are unhappy enough in the transport boxes, and I'm afraid that the stench just might make a few of them sick as hell. We'll wait."

The day passed between drinking paper cups of coffee in the shade and peeking into each of the transport boxes to stare at the beautiful white oryx. They had ample food and water and many more inspections than they actually needed. Truth was, neither Mike nor I could take our eyes off them. The oryx were enchanting.

There was one in particular which fascinated me, a female who would not lie down like all the others. She stood patiently in her transport box, and when I peered in through the ventilation holes, she stared straight back at me. It was a steady, open stare, certainly not timid, but not aggressive either. Somehow we saw each other as equals. And it was, without question, love at first sight.

"Has anyone named them?" I asked Mike.

"Indeed!" he responded. "But those California zookeepers gave them all Arabic names. And I don't think Yoffe will like that very much. I expect he'll insist that they be good immigrants and Hebraicize their names."

"All but one," I replied. "There's a real beauty here, a real fairy-tale princess — and I think she ought to be called Cinderella."

"Then Cinderella it is," Mike agreed. "Let's go to supper."

The white oryx sat at the air terminal for nearly twenty-four hours before they were loaded on the cargo jet and prepared for takeoff. "What do I do with these?" Mike asked, hefting a stack of papers thicker than a Manhattan telephone directory. They included Endangered Species Act documents, veterinary certificates, health and ancestry records, bills of sale and ownership, bills of lading, CITES export certificates, and various other papers — a complete set for each animal.

"Beats me!" I replied. "But I think it's best to keep them with the animals, just in case there's a question somewhere along the way." And thus a herd of eight incredibly rare antelopes sat for a full day at Kennedy Airport, loaded on a cargo jet, and flown out of the United States without a single official looking at one piece of paper. All of those authorizations and contracts and certificates and documents actually meant very little. Nobody ever looked at them.

The El Al Jumbo thundered down the runway and flew off for it's seven-thousand-mile journey to the east. A herd of unicorns and a thousand silly papers were returning to Israel. As they took off, my heart went with them.

One of the first priorities Mike established after returning to Israel was to begin the long effort of teaching the white oryx to be wild again. Through their generations in captivity, these animals had become too tame. If they were released into Nature immediately, Israel's healthy population of wolves and leopards would gobble them up in short order. And even if they managed to avoid predators for a few days, hunger and thirst would claim them. Or the sun would.

Truly wild oryx are pure desert animals. They're tough and resilient. They can stand off packs of wolves, and they can wander for months, even years, without a drop of drinking water — they metabolize enough fluids from the vegetation they eat. But these characteristics are not found in zoo critters. There needs to be a transitional process, a reintroduction.

After a few months in their small enclosure, where they acclimatized and became used to the Negev's heat and the feel of loose desert gravel beneath their feet, the herd of white oryx was released into a larger enclosure of about ten acres. Here, they enjoyed several other elements of their natural habitat — but they seemed totally unaware of these elements. Take acacia trees, for example. The new enclosure was intentionally built to include a small grove of these common desert trees for the oryx to nibble upon. But they didn't.

Somehow, it seemed that the white oryx were unaware that acacia trees should be browsed. Usually, they simply ignored them, except on particularly hot days, when they used the trees for shade. Food, in the minds of these animals, was something that came in bales and sacks — not something that grew on trees.

One day Mike had the idea of entering the enclosure with a bale of hay, opening it, and tossing every last straw up into the acacia trees. The oryx stared at him, confused by his bizarre behavior. But they were very well aware that he was throwing good food up into their shade makers.

As he left the enclosure, the herd moved over and began to stretch upward to eat the hay from the tree. In the process, the animals accidentally nibbled on a bit of acacia, and, evidently found it to be a tasty treat. From that day forward, Hai-Bar's white oryx started to eat natural foods.

When I assumed general responsibility for Hai-Bar, I introduced a number of other manipulations in the enclosure to help the white oryx herd prepare for eventual release into Nature. Water tubs were moved around to help the herd organize a hierarchy — if the tub were set out in an open area, several animals could drink at one time. But if the tub were set into a position where only one animal could drink at a time, there had to be some priority-setting within the herd to determine who got to drink first.

Water was made unavailable for specific periods. First, it was closed off for only a half hour or so at a time, and then, gradually, for longer periods. My plan was gradually to make the oryx less dependent upon available water but to avoid making them completely independent — at least for the time being.

During any reintroduction project, water could be used as a mechanism for controlling the herd. If, for example, we decided to release the herd near a small oasis in the central Negev, and by then the white oryx had become accustomed to living for eight or ten hours without water, we could be rather sure of being able to find them within a four- or five-hour walk of the oasis. This would effectively confine them to an area of about a fifteen-mile radius from their watering site. They'd be reluctant to walk farther because simple thirst would restrain them.

But a fifteen-mile radius gave the animals a very large area indeed for wandering. The area of a circle with a radius of fifteen miles is more than seven hundred square miles — and this would be quite enough for at least the initial stage of any release program.

Keeping the white oryx dependent on drinking water, thereby keeping them within a reasonable distance of their oasis, permits close monitoring and follow-up work. Wildlife researchers can observe the animals and determine how well the reintroduction project is working. They can see whether the herd maintains its social integrity once the animals are free to move about. They can see how the herd defends itself against the predators that also live in the region — and against the many parasites found in the area. Tick infestations, worms, and other parasites can be as deadly as packs of wolves.

If the animals can be monitored and problems observed soon after they appear, there is an opportunity for wildlife workers to intervene and make minor adjustments, or if necessary, mount a major rescue operation.

We also used food in the same way. In restoring the white oryx to Nature, it is important that they become well adapted to their natural diet. Thus, from early in the program, they were exposed to the natural foods of their native environment. They were encouraged to nibble on acacia and on salt bush, wild grasses, and other vegetation growing in their habitat. But we also supplied them with supplementary feeds, for several reasons.

White oryx have a great taste for certain human-provided feeds. Well-cured alfalfa hay is particularly appealing, and particularly nutritious, too. In a reintroduction program, it can be used to draw the animals back to a fixed feeding site at least once a day, allowing wildlife researchers to keep better track of them and monitor their progress in readapting to Nature.

Measured quantities of alfalfa, food concentrate, and other feeds can also assure peak nutrition and thus good health and reproductive capacity. The highest possible reproduction rate simply helps bring this acutely endangered species back from the brink of extinction as quickly as possible.

Good nutrition paid off. In the spring of 1982, our five mature females produced five healthy calves — a 100 percent success rate in reproduction!

Good nutrition helps the animals resist illness and parasites, and this is especially important in the restoration of zoo animals to a natural habitat. For generations, in zoos, they have had the benefit of veterinary care. They are also removed from contact with their natural parasites and infections — many of the protozoan blood parasites carried by ticks in the Negev do not exist in California zoos, and thus is becomes doubly important for zoo animals to have the benefit of peak health when they reencounter these parasites in Nature.

There were many other concerns within the oryx project, and manipulations were all calculated to help with the species' restoration. In Nature, for example, white oryx live in mixed herds with males and females together. But at Hai-Bar, we separated all but one male from the herd. This male was changed periodically, thus giving each male the opportunity to breed and affording a maximum preservation of the gene pool, to avoid, as much as possible, the consequences of inbreeding.

Inbreeding is a serious concern with endangered species. If a male and female have too many common ancestors, their own breeding success tends to decline, and the offspring they produce will tend to be more sickly than the offspring of totally unrelated parents.

Once the initial four pairs of oryx were brought to Israel, the difficulties in obtaining animals from the World Herd ended. Conservationists knew that there would be serious genetic consequences if we continued breeding only the oryx we obtained from Los Angeles, which were themselves descended from a single pair. To break this genetic bottleneck, we then acquired another three male white oryx from the World Herd stock in San Diego, and this broadened the genetic prospects considerably.

Other factors must be manipulated before animals can be released into Nature. The enclosure must have enough space and "cover" vegetation to permit the development of a natural herd hierarchy. In many zoos, space is limited and small enclosures with strict daily routines tend to work against natural herd dynamics and the establishment of a "pecking order." But solid herd integrity is vital to the group's success in Nature and must be established before any release of animals into the wild.

A herd hierarchy develops nearly naturally through the interaction of the animals. It can also be encouraged by manipulating elements such as food and water to a point where a decision must be made within the herd as to who gets to eat or drink first. As a hierarchy develops, so do social strains within the herd, and there must be some compensation mechanisms to prevent the subdominant members of the herd from being bullied all the time by the dominant members.

Cover vegetation is useful in achieving this. This sort of vegetation is the bushy type — we used salt bushes — which spreads out along the ground for several yards and grows to a height of six feet or more. A subdominant oryx that has been pushed around by the herd bully can escape behind cover vegetation and be totally obscured from the more dominant animals. There, it can be at peace.

The availability of several sites that are separate from the main herd area and completely obscured from view helps reduce tensions in the herd, and this also tends to improve health and reproduction.

I took keen interest in the white oryx herd at Hai-Bar, and in addition to daily management chores, I conducted a considerable amount of research on them. Simple measurements offer a good idea of what this animal is like — our Hai-Bar oryx weigh between 143 and 165 pounds, making them the smallest of the four species of oryx antelope that exist in the world. Cows tend to be slightly larger than the bulls. Horns average about twenty-six inches in length, but some grow a few inches longer.

When our oryx came from California, they weren't precisely white. Rather, they were more creamy or ivory in color. But a few months' exposure to the Negev sun changed that, and their coats bleached out to a white that would make a commercial laundry detergent manufacturer envious.

After working with these animals for a while, I learned that their hair is not very well anchored in the skin. Much of it falls out with a simple tug. At first, I looked to nutrition and other environmental factors, but when these all appeared to be proper, I came to the conclusion that this is quite natural for the oryx, and indeed there may be some benefit to it.

I learned this when I had to capture a bull who had suffered a gore wound while fighting. I needed to treat the wound and to prevent it from becoming infested with fly larvae. But in capturing the animal, I learned that it was very difficult to hold on to him. His hair was slick, relatively long, and bristly, and whenever I tried to get a good hold on him, a simple tug on his part would leave me standing alone with a handful of hair. What protected the bull against my grasp, I figured, very likely protects him against the grasp of predators. Thus, an oryx might successfully escape a glancing blow from a wolf or a leopard.

I also put the hair under a microscope and discovered that it was hollow. I knew that polar bears have hollow hair — this was discovered a few years ago when researchers in an American zoo found all their polar bears were turning green. It seems that algae from the bears' fresh-water pool was collecting inside their hollow hair. But in the polar bear's natural arctic habitat, such types of algae do not occur in the cold sea waters and therefore aren't a problem.

The polar bear's hollow hair has been found to have very good insulative value. I presumed that such hair might also be useful for a desert antelope — but instead of keeping the warmth in, it would keep the heat out.

Another interesting feature of the white oryx is its relatively large feet. I made some measurements and calculations and learned that the average foot area of the white oryx is 24.61 square centimeters (times four feet equals 98.44 square centimeters per animal). Dividing this by an average weight of 70 kilograms per animal shows that the white oryx exerts a pressure of about 0.711 kilograms per square centimeter upon the earth — and this is relatively light. The benefit in this is that the oryx won't sink very deeply into loose sand. And when one is aware that, when threatened, the oryx frequently retreats into sand-dune areas, one can appreciate the advantage the animal has in this otherwise inhospitable habitat.

The *carotid rete* is perhaps the oryx's most amazing adaptation. This is a radiator-like assembly of blood vessels located in its sinus cavity. It is a heat-exchange mechanism that cools blood immediately before it enters the animal's brain. With this adaptation, the white oryx can permit its body heat to climb to around 110 degrees Fahrenheit — a level that would be deadly for nearly any other animal. Before blood coming from such a hot body temperature enters the brain, however, it is cooled by the carotid rete to about 103 degrees — feverishly hot for you or me but quite all right for the oryx.

The major concern here is that in the brain there are a number of vital enzymes that break down at high temperatures. When they break down, the regulatory functions of the brain cease to operate properly, and consequently the organism dies. Thus, if the brain temperature can be kept at a safe level, the rest of the body can let its temperature rise without serious consequence — a very useful adaptation for an animal that must exist in an extremely hot habitat.

Some of my most interesting research involved behavior. White oryx herds are matriarchies — that is, they are led by the dominant female. And it so happened that, at Hai-Bar, the dominant female was Cinderella — the cow who stared squarely back at me during our first meeting at New York's Kennedy Airport.

In most herd animals, the dominant individual is normally a critter of substantial capability. But in the white oryx, this aspect is magnified because of its temperamental and aggressive nature. Of course, the oryx's black-and-white coloration is a give-away clue that this is a formidable animal.

Most desert animals have protective coloration. The gazelles and ibex are soft tans, blending into the scenery. But the white oryx, with its bold black facial and leg markings, is as conspicuous as a flashing railroad crossing — and just about as hazardous. Such bold markings are clear warnings in Nature for potential predators to stay away.

Most other horned animals have broad, curved horns, which are normally used in dominance struggles with members of their own species. These fights are usually contests of strength and endurance. The fight is determined by which animal is left standing while the other retires, exhausted and gasping for breath.

The white oryx, however, have a completely different approach. Their horns are straight, narrow, and pointed — like a pair of matched javelins growing from the tops of their heads. When an oryx attacks, it normally lowers its head until its sharply pointed horns are parallel with the ground, and then it charges with a great burst of energy.

The white oryx seeks to impale its adversary. Any fight involving a white oryx is also likely to involve a bit of blood-spilling.

On the other hand, the relationship between mother and calf is incredibly gentle. For the first several days of its life, the calf is usually hidden just inside a low-growing bush. The infant comes out from time to time to nurse and to be nudged gently about by its mother. While the calf is hidden in the bush, its mother stands about twenty yards away, keeping a casual, yet constant, watch. Any intruders venturing too close to the bush will cause the cow to react with an explosive charge.

Once the calf is about ten days old, it can frequently be seen scampering about within the herd. Its aggressive nature is already evident as it lowers its hornless head and charges everything from blowing leaves to full-grown bulls. All members of the herd are patiently tolerant of the youngster, and, if there is ever a threat, any member of the herd will position himself or herself to protect the calf.

Much of the herd's behavior developed only after it came to Hai-Bar. Take Cinderella, for example. When she first arrived, she was as tame as a dairy cow and could be led around just by grabbing the base of her horn and pulling her in the desired direction. Anybody who grabs at her horns today is in for something of a surprise, and most likely a visit to the first-aid station.

Over the years, Cinderella and I have developed an amicable

mistrust. We looked at each other as equals on the Kennedy Airport tarmac more than a decade ago — and we're still on the same terms.

She doesn't trust me because sometimes I did sneaky things to her, like splashing her with a bucket of antitick solution when she wasn't expecting it. The solution got rid of the ticks that had attached themselves to her, but somehow I don't think that she associated the surprise splash with the loss of those tormenting ticks. Instead, she thought I was an ornery human. And that called for a bit of revenge on her part — all perfectly understandable, if not perfectly appreciated. But it kept me on my toes in the presence of this formidable lady.

Cinderella and I get along all right, even if there is an element of mistrust. She's one of my favorite listeners. Sometimes, I like to read biblical passages to her, especially verses that mention her kind.

"Here's a good one," I said to her one morning. "It's actually about the Children of Israel returning to the Promised Land, but the writer needed a good symbol of strength and courage to describe the nation, so he wrote: 'God brought him forth out of Egypt; he has the strength of a unicorn (re'em): he shall eat up the nations of his enemies, and he shall break their bones, and pierce them with his arrows' (Numbers 24:8). They must have been pretty tough! Nearly as tough as you!"

"And here's another one, sweetheart. It describes a time at the end of the Exodus, when Moses gathered all the tribes at the gateway into the Promised Land. Moses turned to Joseph, blessed his tribe, and said to him: 'His horns are like the horns of unicorns (re'em): with them he shall push the people together to the ends of the earth: and they are the ten thousands of Ephraim, and they are the thousands of Manasseh' (Deuteronomy 33:17). Some horns, eh? Just like yours?"

Cinderella always listens, but feigns disinterest. She lowers her head and turns up her lip disdainfully to blare an airy sputtering snort. Then she waves her horns with the same vigor that the late Arthur Fiedler used when he waved his baton while conducting the 1812 Overture.

I've watched a spark of wildness grow in Cinderella during her decade at Hai-Bar. She'll never be truly wild enough to release into Nature — as a general policy, Hai-Bar doesn't release any zoo-bred animals, only their offspring, which have benefited from being born and raised in the natural environments of the desert reserve. Yet, I have seen the spirit of atavism at work — a reappearance of primal behavior, a reemergence of the unbridled, impetuous, and exalted temperament that enchanted prophets and saints, who saw this species as the archetypal symbol of strength and courage.

Cinderella's children will be free in the Land of Israel. Indeed, plans are now being drafted for their release into appropriate wild habitats of the Negev Desert. And with a mother like theirs, growing up in Hai-Bar is giving them the physical and social resources required for successful reintroduction.

Perhaps, in a few years, once these white oryx have been released into the desert and have reestablished their ancient claim to the Land, we may better appreciate the species' unyielding wildness, its absolute refusal to be domesticated: "Canst thou bind the unicorn from his band into a furrow? or will he harrow the valleys after thee?" (Job 39:19).

Of course not. The white oryx is a wild animal, with a place — an ecological niche — in the scheme of life in the desert. It is out there, among the wild hills and blowing sands that this species belongs. And the purpose of Hai-Bar is to get it there.

Onagers

THE GEYSER must have been spouting fifteen feet straight up into the desert air. It was a beautiful sight — a glorious fountain spraying water skyward, shrouded by its own mist. The bright sunshine even threw a small rainbow across the scene.

Ah, so beautiful. It was a shame to put a stop to it. It would also be a lot of nasty work to put a stop to it. There's only one way a geyser spouts in Hai-Bar — the onagers were up to no good, again.

An onager is a type of Asian wild ass, an equine that looks something like a cross between a donkey and a horse — but certainly not a mule. They're big, about the size of a horse, but their scruffy manes stand erect, like a donkey's. They have smallish ears, like a horse, but a donkeylike tail, with hair growing from only the end half. Onagers are light brown or tan, with lighter bellies. They are also the toughest, most independent, smartest animals at Hai-Bar. And I admire them more than any others.

I needed only a glimpse of the water sprouting skyward to know precisely what had happened. I tossed the toolbox on the tractor and started driving a kilometer out toward the desert gusher. When I arrived at the scene of the crime, I found a whole herd of onagers, twelve of them, clustered around the geyser, taking a midday shower.

It looked perfectly enjoyable — even though the water was

scalding hot. The onagers didn't mind. Plenty of H_2O was spouting upward and then spilling back downward, splattering on their heads and backs, and then dripping from their flanks to create a luxurious ooze at their feet.

"Shoo! Get out of here!" I cried, trying to chase the onagers away from their shower. They strolled away, dripping wet. I could see the steam rising from their backs, as they wandered off toward the east.

As I had expected, the geyser was spouting from a punctured hose. Throughout Hai-Bar, there are about ten kilometers of inch-and-a-quarter black hose stretched here and there across the desert. If I had my choice, I would have selected a different color hose, because black absorbs tremendous amounts of heat. So when the desert air in these parts measures about 110 degrees Fahrenheit, the water in the hose can heat up to about 170 degrees. Unfortunately, the Nature Reserves Authority did not consult me when they went to purchase hose. I suspect they consulted their accountant, who told them black hose was the cheapest available to get the job done.

This plastic hose feeds water to four watering tubs that I have placed strategically around the reserve. Once the water spills into the tub and is exposed to the air, it cools down considerably. In fact, an open tub filled with water and standing in the direct sun can be surprisingly cool. This is because evaporation is a cooling process, and the more the water evaporates out of the tub, the cooler the remaining water will be. In the dry desert, where there is high evaporation, water standing in the sun is usually cooler than water standing in the shade.

But, somehow, I suspected the onagers found the cool water in the tubs boring. The tubs are nothing but large plastic basins holding about one hundred liters of quiet water. If they drink some, the valve lets a bit more trickle back into the tub. But there's no excitement to it, no activity, no *pizzazz*. And onagers love *pizzazz*.

To liven things up, from time to time one of these redoubtable equines saunters up to one of the plastic hoses, which are under considerable water pressure, and gives it a strong bite. Presto!

There's a puncture and water spurts skyward. The onagers are worse than juvenile delinquents opening fire hydrants in the city on a hot summer day. When the water starts spouting and squirting all over the area, the whole herd drifts in to enjoy the sabotage. All other species take off for parts unknown. They want nothing to do with the onagers' mayhem.

As usual, when I arrived the onagers were all standing around in the impromptu rain shower, looking as innocent as subway graffiti artists. When I chased them away, they became downright indignant (probably scheming how to get even — which they occasionally do).

Once the onagers were chased away from the scene of the crime, I was faced with some serious repair work. First, I put on a heavy slicker, which was hardly appealing in those temperatures. But it was more tolerable than getting soaked with water that had been brewing all day in that sun-scorched black plastic hose.

Protected against most of the water, I grabbed an old rusty ax and ran close to the spritzing hose. Sure enough, I could see the teeth marks. I swore some day I'd install iron pipes all over the place. Then, with one well-placed (and well-practiced) swing of that old ax, I cut the spouting hose in half, and the geyser collapsed. One end of the hose was lifeless, and the other had a simple flow of hot water streaming out. At least the pressure was broken and the water wasn't spraying in every direction.

Next, a few quick carvings with my keen-edged Buck knife cut away the section of the hose with the teeth-marked puncture. I slipped a few plastic gadgets from the toolbox over each end of the severed hose, pulled them toward each other, and then screwed them together.

The whole job took only about fifteen minutes, and, in the end, the hose was as good as new, with water running properly off in the direction of the next drinking tub. But my feet were soaked, and I felt as if I'd been standing at the bottom of a nearly drained enormous cup of Turkish coffee — in hot ooze.

The onagers, standing about a hundred yards away, appeared to be cursing me. "Sorry, guys," I called to them. "I had to do it. Besides, you guys don't pay the water bill around here!" They snorted a few times, and grumbled like a gang of kids just kicked out of a basketball court.

Actually, Hai-Bar doesn't really have a water bill. But it does have a water ration. There's enough for all the animals to drink, plus a bit of reserve — but that reserve disappears quickly every time the onagers get mischievous.

Onagers have always given me more trouble than any other animals. If they don't like a fence, they'll just back up to it and kick it until it's no longer standing. If they want a shower, they'll break open a hose. If they want anything, they'll work at it until they get it.

Onagers are incredibly tough. They're not the most beautiful animals at Hai-Bar, nor are they the most popular with the tourists. But, somehow, I have deeper feelings for these equines, and I relate to them better. I have a real sense of who they are. I understand them and know the finer subtleties of their ways.

When I made my daily inspections of the animals, I often found myself watching the onagers more closely than any of the others. Their herd dynamics and individual behaviors are, by far, the most interesting. Also, I have a deeper sympathy for the tragic history of the Asian wild ass in the Land of Israel.

The onagers of Hai-Bar are not precisely native wildlife — only close relatives. Israel's native equine was a creature known to biologists as *Equus hemionus hemippus*. It had roamed the deserts of the Land for uncounted centuries and inspired prophets and holy men and shepherd boys who wrote psalms. It had survived right up into the early twentieth century. But then, the introduction of modern firearms to the Bedouin tribesmen in the region sealed this animal's fate.

By the mid-1930s, *Equus hemionus hemippus* was as extinct as the dinosaurs. A living link to Scripture had been snuffed out. A life-form that had inspired prophets and psalmists, which stood in their writings as a living symbol of freedom, had been banished into oblivion. It was a terrible crime.

Three decades later, once the State of Israel had been created and modern conservation had been established, Israeli wildlife enthusiasts decided something should be done to replace the extinct animal. This particular type may be gone, they reasoned, but there are a number of other very close relatives: the kulan of the Russian steppe and the onagers of Iran, the kiang of the Tibetan plateau and the khur of India, the dzeggetai of the Mongol plains — all of these were Asian wild asses of the same species as the extinct native equine. They merely stemmed from different races, or subspecies.

Another factor in their reasoning involved the ecology of the desert. The wild ass's extermination left a vacuum, a vacant ecological niche, which needed to be filled. Equines play a role in arid ecosystems, grazing on desert grasses, loosening the loess crust of the earth, dispersing several types of seeds, and, when they die, serving as significant food sources for birds of prey and mammalian carnivores.

A decision was made to choose the closest living relative of the extinct native equine and bring it to Israel. This was the Iranian onager (*Equus hemionus onager*) — an animal so close to the extinct type that only expert zoologists could tell them apart.

The first onagers brought to Israel came from the Amsterdam Zoo, in The Netherlands, in 1968. During the following year, a second European shipment was received, plus a group coming directly from a nature reserve in Iran. By the 1970s, Hai-Bar boasted of twelve onagers running free within the reserve. Today, they've increased to nearly sixty.

As a matter of conservation interest, it is indeed fortunate that Israel started to breed onagers. Earlier this century, this equine numbered in the tens of thousands in Iran, and despite the many abuses of the shah's rule, the regime did keep a good system of nature reserves. But all that degenerated after the revolution. Today, information coming from very reliable sources in Iran estimates that there can be no more than 660 individual onagers surviving there, and probably fewer. The good wardens have been drafted off to the army in the war against Iraq, and the poachers have relatively free access to the reserves, which they plunder by driving motorcycles or four-wheel-drive vehicles and shooting wildlife with automatic weapons, which are almost freely available in that war-wracked land.

Onagers are fiercely independent animals. Unlike their close relatives, the horses and donkeys, they've never really submitted to domestication. Some people have tried, of course; there are a few records of the ancients' efforts to domesticate onagers, and sporadic attempts have been made right into the twentieth century. But they've all come to naught.

A few generations of captivity can take the fine edge off an onager's senses, however. And that's precisely what the situation was at Hai-Bar. Our onagers were ornery critters, robust, and at times even savage. But they were lacking in other areas. They were what I call "zooified."

The Nature Reserves Authority headquarters in Jerusalem began talking about releasing a test group of onagers into the Negev Desert and gave me about a year to prepare the animals for life in that hostile environment.

In many ways, the animals were nearly ready to be released. They were eating natural foods of the desert, and they were well organized into natural herd structures. They adjusted to Hai-Bar's almost wild habitat quite well over the period of a decade and became very independent. Only in very rare circumstances did the curatorial staff have to interfere with the onager herds — and we believed that even these very rare circumstances would disappear as soon as the animals were given complete freedom.

One such problem, for example, was the stallions' inclination to drive young males out of the herd. Under natural conditions, a stallion will not tolerate one of his male offspring in his herd once that youngster begins to mature. Usually, the young male is driven away, wanders for a while, and eventually joins a bachelor herd, which drifts off on its own. Sometimes, these young males mature a little more and ultimately challenge yet another stallion for control of his herd. This driving-off, wandering, and challenging keeps a measure of interchange within the onager population and ensures a healthy dispersal of the gene pool, thus countering a herd's tendency toward inbreeding.

But in Hai-Bar, the fence that keeps the predators out also keeps the onagers in. And this means the maturing young males really can't run more than a few kilometers away from their angry stallion fathers. Once the onagers were free in Nature, however, a young male could run hundreds of kilometers, if need be, to put a healthy, secure distance between him and the stallion.

The situation was ameliorated at Hai-Bar by a few manipulations that helped wandering bachelors to steer clear of the volatile stallions. Watering tubs were set out in the more remote areas to provide for the bachelors and give them less reason for entering regions controlled by stallions with their harem herds.

At first, the onagers seemed almost totally insensitive to any danger at night, and it was relatively easy for me to sneak close to them — indeed, close enough to touch them before they would snap to their senses. While this general unawareness would not hurt animals that were secure in Hai-Bar, with little danger of serious predator attacks, such insensitivity simply would not do for life out in truly wild parts of the desert. Leopards prowl out there, as do packs of desert wolves, hyena, and other carnivores. In order to survive, the onagers would have to have all their senses functioning, even while sleeping.

I attacked the problem by enlisting the aid of Whyah, my extra-large German shepherd dog, and a long leash. Before we adopted him, Whyah had wandered in the emptiness of the Sinai desert and suffered terrible deprivation. He had survived in a hostile environment, where predators were more common than water holes. His mettle had been tested in one of the harshest proving grounds on earth. But, once he settled in and assumed a position as part of our family, Whyah became a trusted helper.

Out in the field, I learned that Whyah could be recklessly bold, and thought nothing of charging at an onager nearly twenty times his size. He'd even charge at ten onagers which, together, weighed in at about two hundred times his size!

Whyah thought these pursuits were delightful sport, but I knew they could be very useful teaching aids in helping the onagers learn about the real world of a hostile desert.

Those sleepy, zoo-bred onagers had to learn to rest at night but still be sensitive to every scent in the air, and every noise and every unusual stirring upon the desert floor. I had to teach the onagers that they could never let down their defenses — not for a moment. In Nature, they would be either alert or dead.

I planned to approach the problem gradually, using Whyah as a would-be wolf in an education program designed with great detail. I fashioned tough body harnesses for the dog and for myself, similar to the rope outfit I had learned to make a few years before in mountain-climbing school. I linked Whyah's harness to mine with a nylon parachute rope, the length of which could be changed according to need.

This arrangement was devised because I wanted Whyah to surprise the onagers and charge them as a wolf would. But I wanted to restrain him before he could actually come in contact with the big equines. Whyah could charge with all his energy, and if he were tethered only by a simple collar and leash, I knew he could cause some painful and unnecessary injuries. The harness would dissipate the force of his abrupt halt through his entire body. The parachute rope was certainly strong enough to stop the dog's most vigorous charge, but it was also extremely supple and stretched enough to absorb considerable stress.

I fashioned a harness for myself, because I knew trying to restrain the impact of Whyah's charges could be somewhat hazardous to my own health as well. If I tried to hold the dog by grasping the rope in my hand or wrapping it around my arm while he was in a full sprint, I'd be risking a dislocated shoulder, or worse. Thus, I needed a harness too.

I planned to start with very conspicuous mock attacks. As the onagers developed the sensitivities necessary to avoid such attacks, I would gradually increase their sophistication, until we could mimic the highly refined predatory habits of a very hungry wolf.

Our first efforts were merely to create a "presence" about one hundred yards or so upwind from the onagers at nightime. Whyah and I would be quite noisy about this, crashing through brush and kicking stones as we moved along. From time to time I could even coax Whyah to wine and snarl. We were noisy neighbors who kept the onagers awake at all hours of the night. But at least they knew something was going on in the world outside their own nocturnal dreams.

Over a period of months, we gradually became more purposeful

in our activities. We started making mock attacks against the
onagers. I'd choose different hours of the night — but most often
the early hours of darkness or the hour just before dawn — when
most predators are active themselves. Our mock attacks became
increasingly complicated, with assaults being made from a series of
quiet maneuvers downwind.

Usually, we'd maneuver to an appropriate position, from where
I'd encourage Whyah to make his charge. He'd bolt toward the
onagers, growling and snarling as he ran. He'd also quickly
outdistance me. By the time he got to the end of his parachute-rope
leash, the onagers would be fully aware of the attack and turning to
gallop away — and that's just what I wanted.

The attack ended with both Whyah and me tumbling to the
earth, for the force of his weight at the end of a taut rope invariably
yanked me right off my feet. We both loved it. Whyah, I soon
learned, was an incurable adrenaline freak, who relished a rough-
and-tumble game.

Throughout the year, our mock attacks were staged at different
hours of darkness and under different circumstances — moonless
nights, nights when the prevailing wind had shifted, and other
natural variables. Gradually, the herd of onagers, which I could
once sneak up on and smack with an open hand, became so sensitive
to the dangers of the night that neither I nor the dog could get
within two hundred yards of them without some restlessness
developing in the herd. If we moved to within a hundred yards,
using all the stealth we could, the herd would invariably trot off
together into the darkness.

With this accomplished, I set one other sensitizing program
before the herd — ambush. They might be keen enough to sense a
predator approaching them — but were they keen enough to know
when they were approaching a predator lying in wait?

The key to this training program lay around the morning
watering. Every morning, onagers walk as a herd to a watering area
for a drink — this was true at the reserve and later we found it to
be true in Nature. But in Nature, a desert water hole is one of the
most dangerous of places. Predators also know that onagers — and
many other animals — come to the few water holes of the desert to

drink. And so they lie in wait within the vegetation at the water's edge.

I built a hide near one of our water tubs that was frequented by the onagers each morning, and I sat within for several mornings, just to watch how the equines came to drink. It soon became apparent that they approached water with little caution, wandering in as a loosely scattered herd and paying little attention to their environment.

Whyah was enlisted again, and on the first morning, I simply held him within the hide. The onagers came and drank their water, taking no notice of the canine scent or the slight noises of movement coming from within the hide. Perhaps it was the generations of zoo life, where they lived in paddocks only a short distance from lions and tigers and all sorts of other carnivores, that made them insensitive to the scent of a nearby canine.

After a few mornings of studying their undisciplined behavior, I was prepared to act. Using the harnessed dog and the parachute rope, I waited until four onagers were crowded around the watering tub taking their noisy drinks. We sat in the hide, about twenty yards away. With very slight urging, Whyah lunged out of the hide, attacking the equines and sending the entire herd into panicked flight.

A week passed before I staged the second mock attack, which was followed by a third and fourth. Each time, Whyah made an entirely believable surprise attack that put the onagers to flight.

Our ambushes increased in sophistication. At one point, I decided to create a natural water hole by finding a depression in the desert, digging out a small pool, and lining it with heavy plastic sheeting. The sheeting was then buried beneath a few inches of sand and the pool filled with water. It worked quite well, and the plastic prevented the water from sinking immediately into the earth.

At the same time, I built a small hide within a nearby salt bush and then left everything alone for two weeks. The onagers certainly found this water source and began using it each morning. And once they had grown familiar with the site, we started our attacks again.

We attacked at the water hole, and a few days later, we staged another attack along a path leading toward the water hole. Day and night, we harassed the onagers. We surprised them frequently and put them under a disciplined program of stress.

The onagers responded to these attacks by developing greater discipline of their own. At nighttime, they rested with their ears and nostrils sensitized to the slightest change in their environment. When they approached water, the herd would move in single file and then wait a safe distance until the stallion cautiously scouted the water hole.

This and several other modifications of their behavior persuaded me that they would be better able to survive, and thrive, out in the hostile desert. For instance, through the years, I had noticed that the Iranian onagers were becoming more like Israel's now-extinct native race of Asian wild ass. Zoology texts provided definitions of how one race differed from the other: while the Israeli race gave birth to its foals in May, the Iranian race gave birth in July — but at Hai-Bar, over the course of a decade, the onager birthing moved up a month, with most foals born in June. And I expect this trend will continue until they're giving birth in May, which apparently is most appropriate for natural conditions in Israel.

The extinct Israeli type was the smallest of the Asian wild asses, while the Iranian onagers are middle-sized. However, at Hai-Bar, the Israeli-born onagers reach a slightly smaller adult size than their northern-born parents, even though they have excellent nutrition and all the essentials for good growth. Thus, in this aspect, the onagers are also shifting toward patterns established by their extinct cousins.

The Israeli wild ass sheds its shaggy winter coat in April, while the Iranian type doesn't shed until June. And yet again, the imported Iranian onagers are shifting to match the patterns of the Israeli wild ass, and today shed their winter coats in May.

In a few generations, I suspect that it will be virtually impossible for even skilled and observant zoologists to distinguish between the reintroduced onagers and the native type they are replacing, thus confirming a broadly held belief: race is merely a reflection of local environment.

In April 1982, the Nature Reserves Authority informed me that it was time to see if the Hai-Bar education was thorough enough for the onagers. We were to release five bachelor males into the Ein Saharonim area of Makhtesh Ramon, a great crater in the central Negev, about one hundred kilometers northwest of Hai-Bar.

In addition to myself, our team included my helper Nathan Minkovski, wildlife biologist Giora Ilani, veterinarian Motke Levenson, and Motke's helper Rafi. Catching the onagers was actually quite easy. Motke had a dart rifle — that is, a special rifle that shot a syringe loaded with a powerful immobilizing drug. In this case, he used a chemical known as M-99 or Immobilon. These are trade names for etorphine hydrochloride, a synthetic drug which, according to the manufacturer's warnings as well as most wildlife management texts, has about ten thousand times the analgesic potency of morphine sulfate. It is incredibly powerful. Used in the human body, it is just as lethal as consuming arsenic — and thus it has no practical use in human medicine — or drug abuse for that matter. But with onagers, it is just the right chemical.

Onagers, and indeed all equines, have unusual metabolisms, which normally resist other capture drugs. The Hellabruyn cocktail that I've used so successfully on antelopes and ibex is as useless as soda pop when injected into a member of the horse family. The same goes for straight ketamine, which works so well on wolves. There really is only one immobilization drug that can be used with any measure of success on equines today — etorphine hydrochloride.

We climbed into the reserve pickup truck, and I drove slowly toward the small herd of bachelor onagers near the northern fence. We moved in gradually — driving twenty yards, stopping for a moment, and then driving a bit closer. When Motke was certain he was within range, he leveled the rifle at a fine young male, squeezed the trigger, and sent the dart-syringe flying about fifty yards. It landed squarely in the gluteus medius muscle of the animal's rump, causing him to jump a bit as if stung by a wasp — but otherwise quite all right.

Within five minutes we could see the drug beginning to take effect. The animal began to get glassy-eyed and stagger. The herd began to drift away from it. We waited a few more minutes and then called up the rest of the team.

Together, we rushed up to the drugged equine and prepared him for transport. A towel was wrapped around his eyes to protect them from the sun. (The drugged animal's eyes dilate, thus exposing the retina to potentially harmful amounts of sunlight.) A number of ropes and pads were wrapped around the animal. The truck was driven up and the bachelor onager loaded in. Back at the work area, he was unloaded and slipped into a large wooden transport crate — just large enough to accommodate him, but not large enough to let him move around very much — and just as well.

Once the onager was in the crate, Motke gave him an injection of diprenorphine, also known as M50-50 — the antidote to etorphine hydrochloride — and then the crate was sealed.

The onager regained his senses in a couple of minutes and tried his damnedest to break out of the crate. He threw himself against its wooden frame, causing my heart to skip a beat or two. For a moment, I feared he'd kick his way out of that transport box and then go about kicking the daylights out of everyone responsible for putting him in there.

But the crate wasn't large enough to let him kick with all his might. He could throw only short punches, and it became obvious that the crate could absorb them. Had the crate been a few feet longer, the onager could have unleashed the full force of his powerful legs and kicked the walls right out of the box.

We caught three more onager bachelors in quick order that day, and once the four were all in crates and ready to be shipped to Ein Saharonim, we tried a small experiment in capturing the fifth. It is said that if some species of animals are given precisely the right dose of etorphine hydrochloride, they will follow in the direction of any sounds they hear. So, we decided to try with the last bachelor and see if we could just call him to walk right into a transport box, saving us all the labor of lifting him into the pickup truck and lifting him back out for crating.

We drove around among the bachelors until we found our last candidate for liberation. Motke carefully loaded his dart-syringe and set it in the rifle. We moved closer, into range. Motke fired, and once again made a perfect hit. The drug injected itself on impact with the animal's muscle and we had only to wait a few minutes.

It was a weak dose, as we had intended. We wanted the animal just slightly past that indefinable thin barrier between sober awareness and drugged stupor.

And that's precisely where he went. The onager staggered a bit and walked around with a stiff-legged stride, almost like a mechanical toy animal. Perfect! And then we began calling to him. He responded to the noise, but not precisely the way we expected. The noise seemed to have confused him, and it became apparent he was slightly aware of what was happening, and rather frightened. His eyes were wide, his nostrils flared, and his breathing heavy.

The onager tried to run, but the drug restrained him, as if he were tied with hobbles. It was a difficult situation and we had to act fast. Our entire team, carrying pads and ropes and blankets ran hard after the drugged onager, and in a few minutes, we caught up with him.

Rafi reached him first and barely grabbed hold of his tail. I was there next and wrapped my arm around his neck. The rest of the team was there in a moment, heaving blankets over his head and flanks. Ropes were slipped around his legs. We struggled, with a measure of desperation, for several minutes until the onager was dragged to the ground, blindfolded, and bound.

Lifting him into my Peugeot pickup, we rushed him back to the work area and the waiting transport box, shoved him inside, removed all ropes and padding, and then administered the antidote. When the onager regained all senses, he was in a rage and threw his full weight against the inside of the transport box, rocking it on the ground and threatening to knock it, and himself, over.

All five crated onagers were lifted into the bed of a waiting truck and set snugly side by side. The whole lot was then tied down with heavy ropes and cables to prevent the boxes from spilling over.

That night, the five onagers were driven to Ein Saharonim, while a tired work team made it only as far as the Oasis restaurant on Eilat's North Beach. Our sumptuous Middle Eastern meal was liberally irrigated with chilled Israeli white wine.

The onagers were taking their first step toward reintroduction into Nature, the first step toward regaining the freedom they symbolized throughout Scripture.

The test with the five bachelor onagers was successful, although it was marred by a premature escape and a tragedy. We had originally intended to keep the onagers in a large corral at Ein Saharonim for a few months before releasing them. This way, we figured, they would become accustomed to the area and be less likely to run away. If we could keep them in the area, they would be easier to monitor during follow-up studies.

But the onagers had different ideas. The five young bachelors had no intention whatsoever of remaining in that corral any longer than absolutely necessary. The time period defined by "absolutely necessary" was precisely the length of time it took them to kick a hole in the corral fence. They were free within twenty-four hours.

They didn't stay in the immediate area but rather took a fancy to freedom and wandered the desert far and wide. These wanderings brought two of the bachelors toward the east, in the Arava Valley, near the Jordanian border. They were both shot and killed by rifle fire coming from Jordan.

Israeli veterinarians performed postmortem examinations on these animals and found that, until the moment they were shot, they were perfectly healthy. They had lived freely for several months, eating nothing but the sparse, wild vegetation of the desert and drinking from a few brackish water holes. They had lived among wolves, leopards, and hyena, but there was not a scratch to suggest any serious fighting with these carnivores. The examinations also revealed that the natural parasites of the desert — the intestinal worms, ticks, and other parasitical animals that can infest animals in the desert — were essentially nonexistent. In short, we learned that onagers could live quite well in the Israeli desert — if only we could protect them from deadly humans.

The information from the postmortem encouraged us, and the following year a mixed herd of males and females was brought to Ein Saharonim. A repaired and strengthened fence ensured that the equines would remain at the site until we decided they were ready to be released — not when they decided.

We waited until what appeared to be the hottest day of midsummer, after the animals had spent more than four months in the corral. A portion of the fence was opened quietly, and the onagers drifted out to their freedom.

The mixed herd — a stallion, three adult females, and three of their young — produced better herd structural integrity. They stuck together better than the bachelors. And because they were kept at the spring of Ein Saharonim for months, the herd remained in the vicinity permanently and could be monitored.

Other small herds of Hai-Bar-tutored onagers were released in this manner. Together with the foals they bore after their reintroduction into Nature, Israel's wild population of onagers now numbers twenty-eight.

Each time I see a group of these animals released to their freedom, I feel a nervous tremor through my spine — a tremendous excitement, an anxiety, a rejoicing. There is also a great feeling of relief, perhaps akin to making the final payment on a very heavy mortgage loan. And, indeed, it is. Because in being so ruthless with wildlife in these parts, humanity has ransomed and mortgaged its own integrity. In restoring animals to Nature, we are redeeming some of our own honor.

Freedom

SUNRISE. It comes almost as quickly as the word is pronounced. The first invading rays of the new day's desert sun rapidly devour the gray softness of dawn. Laserlike beams of light probe among the rocks and vegetation of Ein Saharonim. In minutes, the light is so harsh that I must dig into my pack for a pair of sunglasses.

The Negev sun is just about as intense as is possible on the face of the earth. Scientists have studied it closely and have learned that on a bright summer day, it can blister every square yard of land surface with six million calories of solar radiation. Temperature measured in the shade hovers around 113 degrees Fahrenheit, but there is no shade except for the little awning over the meteorological instruments. Out in the sun, this kind of radiation can heat exposed stones to 176 degrees.

It's also bright. Surfaces exposed to direct sunlight are flooded with an intensity of more than 130 kilolux hours of light. Your neighborhood physics professor will assure you that this is bright enough to encourage a broad-brimmed hat and welder's goggles.

I lie flat on my belly about three hundred yards northeast of the oasis. The ground here is slightly elevated and affords a good view of the region. There's a 40-power telescope standing on a low tripod just a few inches from my face. It is flanked by a tan canvas bag lying limply in the sand and two *kalkarim* — five-quart insulated

Styrofoam water jugs wrapped in protective burlap. Ten quarts of water should quench my thirst until about noon. To my right, near the telescope, a large-format diary is open to May 25, a black-and-gold fountain pen cradled in its binding.

The day is not yet ten minutes old, and already I feel a trickle of perspiration across my back. But somehow I've grown accustomed to the desert over the years, and its harsh conditions are more than counterbalanced by the appeal of my work.

I've come to this barren landscape to watch "my" onagers — newly-freed princes of the mountainous desert. The herd is bound to turn up within a half hour for its morning drink. But before the onagers arrive, I'm treated to a desert prelude, the opening measures of each day's Symphony of the Negev. In truth, the established patterns of Nature in the desert are as dependable as the printed notes of a classical symphony. The desert has its melodies, harmonies, and rhythms. It has lyrical qualities and precisely organized orchestration. As with a well-known classical score, if there is a single misplaced note, the heedful ear will notice.

For a music lover at a concert, the performance begins with the arrival of the conductor, whose mere presence compels silence and attention. In the desert, the maestro is the sun itself. Sunrise brings stillness. Scores of songbirds that had been flitting about the oasis during the presunrise grayness now retire to their refuges among the reeds, bushes, and tamarisk trees. Their lively chirping ceases. They have eaten and drunk from the brackish water of the oasis. Now they take their places in the shade, sheltered from the burning assault of the sun and safe from the keen eyes of a passing falcon.

I stretch forward a bit and set my right eye against the telescope. Scanning the oasis, I find my opening notes, the overture to today's concert — two russet-colored female dorcas gazelles lapping up the tepid, salty water. These are delicate creatures, lithe and very nervous. Their tails quiver as they drink, and every few seconds, one of them lifts her head to keep watch for lurking predators. Gazelles are well aware that a desert waterhole is a favorite ambush site for leopards, desert wolves, caracals, and hyenas.

Physiologists have proven many times over that dorcas gazelles don't need to drink water. They absorb enough moisture from the vegetation they eat. Nevertheless, the gazelles seem to like water — necessary or not — and they'll risk the dangers of the oasis to take their drink.

One of these gazelles has distended nipples, and I surmise that she is nursing a fawn, which, according to the well-measured rhythms of Nature, should be about seven weeks old right now.

With the precision of the greatest composer, Nature has arranged that the gazelles of the desert are born just after the end of the brief rainy season. This is the time when the vegetation is freshest and high in vitamins and protein. Female gazelles feeding on this vegetation produce the richest milk, helping their fawns grow quickly and in health.

But I don't expect to see the fawn. I don't doubt that the doe has hidden her infant at least five hundred yards away before approaching the oasis.

The two does finish drinking and wander off together toward the north. They walk with infinite grace, like a pair of ballerinas, and disappear behind a large hill.

The next movement of Nature's morning concert is a brisk allegro performed by several male sandgrouse — tan, pigeon-sized birds related to partridge, pheasant, and quail. They come flying in, low over the desert. When they reach the shallow waters of Ein Saharonim, they simply break in midair and plop into the water. They drink energetically and, at the same time, submerge their breasts until they're soaking wet.

The morning ablutions completed, the sandgrouse leap skyward and fly vigorously due east, toward the rising sun. Any marauding falcon seeking to snatch a sandgrouse in the vicinity of Ein Saharonim will have to pursue its quarry right into the blinding sunlight.

These busy desert birds then head for their nests, simple cavities scraped out of the desert floor some two to four miles from the oasis. The sandgrouse is a wary bird, and he won't fly straight back to his nest. Instead, when he comes near it, he'll make a little reconnaissance flight around the area, checking for foxes, falcons, or any other predator that would threaten his family. When he's satisfied that the area is safe, he'll call out *kota-kota-kota* and receive a reply from his mate at the nest. Even then he won't land directly beside the nest but will touch down some thirty or forty feet away and walk the last part of his journey, in order to divert any unseen predator that might be dangerously close to his family.

Finally, as he approaches the nest, the chicks will rush out to greet him and draw every drop of water from his saturated breast feathers with their beaks. At this time of year, the male sandgrouse serves as water carrier for the newly hatched chicks; his specially adapted breast feathers are more absorbent than a household sponge.

In the heat of the day, the hen, which is the color of the rocks around her, spreads her wings to form a canopy that protects the fragile chicks from the scorching sun. Meanwhile, the male stands guard duty, keeping a sharp eye out for predators. If danger approaches, he'll use every trick imaginable to draw the carnivore away from his family. He'll limp and flop and stagger like a Bowery drunk, trying to fool the predator into believing he is unable to fly. After his pursuer has chased him for several hundred yards on the ground, the sandgrouse will suddenly soar into the air and out of reach. The female and the chicks will wait motionless on the ground, trusting that their coloration will camouflage them.

Twenty-two minutes after sunrise, the morning's andante movement begins. For me, this is the most important part of today's concert. Nine onagers appear from the southwest. They march in a strictly organized single file toward the oasis. I uncap my pen and begin to record their activities in my diary.

About seventy yards from the water, the whole herd comes to a halt. The stallion, with his head hung low, advances slowly for another fifty yards and then stops abruptly. He inspects the surroundings meticulously, staring into the thickets, brush, and reeds growing by the water's edge. He swings his head from side to side, focusing sharply on the myriad shapes and morning shadows of the desert beyond. At one point, I am certain that he is staring straight back into my telescope.

But my presence here shouldn't bother him at all. We've been friends for years — ever since he was a frolicking colt at Hai-Bar. I'm here today simply to check up on how the herd is getting along with their new freedom outside the reserve.

The burly equine lifts his head slightly and then draws his chin back. His ears begin to twist methodically, like radar scanners on a fogbound ship. The rest of the herd rivets its attention on this careful and experienced leader, watching him for the slightest hint of danger.

The stallion now juts his muzzle high into the air and draws in a deep breath through his large nostrils. There is no scent of a predator, and he exhales noisily. Satisfied that the area is safe, the stallion strides across the remaining twenty yards of ground to the water. He takes a last, almost casual, glance around him before lowering his head for a drink.

Only now does the rest of the herd — five mares and three adolescents — begin to move in. They maintain their single-file discipline until they reach the water and then fan out along the edge of the pool for their morning drink. In the stillness of the desert, I can hear their splashing and gulping. They love it, even though the water is warm and salty. If I drank a cup of that water, I'd have a stomachache for two days.

I focus the telescope on two of the mares, which drink side by side. They're both pregnant and should be delivering their foals in about a month. These onagers will give birth at the end of June, when the desert is the hottest. The prospect of the birth of these foals brings great happiness to me. I've been waiting for wild-born onager foals for more than a decade.

The herd continues to drink for a little over seven minutes. The onagers are calm, although the stallion pauses every minute or so to monitor the surroundings. Their tails sway to and fro.

But it is not wise to linger very long at an oasis. The dominant mare lifts her head from the pool, swings around to her right, and begins to walk off toward the northwest. The other mares and one of the adolescents trail behind her, lined up in the same order as when they approached the oasis. But two of the youngsters and the stallion remain at the water. The young onagers want to pump as much of the precious fluid as possible into their stomachs before facing another torrid day in the central Negev. I suspect, too, that they like to stand in the soft mud of the shallow pool. Compared to the baking sand and gravel of the desert, it is relatively cool and soothing.

By the time the lead mare is a hundred yards away, the stallion decides the adolescents have loitered by the water long enough. Standing erect, he faces them squarely, lays his ears back, flares his nostrils, and stares at the dawdlers. They bolt off to catch up with the rest of the herd. The onager stallion waits beside the waters of Ein Saharonim until all the members of the herd are together in an open area at a safe distance from any ambusher hiding in the vegetation. The big male then trots off to join them.

The morning's sequence of events at the oasis is perfectly normal for onagers — and that's precisely what makes it so important. It means the many lessons of Hai-Bar have taken hold. It means the onagers have learned enough to be cautious and self-disciplined and competent enough to fend for themselves in the wild. It means that they are well on their way toward replacing Israel's now-extinct native wild ass, that they are fitting quite well into the vacant ecological niche.

The success of a reintroduction usually is not claimed until a "second filial generation" is born in the wild — that is, not until the foals which are about to be born at Ein Saharonim have foals of their own. Biologists usually call this the F-2 generation. But in this program, I believe it is fair to bend the rules a slight bit, because, from one perspective, today's parent generation can be viewed as first filial, or F-1. All of the onagers released in Ein Saharonim were born in the semiwild state of Hai-Bar. None of their parents — the zoo onagers from Holland and Denmark — were ever permitted to run free in Nature. We feared that they would never become truly wild enough to live in this inhospitable region. Only Hai-Bar-born onagers, which never knew a zoo paddock or the close attention of a large curatorial staff or all of the other human influences of a zoological institution, could be let free. Only Hai-Bar-born onagers, which have known only natural herd structures and dynamics, which have been forced to struggle for their positions in the herds, and which have spent their entire lives under the desert sun browsing on natural brush and grasses, were considered proper animals for release.

Hai-Bar is nearly an animal equivalent of the Exodus. A generation had to pass between the departure from Egypt and the return to the Land of Israel. Even Moses, great leader that he was, was destined never to set foot upon the soil of Israel.

Some people have criticized the Hai-Bar program as being overly cautious in using more time than is absolutely necessary to accomplish the reintroduction process. But nobody could complain, when reintroduction did come, that the animals could have been better prepared. Everything imaginable was done to make the passage of the onagers from zoos, through Hai-Bar, and then off into freedom, as certain as possible.

Thus, our Hai-Bar generation was very much like the wildlife biologist's parent generation. But instead of letting such a fragile generation run completely free in Nature, we protected ours and supplemented its nutrition. This generation's tougher, desert-born offspring became equivalent to F-1, and our first candidates for release into a completely wild state. With this reassessment, our first truly wild-born generation then becomes equivalent to that sought-for F-2.

I watch as the Ein Saharonim herd begins to drift off. I gather my gear quickly, shoulder my pack, and follow them. I trail the onagers at a distance of about two hundred yards — any closer and they might spend more time keeping track of me than doing what onagers ought to do when they're alone in the desert. If I follow at a greater distance, I might lose them completely in this difficult desert landscape.

Ein Saharonim is at the eastern end of Makhtesh Ramon, a giant crater in the middle of the Negev. The crater is about twenty-five miles from end to end and walled with sheer cliffs along its rim. Some of these cliffs rise as high as 2,700 feet. The surface of Makhtesh Ramon is rugged, laced with hundreds of ravines, craggy outcroppings, and sharp ridges.

Most of the area is a nature reserve and an excellent habitat for the onagers. A good mixture of desert vegetation grows here — a sparse carpet of acacia trees, tamarisk, salt bush, desert grasses, halophytes, and other plants that are well adapted to this hot, dry, alkaline environment. There are also several springs in the region. Some are only seasonal, but a few — including Ein Saharonim — have reliable water flowing from them every day of the year.

I follow the herd at a leisurely pace across the desert, with the rising sun climbing over my right shoulder and those towering escarpments dead ahead. Some two and a half miles from Ein Saharonim, the herd halts and spreads out to graze on some of the hardy desert grasses.

This gives me an opportunity to open one of my *kalkarim* and swallow about a pint of water. I also take a handful of water and pour it into the top of my hat, soaking its canvas fiber thoroughly. As the sun dries out this moisture, the evaporation process will keep my head a bit cooler than the rest of this sandy oven.

While I watch the onagers, I can't help but realize what a strange and wonderful place this is. I feel very much at home, comfortable despite all the discomforts. Somewhere out here, I fully expect to come across the ghost of Nebuchadnezzar. The Bible tells us that Nebuchadnezzar was the mighty Chaldean emperor who carried the Israelites off to Babylonian captivity. A few decades later, he himself was deposed, and he "was driven from men, and his mind was made like that of a beast, and his dwelling was with the wild asses" (Daniel 5:21).

Eventually the onagers begin drifting back along their original course. I follow and snip several blades of grass from the area where they have been grazing. The sample is slipped into a plastic bag and popped into my canvas sack. At home, I'll take a closer look at these grasses and try to identify them more precisely. An understanding of the type and quality of grass the onagers eat is important to their conservation. Grass, although not particularly nutritious by most standards, is just fine for these wild equines. It has adequate protein, good energy, and plenty of minerals and vitamins. The long grass stems have much cellulose, which, though impossible to digest, is good roughage: it scrubs the onagers' stomachs and intestines, keeping them clean and healthy.

Many centuries ago, the prophet Jeremiah observed the link between grass and nutrition for the onagers: "And the wild asses stood on the bare heights, they sniffed the wind like jackals; but their eyes failed because there was no grass" (Jeremiah 14:6). Modern science has identified grass as having a relatively high concentration of carotene, a biological chemical that is converted to

Vitamin A by the liver. Science has also demonstrated that there is a positive relationship between the absence of Vitamin A and poor eyesight, proving a fact that was known twenty-five centuries ago.

Jeremiah also notes that the onagers "sniffed the wind like jackals." Jackals sniff the wind by pointing their noses toward the sky, just as the coyotes of America do — and just as the onager stallion back at Ein Saharonim did when he was trying to pick up the scent of predators. I wonder how sensitive an onager's nose is, if he can hope to smell grasses in this extremely arid climate, for dry air has little ability to carry fragrances. I also wonder if Jeremiah wandered around the desert as I'm doing today, just to watch the onagers in their own back yard.

The herd comes across another patch of grass in a dry ravine and begins to graze again. I sit down in the shade of a large boulder and observe. On the opposite hillside, two desert ravens stand like silent sentinels, keeping an eye on the strangers who have invaded their little corner of the desert. But they don't remain there very long. Ravens are as curious as cats, and soon they take to the air, flapping their big, broad wings and calling noisily back and forth. They circle over the onagers a few times and then whizz over me. But this lone human is nowhere near as interesting as a whole herd of Asian wild asses, so the ravens fly back to the equines for a closer look. They land among the onagers and strut amid them like Liliputians in the land of giants. Finding nothing to scavenge, the ravens return to their rocky hilltop perches.

As the onagers move on, one of the females leaves me with something to scavenge — a sample of her feces. Once the herd is clear of the area, I move in with a plastic bag and scoop it up. This package is placed inside a second plastic bag, and that into yet a third. The bag is then snugly bound and inserted into a side pocket of my canvas sack. Back home, some of the stool sample will be dissolved and allowed to set for a few hours in a super-dense water solution. This process concentrates the eggs of any worms the onager may be carrying in her intestine. Microscopic study of the worm eggs can determine precisely what type of worms they are and whether they pose any serious threat to the animal.

In Nature, each onager should have a fair number of internal parasites. But a healthy animal should be able to contend with these. If a high concentration of worm eggs is found in the fecal analysis, however, it is a warning signal of poor health. A good fecal analysis offers much more information — what the animal has been eating, how well it's digested, evidence of certain medical problems such as blood in the stool, and other clues to the animal's condition.

There are also ecological clues in those little brown lumps. Equines, unlike the ruminants (gazelles, ibex, deer, etc.), do not have very efficient digestive tracts. Because of this inefficiency, quite a bit of plant material can pass through undigested. And this includes many types of seeds.

Thus, the onager serves as a seed dispersal mechanism for several types of plants. It eats part of a plant, along with a bunch of seeds, at one place, takes a walk while some of it is digested, and then deposits the seeds, with a neat little bundle of fertilizer, somewhere else. Because of this mechanism, onagers help to disperse seeds a good distance from the parent plant. This is very useful in the desert because, unlike more humid habitats, it often doesn't have enough moisture in one place to supply both the parent plant and its growing seedling. Desert plants need relatively great distribution, and the onager assists in this quite nicely.

By ten-thirty in the morning the heat is painfully intense. Of the ten quarts of water I started with, about three and a half remain. It will last until noon, and that's just about as long as I intend to wander around with these onagers. They're slowly moving in the direction of the only road that cuts across Makhtesh Ramon, and along that road is my car, waiting for me with another ten quarts of water.

The herd drifts across a small depression studded by sparse vegetation and open sandy areas. One of the mares casually drops to her knees and then flops over on her side. She lies still for a moment on the hot sand and then, just like a little kitten being tickled, she kicks her legs high into the air. She rolls over, churning up a dense cloud of dust. The lady is taking a sand bath. In a moment, another mare also flops down and stirs up her own dust storm, rolling and kicking and rubbing her back against the coarse, sandy ground.

The end of the sand bath signals the start of "social hour," and the herd lingers in an open area for a rest. Two adolescents lie down, while the third stands close to its mare. The two pregnant mares stand side by side, facing opposite directions. They groom each other about the neck and withers. The grooming is more a means of social contact than a cosmetic activity.

The stallion, however, stands alone, about thirty yards away from the herd. He's their sentry during this midday leisure hour. Throughout the morning, the onagers continue doing precisely what they have been — and ought to be — doing. Most of the time, the herd is led by an older, experienced mare. But when there is a possibility of danger, the stallion stations himself in a position of control.

The stallion himself is a tough and victorious fighter. He has many scars around his neck and shoulders — wounds from battles with other males seeking to take over his harem herd. But he has successfully driven away all challengers. Competition among male onagers for control of a herd can be quite savage. They fight each other with great vigor, and there is little of the ritualized mock fighting conducted by many other species. Onagers go at each other in earnest.

The stallion has also warded off numerous desert wolves, and perhaps even a few leopards. So far, there have been only two wolf-inflicted fatalities among the Makhtesh Ramon onagers — a weak, sickly mare and her foal. But the healthy onagers have stood their ground, even in the face of packs of cunning, efficient, and highly organized wolves.

The onagers of Makhtesh Ramon thrive in a rugged land and a hostile climate. They can outrun just about anything except a cheetah, and there are no cheetahs in this desert. They're also good climbers — something most people don't expect of an equine — and they can scale the faces of some rather steep cliffs. They are proficient jumpers and have well demonstrated their ability to leap over a six-foot fence with relative ease.

The onagers are the great, untamed masters of the desert. An onager will throw a violent fit if anyone attempts to put a harness on it — and many people have tried. Indeed, if onagers could be domesticated, you'd see them at racetracks everywhere, because they can easily outrun the fastest of thoroughbred horses. Scientific measurements have demonstrated that onagers can sprint at speeds of about forty miles an hour and sustain a long-distance gallop at about thirty miles an hour.

For Bible readers, this is old news. Job, one of the greatest naturalists of antiquity, quotes the Almighty: "Who has let the wild ass go free? Who has loosed the harness of the swift ass, to whom I have given the wilderness for his home, and the barren land his dwelling? He scorns the multitude of the city; he rejects the commands of the driver. The range of the mountains is his pasture, and he searches after every green thing" (Job 39:5–8).

By noon my work day is done, and I am tired. Seven hours of desert sun and about fourteen kilometers of itinerant drifting behind the herd have worn me down. I feel that I am a small man in a land of giants.

After a snack and a half-hour rest, I begin a three-hour drive to Jerusalem. And all along the way, my mind lingers on the onagers and their desert kingdom. Certainly the barren lands are their dwelling place, and the range of the mountains their pasture.

There is tremendous ecological advantage in restoring wildlife to Nature. The living fabric of the Land is enhanced by expanded biological diversity of species. And biological diversity tends to stabilize ecological systems. Hundreds of solid biological arguments can be made on behalf of the onagers, and I am firmly persuaded that all the years and all the perspiration have been a good investment in restoring the integrity of the earth.

But they have also been a good investment in restoring the integrity of humanity. Our kind once was (and sadly, still is) very much concerned with the exploitation of Nature for our own enrichment. But a corner has been turned in recent years. People have begun to mend the wounds. The great whales are receiving protection today, as are the lithe gazelles and other creatures. Some of us have learned that we have not inherited the earth from our forebears, nor are we preserving it for our children. We are merely tenants, sharing this planet with many other tenants, whose existence we must respect.